Texas Jack

TEXAS JACK
America's First Cowboy Star

MATTHEW KERNS

TWODOT®

GUILFORD, CONNECTICUT
HELENA, MONTANA

A · TWODOT® · BOOK

An imprint and registered trademark of The Rowman & Littlefield Publishing Group, Inc.
4501 Forbes Blvd., Ste. 200
Lanham, MD 20706
www.rowman.com

Distributed by NATIONAL BOOK NETWORK

British Library Cataloguing in Publication Information available

Library of Congress Cataloging-in-Publication Data
Names: Kerns, Matthew, 1979- author.
Title: Texas Jack : America's first cowboy star / Matthew Kerns.
Other titles: America's first cowboy star
Description: Guilford, Connecticut : TwoDot, [2021] | Includes bibliographical references and
    index.
Identifiers: LCCN 2020054577 (print) | LCCN 2020054578 (ebook) | ISBN 9781493055418
    (cloth) | ISBN 9781493055425 (epub)
Subjects: LCSH: Omohundro, John Burwell, 1846-1880. | Cowboys—West (U.S.)—Biography.
    | Buffalo Bill, 1846-1917—Friends and associates. | Entertainers—United States—Biography.
    | Wild west shows—United States—History. | Scouts (Reconnaissance)—West (U.S.)—
    Biography. | Frontier and pioneer life—West (U.S.) | West (U.S.)—Biography.
Classification: LCC F594.O5 .K47 2021 (print) | LCC F594.O5 (ebook) | DDC 978/.020922
    [B]—dc23
LC record available at https://lccn.loc.gov/2020054577
LC ebook record available at https://lccn.loc.gov/2020054578

To my dad and my mom
who took us West

My dear fellow, sit down. Were I to dare to tell you my adventures, they would fill a stack of books that would reach as high as the Bunker Hill Monument, and be as full of fire as the eruptions of Vesuvius. It is almost impossible for me to give you any idea of scout life; for where shall I begin or leave off? But I'll tell you what I am going to do this summer . . .

—TEXAS JACK

Author's Note

MANY OF THE SOURCES QUOTED IN THIS BOOK USE TERMS AND PHRASES that are rightly considered racist by the standards of today. Racist terminology used to describe Native Americans, including variations on the words "redskin," "Injun," "savage," "squaw," and several others are present throughout quoted text and speak to the prevailing—though thankfully not universal—sentiment of the time. Similarly, slaves on a Virginia plantation are referred to in a quoted newspaper piece as "darkies." The author would like to strongly state that these words are quoted verbatim for accuracy and context and do not express in any way his views on either Native Americans or people of color.

Where possible, Native American people have been identified by tribe and by name in both their own language and in English, and the names of historic conflicts such as the Battle of the Little Bighorn are also referred to by the English versions of their native names, i.e., the Battle of the Greasy Grass.

Contents

ACT III

INTRODUCTION

IT COULD BE A SCENE IN ANY HOLLYWOOD WESTERN. BEFORE THE break of dawn on a cool spring morning, a civilian scout and his cowboy friend ride out of a frontier army fort in pursuit of a party of Indian raiders. The raiders absconded with the horses from the army's telegraph station the night before and raced north, across the prairie toward relative safety beyond the river's northern branch. Close behind the scout and the cowboy rode two squadrons of soldiers. Their captain assured his men that the pair at the lead could read the signs and follow the trail of their enemies.

After breaking camp in the cold predawn hours and a hard ride of many miles across the unbroken prairie, the scout and the cowboy abruptly stopped ahead of the troops, conversing as they pointed into the distance. They rode back to tell the captain that the Indians and their stolen horses were just on the other side of the river. The scout proposed to proceed with a small number of men toward the enemy encampment while the cowboy took the larger force around from the north, surrounding the natives and cutting off their escape. Soon the cavalry was split, and as the flanking column led by the cowboy wended its way into position, gunfire erupted from the direction of the camp. The cowboy immediately put heel to horseflesh, charging toward the sound of rifle shot, followed by the pounding hooves of the troops' mounts as they rushed toward the scout and his smaller contingent now engaged in combat.

The scout had just fired his .50 caliber trapdoor needle gun at one of the mounted braves when he felt fire blaze across his scalp, followed by the blinding flow of blood pouring across his forehead. Frantically wiping the warm blood from his eyes, he looked in the direction of the shot. There he saw the warrior who had pulled the trigger falling to the earth, a bullet fired from the weapon of the mounted cowboy lodged in his brain. Had the cowboy fired a second later, the scout knew, the shot meant to end his life would not have missed. The cavalry troops rounded up the remaining braves, and the scout bandaged his wound while the cowboy showed the ranking officer the tracks indicating the larger force of Indians that had recently camped in the area.

The captain's report to his superior officers about the incident noted that the scout's "reputation for bravery and skill as a guide is so well established that I need not say anything else than but he acted in his usual manner." The cowboy, he said, "is a very good trailer and a brave man, who knows the country well, and I respectfully recommend his employment as a guide should the service of one . . . be needed."

The idea of encounters like this—of cowboys fighting Indians on the outskirts of civilization—is so ingrained in the collective conscience that the scenario seems not merely plausible but possibly clichéd. The tropic cowboy captures all of American history and virtue reduced to a central mythic figure comprising a set of beliefs: The cowboy fought Indians. The cowboy was a rugged individualist. The cowboy played a significant role in American history. The cowboy fought in gunfights. The cowboy's life was full of excitement.

The reality of the cowboy stands in contrast with romantic depictions in stories and movies. By the time of the big Texas cattle drives of the late 1860s, herders meticulously avoided native territories, despite the decimation of native populations between Texas and Kansas by disease and the relegation of Native Americans to reservations. Ranch owners entrusted their cowboys with the care of their valuable stock. Ensuring the value of their charges during transportation made cowboys more akin to modern truck drivers than leather-clad knights. Cattle drives along the Chisholm Trail, Goodnight-Loving Trail, and others lasted only from 1866 until the mid-1880s when a combination of rail lines and hundreds of miles of barbed-wire fence rendered the job of trail-driving cowboy obsolete. During the scant twenty years of cowboy primacy, swift streams swollen by rain, lightning, falls from horseback, and disease accounted for the majority of cowboy deaths. A cowboy was more likely to draw his gun on a farmer than on another cowboy or card cheat across a town square at high noon—more likely to fire his rifle at a coyote than a Comanche (Numunuu) brave. Dust and tedium were the rule of a cowboy's work, as was enduring the worst of conditions to ensure top dollar for beef.

Why, then, do stories of cowboys and Indians fighting in the American West ring so true? How did this virtually nonexistent conflict come to form the basis of the Western, America's most enduring mythology, both in print and on-screen? Is there some foundational truth upon which this myth is built? In looking for answers to these questions, one must start with the man most responsible for shaping the popular understanding of the American West, Buffalo Bill Cody.

It is impossible to overstate the enormous impact of Buffalo Bill and his Wild West entertainment upon the American public consciousness from the show's inception in 1883 until well beyond his death in 1917. During those thirty-four years, no entertainer was as successful, no American as widely known, as William Frederick "Buffalo Bill" Cody. Today, in Cody, Wyoming, visitors to the town named after its famous founder and situated on the Shoshone River at the entrance to Yellowstone National Park can visit the Buffalo Bill Center of the West. Patrons are greeted by a helio-display of the scout, welcoming visitors the same way the genuine article welcomed hundreds of thousands to the enormous spectacle of his traveling Wild West exhibitions. Now, as then, Buffalo Bill serves as a primer on and cornerstone of America's fascination with the American West, as he has from the moment he stepped from the frontier and the yellowed pages of dime novels and onto a Chicago stage in the winter of 1872. As biographer Louis Warren notes in his book *Buffalo Bill's America*, "For generations of Americans and Europeans, Buffalo Bill defined the meaning of American history and American identity.... [The] crowds who came to see Buffalo Bill's Wild West show spoke so widely and fervently about it for years afterward that it became a defining cultural memory—or dream—of America."[1]

Central to Cody's vision of the Wild West was what would become the defining icon of the Western man—the cowboy. Indeed, for over twenty years the culminating act of the show was listed in the program as "Attack on a Settler's Cabin by Hostile Indians. Repulse by Cowboys, under the Leadership of Buffalo Bill." With civilization at stake and the fate of the emblematic white family on the line, the group of heroes riding to the rescue was not comprised of professional soldiers, but of cowboys. At their head was Buffalo Bill, a man who Warren notes was "an absentee [ranch] owner who was never a cowboy."[2] When Cody, celebrated as a civilian scout for the military well before taking to the stage in 1872, rode toward engagements with hostile Sioux (Očhéthi Šakówiŋ) or Cheyenne (Tsêhéstáno) on the plains of Nebraska and hills of the Dakota territory, it was never in the company of cowboys, but of trained soldiers. Why, then, did Cody present the cowboy as the savior of the white family—of civilization itself—from the threat of savagery?

One important clue lies in the programs handed out to the millions of men, women, and children visiting the Wild West at stops in cities across America and throughout Europe. From its inception as *The Wild West: Buffalo Bill and Dr. Carver's Rocky Mountain and Prairie Exhibition* in 1883 and in long stands at New York's Madison Square Garden in 1886, Queen Victoria's 1887 Diamond Jubilee in London, and Chicago's Columbian Exposition in 1893, these programs contained a section titled simply "The Cow-Boy."

"The cow-boy!" began the piece that introduced the profession to so many eager spectators, "How often spoken of, how falsely imagined, how greatly despised (where not known), how little understood! I've been there considerable." With descriptions of stampedes and storms, cowboys singing to restless steers at night, and "cow sense," the piece describes a profession requiring the patience of Job and peopled by ambitious, adventurous, and rebellious young men, "taught at school to admire the deceased little Georgie [Washington] in exploring adventures, though not equaling him in 'cherry-tree goodness.'"

How many of these brave cowboys "never finish," the author wonders in conclusion, "but mark the trail with their silent graves, no one can tell. But when Gabriel toots his horn, the 'Chisholm Trail' will swarm with cow-boys. 'Howsomever, we'll all be thar', let's hope, for a happy trip, when we say to this planet, *adios*!"

This piece, explaining the origins and extolling the virtues of the cowboy to audiences amassed to experience a group of the same gallantly riding to the settler family's rescue at the heels of Buffalo Bill Cody, bore the signature of one of that man's oldest friends and earliest associates, Texas Jack. In looking at Cody's life for a significant example of the kind of man that Buffalo Bill—jayhawker, soldier, hunter, and scout—would raise above all other professions in his simulacrum of the real West, presented as absolute historical truth to huge audiences across the world, one need look no further than John B. "Texas Jack" Omohundro, cowboy.

Thousands of men and women shared stage or stadium with Bill Cody. Wild Bill Hickok, Doc Carver, Annie Oakley, and Sitting Bull each appeared with the scout in various permutations of his ever-evolving entertainment career. Alone among his fellow scouts, soldiers, shooters, and stars, Texas Jack was perhaps the only person in Bill Cody's life who qualified fully as partner. On stage and trail, the men stood as equals, shared equal billing, and split equal revenues. They were friends and scouting partners in frontier Nebraska for three years before stepping together onto the stage in Chicago as actors for the first time. The pair would tour together in the East and hunt together in the West for four years before separating to establish their own touring companies.

During their years together onstage, Buffalo Bill impressed crowds with tales of buffalo hunting on horseback while Texas Jack thrilled with stories of cattle stampedes told in his baritone Virginia drawl. He entertained packed halls, auditoriums, and theaters as he whirled his lasso overhead, the first to turn that tool of the cowboy trade into an object of entertainment for fascinated audiences. More than stage costars and business associates, the men were friends and partners. Cody referred to the relationship as "Pards of the Plains for life."[3] In Nebraska, while Cody spent long weeks away from his North Platte home scouting with the Third Cavalry, Texas Jack slept in a spare room at the Cody house to ensure the safety of Bill's wife, Louisa, and their children, Arta, Kit Carson, and Orra.

Louis Warren points out that "William Cody seldom spoke of death, or of people who had died. In all his correspondence there is barely a mention of any deceased friends or acquaintances. He wrote no poignant words about Wild Bill Hickok, Sitting Bull, or Nate Salsbury. No matter how tragic their deaths, he seldom spoke of the loss."[4] The exception to this rule is John Omohundro. On September 5, 1908, twenty-eight years after Texas Jack's death in Leadville, Colorado, the loss still weighed heavy on Cody's mind. That evening, Cody assembled the entire cast of Buffalo Bill's Wild West at the grave of his cowboy friend.

With the sun setting behind 14,000-foot Mount Massive, Cody and his Wild West troupe gathered under the tall pines of Evergreen Cemetery in Leadville to pay tribute to Texas Jack. A reporter for the local *Herald Democrat* wrote that "If the spirit of Texas Jack were able to hover over the little mound that contains his mortal remains he would have been gratified by the ceremonies in honor of his memory. They were the kind of ceremonies that his plain, rough, honest character would have asked could he have chosen—brief, simple, and unaffected, but oh, how impressive!"[5] A reverend offered a prayer, and Cody stepped forward to say a few words about his friend.

Picture the scene: The silver-haired showman stands next to the pine slab marking his old partner's final resting place. Around him are hundreds of Leadville locals, and next to him stands the reverend who conducted the service and the professor who led the brass band at Omohundro's funeral procession twenty-eight years earlier. Members of Cody's Wild West show stand arrayed in their costumes. A dozen cavalrymen form a rough semicircle. Some of these men, like their leader Buffalo Bill, served the Union during the Civil War, fighting on the opposite side of the battlefield from the former Confederate soldier they now commemorated. Representatives of the Ute and Sioux tribes, also part of Cody's entourage, stand tall in war paint and feather headdresses as they listen to words spoken about a man who claimed Powhatan (Wahunsenacawh) lineage, hunted with the Pawnee (Chaticks si Chaticks), and fought against Comanche, Sioux, Nez Perce (Niimiipuu), and Cheyenne. Russian Cossack hunters, Japanese warriors, British cavalry, Arab riders, and German horsemen, each in full show garb, have come to pay their respects.

A report in the local newspaper captures best the largest constituent group of men gathered for the ceremony. "Impressed by the ceremony second only to Col. Cody himself was the crowd of cowboys, whose experiences on the plains have been similar to those of the dead friend of their present day chieftain. These men felt that the old scout was one of them. To them the service was of greater import than to those whose life has been spent in some other pursuit. Tears welled to the eyes of many of these strong-muscled, large-hearted men. It was one of their comrades whom they were honoring, a man whom they knew and whose life was their life, though they had never seen him."[6]

Here, then, are the cowboys of the Wild West, come to honor one of their own, the first of their kind. These men shared with Texas Jack the common bond of the trail: hours spent breathing the dust of the herd, nights filled with stories shared by campfire and invented verse sung to restless doggies, tedious days and weeks broken only by the adrenaline rush of high river crossing, murderous rustler, and deadly stampede. Here stood the second generation of cowboy stars, held dear in American hearts as the rescuers of embattled settlers and the embodiment of the frontier man, acknowledging the first of their kind.

Cody removes his ever-present wide-brimmed Stetson, his famous locks now silvered and significantly thinned with age. He clutches the hat before him and begins to speak:

> *My friends, perhaps many of you do not know this man whom we have gathered to honor. No doubt you would like to know something of him, who was one of my dearest and most intimate friends.*
>
> *John B. Omohundro, better known as Texas Jack, was a Virginian by birth. The blood of the Powhatan Indians flowed in his veins. He was of proud and noble birth.*
>
> *During the Civil War he was a member of the cavalry command under Col. "Jeb" Stuart of the Confederate Army. He was one of his most trusted and faithful scouts and performed almost invaluable service for him.*
>
> *After the war he drifted westward and located in Texas, where he took up the hazardous work of a cowboy. He was one of the original Texas cowboys, when life on the plains was a hardship and a trying duty.*

When they began to drive the cattle to the northern country, he engaged in that occupation, following the herds northward, and returning after each trip for another herd.

Finally, he located at North Platte, Nebraska. It was there that I first met him. He was an expert trailer and scout. I soon recognized this and tried to secure his appointment in United States service. But the authorities were unwilling to hire discharged Confederate scouts, so I had to take the matter to the Secretary of War. After much persuasion I was given permission to hire him.

Here Cody's voice breaks.

In this capacity I learned to know him and to respect his bravery and ability. He was a whole-souled, brave, generous, good-hearted man.

Later he and I went East to go into the show business. He was the first to do a lasso act upon the stage.

After a short career with the show we again went West. That was in 1876, when the Sioux War was being fought. About the same time General Custer was killed and we had to take part in many important engagements. After the Indian Wars we returned East and again went on the stage. It was during tours of the large cities that he met and married Mademoiselle Morlacchi, the famous dancer, who later traveled with him.

After I left him, he and she continued to travel. They came to Leadville, where she was engaged as a performer. Becoming attached to the place, my friend and his wife remained for a while.

It was while here that he was stricken with pneumonia, which was then prevalent. He succumbed, and was buried here under this mound by his many friends.

Among those who contributed to the ceremony at that time was Mr. Kerns, who is here now, and who remembers the manly traits of poor Jack.

Cody pauses to gather himself before continuing.

Jack was an old friend of mine and a good one. Instead of this board which now marks his grave, we will soon have erected a more substantial monument, one more worthy of a brave and good man.

Cody's eyes follow the sweep of his hand past the board, beyond the pine trees, and toward Mount Massive towering in the fading orange sunset. A slight breeze plays through the tops of the trees as they cast long shadows over the assembled party. Cody takes a moment to wipe his brimming eyes with his handkerchief. He looks out over the assembled citizens of Leadville and then to the cast of his Wild West show, the dozens of Native Americans, soldiers, scouts, and cowboys that are employees, cast members, and friends. He places a hand on the grave marker he means to replace and returns the Stetson once again to his head.

May he rest in peace.[7]

As the band plays "Nearer My God to Thee," Cody places a wreath of flowers on the grave of his old friend. He mumbles a few brief words of his own before mounting his horse and riding away.

Show programs and graveside eulogies are not the only places where it is readily apparent that Buffalo Bill remembered his closest friend. In 1883, a decade after his first tour with Texas Jack and three years after his death, Cody wrote and published a story about his friend titled "Texas Jack, the Prairie Rattler." That same year Omohundro's writings about his first buffalo hunt with the Pawnee were likewise printed in material from the Wild West show, where they remained for the rest of Cody's life. Cody mentions Texas Jack fondly in each of his autobiographies. In her book about her late husband, Louisa Cody paints Jack as an ever-present fixture in Bill's life, both at their home in Nebraska and as they began their stage venture in Chicago. Texas Jack and Buffalo Bill didn't just hunt and scout together; they hung wallpaper and shared dinner; they fought hostile Sioux and entertained royalty.

When one reporter was granted an interview with Cody during the height of his fame at his Scout's Rest Ranch home west of North

William F. "Buffalo Bill" Cody at the grave of John B. "Texas Jack" Omohundro, September 5, 1908, Leadville, Colorado. (BUFFALO BILL CENTER OF THE WEST, CODY, WYOMING)

Platte, Nebraska, he spent a portion of his article describing the home. The reporter mentions that on the wall opposite the entrance, visible immediately when a guest walked into the home, was a color drawing of Texas Jack. In the same way, an image of Texas Jack is imprinted on the cowboy as presented to America and the world by Buffalo Bill and his Wild West show. In Texas Jack, we discover the foundation of both common perception and tropic ideal. If in Texas Jack we see the cowboy, then perhaps in the cowboy we will find Texas Jack.

ACT I

[Buffalo] Bill had, I think, always been in Government employ as a scout, but Texas Jack had been a cowboy, one of the old-time breed of men who drove herds of cattle from way down South to Northern markets for weeks and months, through a country infested by Indians and white cattle thieves. With the settling up of the country that type has disappeared . . .

—Windham Thomas Wyndham-Quin,
Fourth Earl of Dunraven
Past Times and Pastimes

CHAPTER ONE

Cowboys and Indians

THE FAMILIAR STORY OF THE BRAVE COWBOY FACING HOSTILE INDIANS on the plains does indeed have a foundation of truth. On April 26, 1872, Bill Cody rode out of Fort McPherson, Nebraska, in pursuit of a party of Miniconjou Sioux raiders and horse thieves. In his 1879 autobiography, Cody recalled that the Miniconjou "made a dash on McPherson Station, about five miles from the fort, killing two or three men and running off quite a large number of horses. Captain Meinhold, Lieutenant Lawson, and their company were under orders to pursue and punish the Miniconjou raiders if possible. I was the guide of the expedition and had as an assistant J. B. Omohundro, better known as 'Texas Jack' and who was a scout at the post."[1]

The day's events, which would earn Cody the Congressional Medal of Honor, are worth exploring further as foundational to the portrayal of the cowboy in Cody's later dramatic endeavors and subsequently in depictions of the cowboy in American literature, television, and film. The incident became one of the milestones of Cody's life, occurring just on the border between his twin careers as scout and showman. The episode would be recounted, with various degrees of accuracy, as a part of every subsequent Cody biography.

The Miniconjou and the recently rustled horses were spotted near the convergence of the Dismal and Middle Loup rivers. Omohundro discovered their trail going north and determined that they would probably make camp between the rivers, where they could water the stolen horses. Cody decided to set out at night, leaving the expedition in Texas

Jack's capable hands, informing the commander that "Texas Jack knew the country thoroughly and that he could guide the command to a point on the Dismal River where I could meet them that night." Before leaving, Cody told Omohundro that "the general wanted him to guide the command to the course of the Dismal. When he got there, if he didn't hear from me in the meantime, he was to elect a good camp."[2]

Confirming Omohundro's report that the Miniconjou were camped on the Dismal, Cody returned to meet the command:

> *I found the scouts first and told Texas Jack to hold up the soldiers, keeping them out of sight until he heard from me.*
>
> *I went on until I met General Reynolds at the head of the column. He baited the troop on my approach; taking him to one side, I told him what I had discovered. He said:*
>
> *"As you know the country and the location of the Indian camp, tell me how you would proceed."*
>
> *I suggested that he leave one company as an escort for the wagon-train and let them follow slowly. I would leave one guide to show them the way. Then I would take the rest of the cavalry and push on as rapidly as possible to within a few miles of the camp. That done, I would divide the command, sending one portion across the river to the right, five miles below the Indians, and another one to bear left toward the village. Still another detachment was to be kept in readiness to move straight for the camp. This, however, was not to be done until the flanking column had time to get around and across the river.*
>
> *It was then two o'clock. By four o'clock the flanking columns would be in their proper positions to move on and the charge could begin. I said I would go with the right-hand column and send Texas Jack with the left-hand column. . . . I impressed on the general the necessity of keeping in the ravine of the sandhills so as to be out of sight of the Indians.*[3]

The two columns approached from the cover of the ravine, with the main force waiting and then initiating a charge. After a brief resistance, the raiders realized that they were surrounded and largely cut off from their mounts and surrendered. Cody, Omohundro, and Captain Meinhold's troops had captured a band of Miniconjou Sioux (Očhéthi Šakówiŋ) from the southern agency at Whetstone Creek, which would soon bear the name of Brulé Sioux leader Spotted Tail (Siŋté Gleška).

In Captain Meinhold's official description of the days' events, he notes that "Mr. William F. Cody was the guide aided by Mr. Omehendev [*sic*] who volunteered his services." At the end of his description, Meinhold mentions four men. The first is William F. Cody, whose "reputation for bravery and skill as a guide is so well established that I need not say anything else than but he acted in his usual manner." Next are Sergeant John H. Foley, "who in command of the detached party charged into the Indian camp without knowing how many enemies he might encounter," and First Sergeant Leroy H. Vokes, "who bravely closed in upon an Indian while he was fired at several times and wounded him." The last is Texas Jack Omohundro, "a very good trailer and a brave man, who knows the country well, and I respectfully recommend his employment as a guide should the service of one in addition to Mr. Cody be needed." Cody, Foley, and Vokes were each awarded the Medal of Honor for "gallantry in action."[4] Texas Jack, perhaps because of his former allegiance to the Confederacy, was not.

In their description of the encounter, a reporter for the local *North Platte Democrat* newspaper wrote that after Cody began firing at the Miniconjou raiders,

> [t]he remainder of the command, hearing the fire, came up at full jump—"Texas Jack" at the head. "Texas Jack" immediately let drive and brought his Indian down, and he finished by adorning his belt with his victim's scalp-lock. . . . Too much praise can not be awarded to Captain Meinhold for his successful efforts. . . . Lieutenant Lawson, with the gallant members of "B" Troop, did their duty nobly and well, for which they have justly earned the thanks of the community. In this connection we would mention the efforts of our heroic friend "Texas Jack." Beside enjoying the reputation of a "dead shot," he is well skilled in the ways of the red man, and we are glad to know that his services have been retained by the Government.[5]

Another newspaper called the skirmish "a lively little Indian fight out at McPherson station. 'Buffalo Bill' and 'Texas Jack' each brought down a redskin. The Indians then left."[6] In what would prove to be a characteristic display of modesty, Texas Jack deferred praise to Cody when asked about the incident. However, he would be referred to as "the hero of the Loup Fork" by Nebraska newspapers for having shot a Sioux just as that warrior fired at Buffalo Bill, causing the shot to merely graze the famous scout's scalp rather than ending his life altogether.

Cody later wrote that "two mounted warriors closed in on me and were shooting at short range. I returned their fire and had the satisfaction of seeing one of them fall from his horse. At this moment I felt blood trickling down my forehead, and hastily running my hand through my hair I discovered that I had received a scalp wound."[7] Another newspaper reported that "to [Texas Jack] was Buffalo Bill indebted for his life. . . . The red thieves were pursued and overtaken by Bill and Jack, who each killed an Indian. A third redskin had just drawn a bead on Bill, when Jack's quick eye caught the gleam of the shining barrel, and the next instant 'the noble red' was on his way to the happy hunting ground, his passage from the sublunary sphere being expedited by a bullet from Jack's rifle, at a distance of one hundred and twenty-five yards."[8]

Here then is Buffalo Bill Cody, the man who more than anyone else would shape the public perception of the cowboy as the paragon of American courage and virtue, fighting Miniconjou Sioux braves alongside Texas Jack. Here is the great scout saved from death at the hands of "villainous Indians" by a lone cowboy. Tall and lean, a natural horseman, deadly accurate with pistol and rifle, brave and loyal to a fault, this man would be all of the things Cody would urge audiences to believe about the cowboys he led to the rescue of embattled settlers in arenas across the world, as well as in their counterparts working the ranges of the American West. In the cowboy, Bill Cody presented a hard worker, an enduring spirit, a man of principle, an American knight. In sharing this version of the cowboy with audiences, Buffalo Bill was sharing with them his old friend, Texas Jack.

Soon after the encounter with the Miniconjou Sioux raiders on the Loup Fork, a report on the battle from the pages of the *North Platte*

Democrat appeared in full in the June 10 issue of Street & Smith's *New York Weekly*, the publishing house that printed the dime-novel stories of novelist and frontier celebrity Ned Buntline. "Why should the novelist weary his imagination in drawing fictitious characters," the preface asks, "when even our own land contains *living heroes* whose noble deeds are as marvelous as any that the mind could conceive? Ned Buntline takes his characters from life—paints them as they are; and his admirers, aware that they are reading history, peruse his stories with an interest impossible to be aroused by mere works of fiction."[9] The article closes with a promise that "Texas Jack, the Hero of the Loupe" [*sic*] is another story which Ned Buntline has promised to place in our hands at an early day. He is now hard at work upon it, and our readers will find that Texas Jack is a hero worthy of the esteem in which he is held by his comrade, Buffalo Bill."[10]

William F. Cody and John B. Omohundro were fighting enemy Sioux far from the fort on the Nebraska frontier in April and appearing in stories about fighting Indians in New York papers in June. By December, they would stand together onstage, portraying Buffalo Bill and Texas Jack in a play based on the stories inspired by the reality they had lived mere months earlier. There was no "Wild West" before the night of December 16, 1872. Gamblers and lawmen, thieves and cowboys, braves and banditos roamed the plains, canyons, and mountains west of the Mississippi, but the Wild West of popular imagination, with high-noon shoot-outs and hammer-fannin' heroes, hadn't been boiled down to its essence until Ned Buntline's play *The Scouts of the Prairie; and Red Deviltry as It Is!* premiered at Nixon's Amphitheatre in Chicago.

The *Chicago Tribune* issued a warning that the theater—in reality, no more than a large canvas tent with wooden boards for walls—would reek with the bad breath and unwashed feet of two thousand audience members. The warning did little to dissuade Chicago's theatergoing public, as on that cold winter evening, Nixon's floors and balconies exceeded capacity, and eager patrons were turned away.

After an entertaining opening piece by a world-famous Italian ballerina who had delighted Chicago audiences for weeks, the footlights rose, and the packed house quieted. Onto the stage walked a man with a rifle, greeted with thunderous applause. He warned the audience about

TEXAS JACK

Advertising poster for *The Scouts of the Prairie*, featuring Texas Jack. (BUFFALO BILL CENTER OF THE WEST, CODY, WYOMING)

the savage warriors he was sure were on the prowl just over the next rise, wondering when his two friends would arrive to aid him. He clapped the butt of his rifle onto the stage boards to signal those friends, waiting with apprehension in the wings. A man stumbled from the audience onto the stage and offered the remaining contents of a whiskey bottle to the speaker standing there. Perhaps the offender meant it as an offering, a new kind of bouquet for a new kind of show. After a moment of breathless suspense, the buckskin-clad speaker grabbed the offender by his neck and tossed him into the orchestra pit, smashing half a dozen stage lights on his way.

"Let any renegade paleface dare to cross this red line, and he shall thus feel the weight of my strong arm!" the man exclaimed, to a hail of rapturous applause. An orchestra member retrieved the luckless admirer from inside the contrabass where he had landed and handed him over to a policeman. As the offender was escorted out of the theater, the man onstage warned his audience at length about the dangers of strong drink. Finishing his impromptu temperance speech, he again banged the butt of his rifle on the rough boards of the stage. Two men nervously joined him onstage.[11]

Before a painted forest backdrop, the three men now stood resplendent in fringed buckskins lined with fur. The next lines belong to the tall and handsome man standing in the middle of the trio, but for perhaps the first time in his twenty-six years, his nerves got the better of him. He stood nervously, looking into the anxious crowd. Someone coughed. The silent moment stretched until the older and shorter man to his left spoke.

"Bill . . . you been out buffalo huntin' again?" The shorter man's voice was low and full of gravel.

The tall man turned and stared. The question was repeated.

"Buffalo Bill! You been huntin' those buffalo again?"

"Yeah," came the stuttering reply, "with Milligan."

Cody looked out into the sea of faces packing the theater and pointed toward the spot where Mr. Milligan and his friends were sitting. William F. Milligan—a wealthy paint merchant who had made a fortune selling to a town rebuilding after the Great Chicago Fire of the preceding year—was well known to the Chicago crowd, who now erupted in laughter and

Advertising poster for *The Scouts of the Prairie*, featuring Buffalo Bill. (BUFFALO BILL CENTER OF THE WEST, CODY, WYOMING)

Left to right: Buffalo Bill Cody, Ned Buntline, and Texas Jack Omohundro in their *Scouts of the Prairie* costumes. (BUFFALO BILL MUSEUM AND GRAVE, DENVER, COLORADO)

cheers. Milligan had indeed been buffalo hunting with Cody that summer, publicly expressing how desperately he wanted to face a Sioux warrior in combat until the moment the party spied a brave in the distance across the Nebraska prairie. At this sight, Milligan had experienced a sudden change of heart. "I don't believe this is one of my fighting days," he expressed in sudden realization to the other men in the party, turning his horse away from the native warriors, "and it occurs to me that I have urgent business at the camp."[12]

Audience members had heard accounts of Milligan's hunting adventure with Cody, and their hearty response was all the encouragement Buffalo Bill needed. He spoke to the audience about the hunt and the crowd as one leaned forward, hanging on his every word. Here was the scout they had read about in the dime novel *Buffalo Bill, King of the Border Men* by Ned Buntline, the man asking the questions and standing to Cody's left.

On Buffalo Bill's right stood the cowboy, wearing now a wide-brimmed Stetson hat, a fringed buckskin jacket, and pants tucked into tall black cavalry boots. These men had ridden into hostile territory together eight short months earlier. They had stalked buffalo and elk together within the last four weeks. Now they stood in the glaring calcium light before a standing-room-only crowd.

Having listened patiently to minutes of Cody's talk, the man at his right now let loose a bloodcurdling war whoop and yelled, "Injuns!" as ten Chicago supernumeraries dressed as natives rushed onto the stage. The three buckskin-clad men fired blanks from their pistols, vanquishing with haste the oncoming "red threat" to the thunderous applause of the Chicago audience. Cody's wife, Louisa, would write in her memoir that it was at this moment that her husband—who had been a Pony Express rider, a teamster, a soldier, a hunter, and a scout—became a star. "He was back at home now, with Texas Jack at his side, pulling the triggers of his six-shooter until the stage was filled with smoke, and until the hammers only clicked on exploded cartridges. They yelled. They shouted. They roared and banged away . . ."[13]

Texas Jack was as well-known that night to the Chicago crowd as his partner on stage and trail, Buffalo Bill. The same readers that voraciously tore through the pages of Buffalo Bill stories were fascinated by the man that the dime novels and newspapers would call the "White King of the Pawnees," the "Mustang King," the "Hero of the Loup Fork," and the "Lasso King." Unlike the name Buffalo Bill Cody, however, the name Texas Jack Omohundro has largely faded into the depths of history. There is no Texas Jack Center of the West. There was never a Texas Jack movie. No NFL team bears his name. And yet, while John B. Omohundro's name isn't spoken of in the same hushed tones as his friends Buffalo Bill Cody and Wild Bill Hickok, his contribution to the lasting legacy of the American West remains indelibly woven into the popular idea of the Western hero: loyal and brave to a fault, lasso and revolver in hand, Stetson pulled low, riding west into the setting sun. Though Buffalo Bill's cognomen graces the professional football team from Buffalo, New York, in a very real way, we will learn that without Texas Jack, there might not be a Dallas Cowboys.

While his friends Buffalo Bill and Wild Bill were rendered iconic as the preeminent scout and lawman of the American West, Omohundro's legacy as the first cowboy on the American stage is fundamental to the mythologized Western hero later introduced to the world by Buffalo Bill and personified in the stories of Ned Buntline and Prentiss Ingraham, the books of Zane Grey and Louis L'Amour, and the movies of John Wayne, Ronald Reagan, and Clint Eastwood. If the idealized American man is the frontier cowboy, then the genesis of the American cowboy in popular culture is Texas Jack Omohundro, a man who, despite his moniker, was not from Texas.

CHAPTER TWO

The Virginian

TEXAS JACK'S TRAIL FROM HIS CHILDHOOD HOME IN VIRGINIA TO FORT McPherson, near North Platte, Nebraska, was far from a straight one. Readers of Texas Jack's words on the cowboy in those Wild West programs learned that many of the young men that found themselves situated on a tall horse and watching over a restless herd were "to the manor born." The manor, in this case, was "Pleasure Hill," where John B. Omohundro spent an idyllic childhood playing, fishing, and hunting along Cunningham Creek and the Rivanna River.

In that big house, situated in a cluster of tall and sturdy oaks on the well-maintained fields of the big farm just a mile west of the Fluvanna County seat of Palmyra, the Omohundro family was a large and a prosperous one. A full-time overseer lived on the property and managed the twenty-five slaves that toiled the fertile fields full of wheat, tobacco, and corn, as they were on June 28, 1846, when the senior John Burwell Omohundro and his wife, Catherine Salome (née Baker), welcomed the fourth of their eleven children into the world. Their oldest son, Orville, was a studious child whose academic interests would eventually lead him to study the law and medicine. Young Johnny was his brother's opposite, rejecting the classroom in favor of the fields and streams of the Virginia countryside, often arriving home well after the setting of the sun with a line full of fish or sack full of rabbits replacing his neglected schoolbooks. Seeking to mediate the damage that might be done by their younger son's academic disinterest, John and Catherine soon hired a full-time tutor to augment their children's education.

"He was not very fond of work or walking," remembered his youngest brother, Malvern, "but from his youth he seemed to have been a natural-born fisherman, huntsman, horseman, and 'crack' shot. He could catch fish when no one else could. While only a boy he had more dogs and horses, could ride better, hunted more, could find and kill more game than anyone else, even more than men of greater experience. Any kind of danger or adventure was his delight, and he was an inveterate lover of all the out-of-doors."[1] For the man that would become Texas Jack, there could be no better education.

Dime novels mythologizing Jack's life often have him setting off as a young man, heading out into the world bound by the machinations of fate for Texas. Ned Buntline's stories said that Jack "originally evinced a disposition for the sea," and that "as a sailor he visited Australia, South America, the West Indies, etc., and was finally wrecked upon the coast of Texas." Prentiss Ingraham wrote that Jack set off for the Lone Star State alone at the age of fourteen, his personal property consisting of but "ninety dollars, a good horse, saddle, bridle, halter, a rifle worn at his back with a strap, a Colt's revolver and hunting knife in his belt . . . and a pair of saddle-bags to contain his stock of wearing apparel."[2]

Buntline and Ingraham were friends of Omohundro and may have heard stories of adventures in Texas from him, but documentation placing Jack in the land of his future moniker before the Civil War does not exist. In his exhaustive chronicle of the Omohundro family, Jack's brother Malvern fails to mention any childhood treks to cattle country. Yet the question remains because of comments made by Jack himself, who once began a written piece by mentioning that, after the Civil War, "I picked myself up, and lit out with all speed *back* toward the 'Lone Star' State."[3]

As Jack continued to shirk his studies for the sake of tracking deer through the Virginia woods, his older brother Orville enrolled at the Norwood Military Institute, where he must have grown acutely aware of the rising tensions among his fellow cadets. These tensions came to a boil when federal troops fired on Fort Sumter on April 12, 1861. Too young for regular service, both Omohundro brothers were rejected when they immediately volunteered. Orville left school to join a branch of the Confederate Army in Southwest Virginia, where officers not familiar with his family overlooked his age. Jack likewise refused to accept rejection in his determination to serve his state.

For these two young men, the question of slavery was an existential one. They shared their father's fears that the loss of his slaves would mean the loss of his farm, his home, his livelihood—fears that would prove well-founded. Rejected twice as a regular soldier, Jack volunteered as "headquarters courier" for Major General John Buchanan Floyd, the man whose decisions as Secretary of War under President James Buchanan and subsequent defection to the Confederacy brought accusations of outright treachery.[4] Ulysses S. Grant would write that, "Floyd, the Secretary of War, scattered the army so that much of it could be captured when hostilities should commence, and distributed the cannon and small arms from Northern arsenals throughout the South so as to be on hand when treason wanted them."[5]

Jack Omohundro carried Floyd's recommendation with him after the general was dispatched to the Western Theater of the war. The young Virginian offered his services as a scout to James Ewell Brown Stuart, the Confederate general in command of the 1st Virginia Cavalry Corps in the Army of Northern Virginia. Orville Omohundro had joined Stuart's Corps the moment he turned eighteen, rising to the rank of second lieutenant by the time Jack enlisted as a private in Company G of the Fifth Regiment Virginia Cavalry on February 15, 1864. Here the younger Omohundro quickly brought attention to himself through his horsemanship and scouting skills, proving himself to be both shrewd and trustworthy.

Receiving favorable reports on Jack's service initially from General Lunsford Lomax and later, from General Fitzhugh Lee, Major General James Ewell Brown Stuart, known as "Jeb" to his friends and soldiers, began using Omohundro as a courier, entrusting Jack to carry battle plans and dispatches for urgent delivery to various commanders. Jack grew to respect the cavalier Stuart, who often wore a red velvet–lined cape and yellow sash in the saddle, ostrich plume in his hat brim blowing in the breeze. This dashing image would leave a lasting impression on the teenage Omohundro, who would occasionally adopt the ostrich plume in the wide-brimmed hats he wore onstage with Buffalo Bill.

Jack's youth caused him to stand out among the scouts of Jeb Stuart's Cavalry, who soon branded him the "boy scout." A title given out of derision, Jack would come to wear it with pride, eventually earning widespread recognition as "the Boy Scout of the Confederacy."[6] Jeb Stuart must have seen utility in his scout's youth, often sending him on reconnaissance missions behind enemy lines. Jack would enter Union encampments disguised as a peddler, selling bits of chicken or ladles of soup to Union soldiers as he took careful note of enemy numbers and camp positions. *Uncle Remus* writer Joel Chandler Harris included Omohundro as a character in his Civil War spy story, *On the Wing of Occasions*. He describes Jack disguised, under cover, and behind enemy lines:

> *He wore brogans of undressed leather, his copper colored breeches were short enough to show his woolen socks, and, as the day was warm, he carried his jeans coat on his arm, which enabled all who glanced at the droll figure to see that he had but one suspender, and that made of twine. His wool hat had seen service so long that it was as limber as a dish-rag. He was driving a rugged-looking mule to a small cart which contained fresh vegetables, a basket of eggs, and a few chickens. He was chewing a straw, and his face wore a most woebegone expression. He walked with a slight limp, and this circumstance, simple as it was, preserved the figure from exaggeration. You knew at once that here was a droll specimen of the poor white common to all parts of our common country, as familiar to Maryland, Virginia, and Pennsylvania as it is to Georgia and Florida, or to Maine or Vermont.*[7]

Jack remained with Jeb Stuart's Virginia Cavalry throughout the summer of 1864. He was with them that May during the Wilderness Campaign and at the Battle of Yellow Tavern, where he carried a final scouting dispatch from General Lomax to General Stuart. Arriving on horseback, Omohundro brought news from Lomax that his troops were in danger of being overrun, along with an urgent request for Stuart's assistance. Thanking his scout for his courageous ride through enemy fire to bring the dispatch, Stuart wheeled his force about to launch a countercharge that would successfully push the Union troops back from their hilltop position. Stuart was on horseback, firing his twin pistols at retreating Union soldiers, when he was struck in the left side by a .44 caliber revolver shot. He died the next day. His widow, Flora, daughter of Union general and "Father of the US Cavalry" Phillip St. George Cooke, famously wore black for the rest of her life.

Jack was at Cold Harbor in early June, where more than twelve thousand Union troops were killed or wounded in a hopeless assault against fortified Confederate soldiers in one of Robert E. Lee's final victories of the war. On June 11 and 12, 1864, he fought in the Civil War's bloodiest all-cavalry battle, the Battle of Trevilian Station. Here, Union cavalry under Major General Philip Sheridan attempted to destroy major sections of the Virginia Central Railway but were fought off by Confederate cavalry under Major General Wade Hampton.

In his role as a scout, Omohundro passed word of Sheridan's movements to Hampton, and, on the morning of June 8, the general determined that his scout's information was good, correctly surmising that the Union planned to attack railroad junctions at both Charlottesville and Gordonsville. Hampton's troops and Omohundro, under the command of Fitzhugh Lee, were able to arrive at both points before the Union cavalry. In the early dawn hours of June 11, Hampton woke to bugles sounding the attack of opposing Union forces. When one of his men asked, "General, what do you propose to do today, if I may inquire?" Hampton replied, "I propose to fight!"[8]

During the day's fight, Union brigadier general George Armstrong Custer managed to take control of Hampton's supply train for a short time before being completely surrounded in what historian Eric J. Wittenberg describes as "Custer's First Last Stand."[9] Believing his command overrun, Custer tore the battle standard from its staff after his flag-bearer was wounded and stuffed it into his coat pocket, not willing to surrender it to the Confederate troops that now surrounded him. Hearing gunfire from Custer's direction, Sheridan turned his troops to charge the Confederates, rescuing Custer only after his 5th Michigan Cavalry was devastated by the loss of fully half of its men. When Sheridan reached Custer, he asked if his unit's colors were lost. Custer pulled the flag from its hiding place in his coat pocket and offered it to his commanding officer, exclaiming, "Not by a damned sight!"[10]

During the second day of fighting at Trevilian Station, Jack suffered a combat wound while taking fire from withdrawing troops as Confederate forces mounted a strong counterattack on the Union's right flank. He was shot through the left thigh by a musket ball and admitted to the Confederate States General Hospital at Charlottesville on June 20 to recuperate before returning to active duty.[11] During his convalescence, Omohundro received leave to return to his father's plantation, Pleasure Hill. He had been away since he became a headquarters courier, and newspapers later described his return to the family home:

Soon after the commencement of the war he enlisted in the Confederate Cavalry, and in course of time reached his old home, having obtained leave of absence to visit it. From a stripling boy he had developed into a powerful man, and his adventures in reaching his home were romantic in the extreme; in fact, his whole life has been replete with such incidents as dime novel writers love to elaborate and dish up in sensational form.

His family, who had not heard from him since he had left home, were engaged in festivities in the old homestead, and the darkies were flitting about in their gayest attire when a man wearing the much dreaded gray uniform appeared, causing consternation among the colored folks, who supposed him the advance guard of some awful visitation. The effect of the sudden advent of a Confederate soldier fully equipped where naught but merry-making was in progress can be easily imagined. All were speechless at the apparition—and it was only when his voice broke the silence with, "Well, anybody here know me?" that harmony was restored, and the festivities gained greater zest from the return of the prodigal son.

He subsequently made his way back to the Confederate lines and became one of the South's most reliable scouts. Like all who have figured in this capacity, his experience contained much of interest, but he was very reticent and could seldom be induced to talk about himself.[12]

Returning to the battlefields of rural Virginia by late summer, Jack fought alongside his brother Orville at the Third Battle of Winchester, considered by some historians to be the most important conflict in the Shenandoah Valley during the war. During an attack on the Confederate army's right flank, Orville took a ball to the ankle, his third and final wound of the war. The battle proved devastating for the Confederacy, with General Robert E. Rhodes killed and generals Fitzhugh Lee, William Terry, and Archibald Godwin injured. Among the Confederate dead of the battle was Colonel George Smith Patton Sr., whose grandson and namesake would follow him into military service and achieve great fame in World War II.

Because of Orville's injuries, Jack Omohundro was for the first time in the war without the company of his brother for the humiliating defeat of the Confederate cavalry at the October 9 Battle of Tom's Brook, where the Confederates retreated with such speed that locals referred to the battle as "The Woodstock Races." Less than two weeks later, the 5th Cavalry and Jack Omohundro were involved in the Battle of Cedar Creek. Confederate general Jubal Early launched a surprise attack against the encamped army of Union general Phil Sheridan. Early success turned into disaster when Sheridan rallied his troops for a counterattack, routing Early's forces. The Confederate Army would never again threaten Washington, DC. The Union victory, just weeks from the 1864 presidential contest, assured Abraham Lincoln's reelection.

In November of 1864, Jack received a rare letter from his brother Orville, recuperating from his wounds at the family home. The letter brought grave news, informing Jack that his mother Catherine Salome Baker Omohundro had died following a brief respiratory illness, likely tuberculosis. She was only forty years old, and her death came as a devastating shock to her son, then just eighteen years old. He rushed home to be with his family as they buried their beloved matriarch. One likely explanation for the discrepancy in Jack's middle name is that after his mother's death, Jack used her maiden name Baker at the expense of the given Burwell, as a token of his affection for his late mother.

Jack remained with Lomax's Brigade as a scout for the remainder of the war, seeing action at Dinwiddie Court House and Five Forks before again being assigned as a scout under Fitzhugh Lee for the duration of the Appomattox Campaign. On April 9, 1865, Jack cut through Union lines rather than waiting near the home of Wilmer McLean while Robert E. Lee surrendered his Army of Northern Virginia to Ulysses S. Grant, who had scored a decisive victory with the help of generals Sheridan and Custer. As Lee left the house and rode away, Union soldiers cheered, only to be silenced by Grant, who told them, "These Confederates are now our countrymen, and we will not exult in their downfall."[13]

Years later, Jack's sister Elizabeth told her nephew that a few days after Lee's surrender, "about the middle of April 1865, Jack came riding up to the house. He looked tired and was hungry. He told me Lee had surrendered at Appomattox. I told him to get down off the horse and tie it. Then I fed him and took all his clothes and burned them. I loaned him some of my husband's clothes. Jack told me he was going home to see his other folks and then would probably go to Texas because there was little to be done in Virginia after the war ended."[14]

Like many soldiers, Jack Omohundro was uneasy speaking of his wartime exploits after the end of the war. His words on deer and elk hunting with English aristocrats, early explorations of Yellowstone Park, tracking buffalo alongside Pawnee warriors, and cowboy adventures in Texas would soon fill column space in newspapers and magazines. On the subject of the Civil War, on the other hand, the former Confederate remained forever quiet.

The battlegrounds of the Virginia wilderness would not be the last time he interacted with Union soldiers, however, including generals Sheridan and Custer. The war that had ended slavery, and with it the fortunes of the Omohundro plantation on Virginia's Cunningham Creek, would soon send Jack west, to Texas.

Chapter Three

Texas Jack

The Civil War began eighty-five miles northeast of Jack's Pleasure Hill home at Bull Run and ended fifty-five miles to the southwest at Appomattox Court House.

Allowed to keep his horse to assist with the coming season's harvest, Jack rode home to his father's plantation, likely knowing that his days of dodging enemy fire while riding reports between generals would not simply give way to afternoons balancing the books in the counting-house of the Pleasure Hill plantation. The war, fought largely on Virginia farmland, spelled the end of Virginia's plantation farms like the one owned by John B. Omohundro. The emancipation of his slaves dealt a major blow to the senior Omohundro's operations, one that his youngest son Malvern wrote would ultimately leave him "utterly unable to adapt himself to the new condition of things, and as [Pleasure Hill] had to be abandoned his large family of boys and girls scattered, to seek what fortune had in store."[1] Having come into contact with fellow Confederate soldiers from Texas during the war and hearing of fortunes to be made working the herds of Texas cattle bound for Eastern markets, Jack determined to set off to Texas to pursue life as a cowboy.

Mere months separated from his life as a soldier, Jack boarded a ship in New Orleans bound for Galveston, but it was badly damaged in stormy seas, leaving Jack shipwrecked on the west coast of Florida. "The sailor boys struck up the coast to Pensacola, and were soon on deck again, back to the Crescent City," wrote Jack, "but as I had weakened considerably in regard to 'a life on the ocean wave,' hearing there was good hunting in the country, and as I had never starved at that business, it being just my long suit, I concluded to camp on the Peninsula, and struck up country to the northwest portion."[2] Hunting as a profession was an employment Jack would continue to fall back on throughout his life, sometimes through necessity, as was the case in Florida, but often simply because he enjoyed the time spent outdoors and the companionship on the trail of a few good friends.

During his time on Florida's Gulf Coast, Omohundro subsidized his hunting by working as a schoolteacher, an occupational irony not wasted on Jack, a rebellious student throughout his youth. Writing for the *Spirit of the Times* in 1877, Jack recalled his days as a schoolmaster:

Once upon a time, when I was out in the interior of Florida, circumstances obliged me to seek the position of school teacher. The schoolmarm was about to retire, and I was anxious to take her place. The young idea is taught how to shoot out there promiscuously, and a he is as good as a she in teaching it. The schoolmarm was said to be of great erudition, and pronounced likely to "smash" any man at larnin'. [This is a quote from the 1728 poem "Spring" by James Thomson.]

I addressed her a letter, in consequence, in which I used the biggest words I could think of. I styled her "honored madam" and beat heavy on "construction," "promiscuous," "retard," the "affinities," and all the ten syllables in general. The letter was profoundly respectful.

The next day I was mobbed. The schoolmarm could not read my letter. The big words stuck in the throats of her admirers, and it was with difficulty I persuaded them I meant no harm. They apologized, and I was accepted as teacher.

The first day I told the little boys and girls the world was round, and the sun stood still to warm it. The children were amazed. In the evening in came the father of a promising young family, the majority of which flourished amongst my pupils.

"What do you mean by tellin' a lot of damned lies to my youngsters?" says he.

"What do you mean?" cried I.

"Why, you idiot, don't you be a tellin' of 'em that the sun sticks stock still, and this 'ere earth goes round him? That's a lie, and you

know it. Don't I see the sun a-gettin' up every blessed morning in one place, and a-going to bed in t'other, and you idiot you, you keep on a tellin' them 'ere youngsters it sits there all day long, contrary to evidence. You go home, young man. You are dangerous, and'll be a-tellin' of 'em I ain't their own father next, you will. Go home, young man."

With this, the irate pater familias bounced out of the room, sweeping his offspring before him like ducklings in a whirlwind.[3]

Eventually tiring of both the defense of Copernican heliocentrism and life as a schoolmaster, Omohundro set off again for Texas, this time sticking to a land-bound route to avoid further maritime disaster. His months of hunting, living, and teaching in Florida now behind him, Omohundro and his horse stepped from the fertile Arkansas soil and into the waters of the Red River, emerging onto the western riverbank and linking forever the man with the place he now stood. Jack Omohundro was in Texas.

Being a young man, as Omohundro was when he arrived in Texas, was not necessarily a detriment when faced with the challenges of working stock. Jack would later write that "youth and size will be no disadvantage for his start in, as certain lines of the business are peculiarly adapted to the light young horsemen."[4]

Jack's first job in Texas was not as a trail boss or ranch foreman, but as a cook at Sam Allen's Ranch near Galveston.[5] Started just after the Texas Revolution, by the time Omohundro arrived at the ranch after the Civil War, Samuel W. Allen and his partners had gone from rounding up a few stray longhorns to controlling the state's largest cattle operation. The Galveston, Houston, and Henderson railroad had been built crossing Allen's land in the 1850s, and multiple other rail lines followed suit, giving Allen better access to transportation than any other ranch in the state. A private railway station called "El Buey" was eventually added and docks were built along Buffalo Bayou, the river that flowed slowly through Allen's property in Harris County near present-day Houston and emptied into Galveston Bay. Allen's agreement with the Morgan Lines, the first steamship company in Texas, provided him exclusive shipping rights to supply cattle to both New Orleans and Cuba.

Quickly leaving behind the kitchens and mess wagons of Sam Allen's ranch and finding work as a ranch hand, Jack initially assisted more experienced men with their day-to-day tasks, but over time gained the confidence of his employer, taking on additional responsibilities. His ease on horseback and natural athleticism meant quick advance, and, as the other men taught him how to make and throw a lasso properly, birth a calf, and brand a steer, he gained their respect. The same skills that had so impressed his commanding officers on Virginia battlefields now proved to the trail bosses of Texas that Jack Omohundro was intelligent and industrious. His penchant for colloquialism and storytelling made him an easy companion, and he was noted for his optimism and happiness, earning the nickname Happy Jack among the other cowboys.

As Jack rose to prominence within the ranks of his fellow cowboys, he came to the attention of a ranch owner named John Taylor, whose operation was remembered by Malvern Omohundro as being "the largest in Texas." Taylor's Bexar County ranch had grown from an initial grant of 1,476 acres in 1845 to incorporate over 18,000 acres across seven counties.[6] Across Taylor's vast holdings, Jack was responsible for assisting with and eventually managing the large numbers of horses that Taylor trained for stock work and sold to cattle ranchers across Texas. Here Jack's natural abilities as a horseman, combined with his experience in Stuart's cavalry, provided a distinct advantage, both in managing the animals themselves as well as in protecting them from inevitable trouble.

Horse theft and cattle rustling were both widespread problems across the West, where a horse and a cow were often the most valuable pieces of property for miles. Mexican rustlers are said to have stolen an estimated 145,298 Texan cattle from 1859 through 1872, along with an unknown number of horses.[7] Even with those numbers, Mexican rustlers were no match for the depredations of white thieves. Often cowboys themselves, these men adopted the practice of branding strays, stealing unbranded calves, and swimming large herds of "wet stock" stolen from Mexican ranchers across the Rio Grande and up the Chisholm Trail to Kansas, significantly impacting every rancher and cowboy in the West. While more likely to steal horses and rustle cattle south of the Mexican border, Comanche (Nʉmʉnʉʉ) warriors riding from the Comancheria were not averse to occasionally adding Texan cattle and horses to their numbers. One of Omohundro's principal responsibilities was protecting Mr. Taylor's horses and cattle from just such incursions.

The *Historical and Biographical Record of the Cattle Industry and the Cattlemen of Texas and Adjacent Territory* notes that "we could fill a large-sized book with but a summary of the fights between cattlemen and redskin cattle thieves, but space forbids. A few lines in reference to 'Texas Jack,' the great Indian fighter, who rescued thousands of cattle, may not, however, be out of place." The *Record* goes on to report that Jack was stationed at a part of Taylor's vast holdings near the Texas Panhandle, near the border of Indian Territory, when "a large body of redskins came down upon him and his partner, with whoop and weapons, intent upon capturing the horses under Jack's charge."[8]

While his partner drove the horses away from the approaching Comanche, Jack dismounted his horse and took careful aim before pouring fire into the oncoming warriors. Quickly realizing that this man was unlike the majority of cowboys they accosted, and would not retreat and leave them to pick through his horses, cattle, and supplies, the band retreated.[9] Grateful for the stalwart defense of his property, Taylor rewarded his cowboy, who turned the reward into an interest in a herd of cattle to drive north to Abilene.

Texas cattle at the time were worth only four dollars a head, a tenth of the price they might fetch in New York or Washington, DC. The low cost of Texas beef meant plenty of work for cattlemen like Jack Omohundro rushing their herds north to be loaded onto trains and sold to hungry postwar cities back East. Joseph G. McCoy—who by dint of his reputation for reliability in his business ventures inspired the phrase "the Real McCoy"—in 1867 established a hotel, office, and large stockyard just north of the small railroad village of Abilene on the Kansas Pacific Railway. The most prominent cattle trail out of Texas and toward McCoy's stockyard followed the route established years earlier by its namesake, a Cherokee (DhBƟⱷT) fur trader named Jesse Chisholm. During the Civil War, Chisholm used his trail to trade with the Cherokee and to supply beef to the Confederate Army. By the late 1870s, as many as five thousand cowboys a day were receiving their payouts for pushing huge herds of longhorn north along the trail.

Cowboys eagerly spent the money they earned on these cattle drives drinking and gambling in the many saloons that sprang up to cater to the wealth now passing through the cowtowns. As money flooded the streets, gamblers and outlaws followed. Their presence necessitated strong lawmen like Wild Bill Hickok in Abilene and Hays City, and later Wyatt Earp and Bat Masterson in Dodge City. Though McCoy had once bragged that he might be able to handle 200,000 head of cattle north in a decade, within the first four years, his stockyard saw a staggering two million animals reach Abilene.

Most of the Chisholm Trail wound not through Texas proper, but through Indian country in what would become Oklahoma. President of the Old Trail Drivers Association, George W. Saunders, said that "The famed Chisholm Trail, about which more has been written than any other Southwestern Trail, cannot be traced in Texas for the reason that it never existed in this State."[10] Starting west of San Antonio, the trail was a wide delta of cattlemen ranging east toward Houston and Galveston Bay. They drove their herds north through Austin and Waco toward the mouth of the Salt Creek at Red River Station, where they passed into Indian Territory on their way to the rail hubs of Kansas.

The cowboys themselves were made up not only of "manor-born" young men like J. B. Omohundro, but also Mexican vaqueros, mixed-race Native Americans, and increasingly large numbers of former slaves seeking gainful employment far from the Reconstruction-era South. "As the rebellious kid of old times filled a handkerchief (always a handkerchief, I believe), with his all, and followed the trail of his idol Columbus, and became a sailor bold," wrote Texas Jack, "the more ambitious and adventurous youngster of later days freezes onto a double-barreled pistol, and steers for the bald prairie to seek fortune and experience. If he don't get his system full, it's only because the young man weakens, takes a back seat, or fails to become a Texas cow-boy."[11]

Life on the cattle trail was a hard one, filled with toil, trail dust, tedium, and terror. Weeks of slowly guiding herds toward their destination could be interrupted by bouts of extreme weather. The cow-boys, who normally spent nights calming the cattle by riding in circles around the herd while singing improvised verses to soothe the fears of the restless bovines, often found their voices unable to penetrate the fury and thunder of storms rushing across the plains. "On nights when old 'Prob.' [Old Probabilities was the nickname given to forecaster Cleveland Abbe by Mark Twain. Over time the nickname became slang for any bad weather] goes on a spree, leaves the bung out of his water barrel above, prowls around with his flash box, raising a breeze, whispering in tones of thunder, and the cow-boy's voice, like the rest of the outfit, is drowned out," warned Jack, "steer clear, and prepare for action. If them quadrupeds don't go insane, turn tail to the storm, and strike out for civil and religious liberty, then I don't know what *strike out* means. Ordinarily, so clumsy and stupid-looking, a thousand beef steers can rise like a flock of quail on the roof of an exploding powder mill, and will scud away like a tumbleweed before a high wind, with a noise like a receding earthquake. Then comes fun and frolic for the boys!"[12]

The fun and frolic came in the form of three thousand nervous steers, frightened by sounding thunder and flashing lightning, tearing across a plain full of "hog wallows, prairie dog, wolf, and badger holes, ravines and precipices." Adding to these dangers was the necessity of crossing streams and rivers invariably swollen by rains during driving season. "When cattle strike swimming water they generally try to turn back, which eventuates in their 'milling,' that is, swimming in a circle, which if allowed to continue, would result in the drowning of many," explained Jack. "There the daring herder must leave his pony, doff his toggs, scramble over their backs and horns to scatter them, and with whoops and yells, splashing, dashing, and didoes [mischievous tricks or deeds] in the water, scare them to the opposite bank. This is not always done in a moment, for a steer is no fool of a swimmer; I have seen one hold his own for six hours in the Gulf after having jumped overboard. As some of the streams are very rapid, and a quarter to half a mile wide, considerable drifting is done."

Even with the cattle now safely moved across the raging stream, "the naked herder has plenty of amusement in the hot sun, fighting green head flies and mosquitoes, and peeping around for Indians, until the rest of the lay-out is put over—not an easy job. A temporary boat has to be made of the wagon box, by tacking the canvas cover over the bottom, with which the ammunition and grub is ferried across, the running gear and ponies swam over after."

The occasional Comanche fight, trouble with horse thieves and cattle rustlers, the search for water for cattle to drink between streams, mixing with other herds, and subsequently ensuring no loss of cattle in the process were all part of the routine of the cattle drive. Forced to use dried buffalo chips as a poor fuel source to provide some meager warmth on cold nights, the cowboys were also invariably faced with prairie fires as they crossed the vast plains of Indian Territory. The rigors of trail life proved too much for many would-be cowboys, with a majority giving up the profession as soon as they reached trail's end and their first payout. And yet for others, the money proved irresistible. "It would fill a book to give a detailed account of a single trip," wrote Jack, "and it is no wonder the boys are hilarious when it ends, and, like the old toper [drunkard], 'swears no more for me,' only to return and go through the mill again."

Bustling rail hubs in Kansas were far from the only destination for the vast cattle herds. Jack drove beef to Missouri, Nebraska, Colorado, Montana, Idaho, Nevada, and California on trips varying from five hundred to two thousand miles, with as many as six months at a time spent with a watchful eye on outward-bound cattle trains. One of these trips saw Jack at the head of three thousand head of cattle, bound east across Arkansas to a meat-hungry and drought-stricken postwar Tennessee. The route from Texas to Tennessee passed through Indian country, and Omohundro and his associates were under no false impressions of safety. During one attack, Choctaw (Chahta) warriors killed seven of the cowboys in Jack's employ.

Starving Tennesseans in town after town watched as Omohundro's herd approached, bringing with it the promise of meat. These citizens were grateful, and soon whispers of the procession reached towns before the cowboys could. Jack's outfit neared one of these towns, and local officials met the cowboys, eager to buy a share of the crew's beef. One man asked who was in charge of the operation.

"Jack," answered the nearest cowboy, pointing to the tall man on horseback.

"Where you from, Jack?" asked the man.

"We're in from Texas," replied Jack, nodding to the herd.

"Well, boys," the man shouted to the crowd, which had by now assembled to inspect the cattle, "here's Texas Jack, who has saved us!" As the appreciative crowd cheered, men walked up to shake the hand of Texas Jack, the cowboy bringing their starving families meat from Texas. The other cowboys began referring to Omohundro as "Texas Jack" as they reached towns along their journey, and the name remained with him for the rest of his life.

Years after Texas Jack's death, a young man showed up at the Omohundro home in Virginia. The young man told the family that on a cattle drive into Kansas in the 1860s, Jack chanced upon a group of ransacked wagons with an escort of soldiers dead and scalped nearby. Inspection of the wagons revealed dead settlers who had come with this military escort bound west across the plains. Following the tracks of horses leading away, Jack came upon a group of Comanche warriors. Getting the drop on the Comanche, Jack rescued a boy and two unrelated girls who had been taken captive by the warriors.

Omohundro escorted the children to safety on the backs of the Comanche ponies he took with him, and according to the young man's account, took the children to a Fort Worth orphanage where he sold the ponies and generously offered to fund their education with the proceeds. The young boy's family was dead and his name unknown, and for the rest of his life, he called himself "Texas Jack Jr."

The younger Jack would later take up his benefactor's mantle as an actor and showman. He starred as Frederick Russell Burnham, American chief of scouts, in an early British film called *Major Wilson's Last Stand*, which depicted battles between the British South Africa Company and native Ndebele warriors in present-day Zimbabwe.

Having made his mark on cinema, he started "Texas Jack's Wild West Show & Circus." As part of a poem he included in his own show's program, Texas Jack Jr. wrote:

I was rescued from the Indians
By a brave and noble man,
Who trailed the thieving Indians,
And fought them hand to hand;
He was noted for his bravery
While on an enemy's track;
He has a noble history
And his name is Texas Jack.

The show traveled the world and was playing in Ladysmith, South Africa, in 1902, where a young man approached Texas Jack Jr. to ask him three questions. Was he really from Texas? Was he related to the famous Texas Jack Omohundro? Were there any jobs wrangling horses or setting up tents for his shows? Demonstrating his namesake's keen eye for showmanship, Jack Jr. asked the young man if he could put together a rope trick act. The young man said he believed he could. He accepted a lasso and began twirling it overhead. Texas Jack Jr. hired him on the spot, suggesting the young performer adopt the nickname "The Cherokee Kid" in homage to his Native American heritage. Performing the same lasso act that Texas Jack Omohundro had introduced to the world thirty years earlier, this was the first job in show business for a young Will Rogers.

At the end of many of his cattle drives, the senior Texas Jack found himself in the cowtowns of Kansas. Charles and George Marlow, the brothers whose autobiography *Life of the Marlows* inspired the John Wayne movie, *The Sons of Katie Elder*, recorded that, "Texas Jack was marshal [in Wichita] for a time, and it was not at all infrequent for it to be necessary for him to kill a man in the discharge of his duty. He got quite a wide-spread reputation in this way, and started a good-sized private burying ground of his own."[13] Jack didn't record in any of his surviving letters or newspaper stories a career as a lawman, if he was so employed. It is more likely that he was occasionally hired by lawmen who had heard of his marksmanship, tracking skills, and ability as a horseman to assist in returning stolen horses and apprehending thieves. The lawman most likely to have enlisted Jack's assistance was the most famous peace officer west of the Mississippi River, James Butler Hickok.

On one of his sojourns through Kansas at the end of a cattle drive, Omohundro found himself near Fort Hays, where he met and befriended Moses Embree Milner, better known as "California Joe." A scout in the Mexican-American War, Joe had later been kidnapped by and subsequently escaped from a band of Utes (núuchi-u). Returning home, Joe married a thirteen-year-old beauty and convinced her to honeymoon some two thousand miles away in California, where he could prospect for gold. Milner fathered four children with her before deciding that domesticity was perhaps not a lifestyle he was well suited for and heading for Kansas.

Joe traveled throughout the West, prospecting in Montana and Idaho, killing men in Texas (a dispute over cards), Montana (for jumping Joe's claim), and Virginia (for kicking his dog). In 1867 Joe was hired as chief scout for Lieutenant Colonel George Armstrong Custer on an expedition with General Winfield Scott Hancock—known to his troops as "Hancock the Superb." Custer was instantly taken with Joe, promoting to chief of scouts this funny and talkative man who smoked his briar pipe atop the back of his mule as he rode in line with the 7th Cavalry's fine horses.

California Joe was eventually demoted from chief scout to common scout after one particular losing battle with a whiskey bottle. He fell in with another scout he would quickly befriend, James "Wild Bill" Hickok. Milner would later describe Jack Omohundro as "a pleasant man who made friends easily, a man with a smile and a joke for all, but very dangerous when his anger is aroused. During those days at Fort Hays [we] became warm friends."[14] One interviewer recounted a story from Jack's cowboy days that attests to California Joe's assessment of Omohundro:

On one occasion, some five years ago, in Texas, a man attempted to bully him in a bar-room, and bandied words with him insultingly. Jack took no notice of his jibes at the time, and people thought the matter had "blown over." About seven months afterwards the two met again in another bar-room in another State. Jack thereupon stepped up to the man who had goaded him nearly a year before, and asked him to take a drink. The man complied; as they were drinking, Jack said in his characteristic way to the other: "See here, the last time we met you blew your tongue out on me. Now, I give you fair notice I am going to blow out something besides cheek. So take care of yourself, d—n you," and thus putting his adversary on guard, and giving him time to prepare for his defense, Jack drew his revolver and fired at his insulter, who escaped with his life this time. But "Texas Jack" ultimately wiped out the insult in the life-blood of the man who uttered it, in "a fair fight" two years afterwards in the Indian Territory.

The same spirit differently applied, led Texas Jack to befriend, several times at the hazard of his life, an Indian who had once done him some slight service, and to make "Texas Jack" your friend once is to make a friend forever.[15]

California Joe wasted no time introducing his young cowboy to Wild Bill, then acting sheriff of Ellis County. Hickok seems to have taken an immediate liking to the younger man, following the example of some of Jack's cowboy friends by calling him "Happy Jack," because of Omohundro's good nature and carefree attitude.[16] With a shared fondness for drinking and playing cards, the pair began a friendship over whiskey and poker that would last until Hickok's death. As they shared whiskey bottles, laughed over hands of cards, and perhaps pursued horse thieves together, Hickok told Jack about the money to be made for hunters and scouts out of frontier forts in Nebraska and Wyoming. He advised Omohundro to seek out Bill Cody, whom Hickok had known since their time in the employ of Russell, Majors & Waddell in Leavenworth. Cody had earned a reputation, a living, and his famous sobriquet hunting buffalo to supply meat for railroad workers in Kansas, and later, as a scout for the army at Fort McPherson. The twin prospects of hunting and scouting must have appealed to Jack, who in 1869 took the opportunity to drive a herd of government cattle north to Nebraska.

Trailing four thousand cattle from Texas to North Platte, Nebraska, Jack saw success selling his steers to local ranchers. Local rancher M. C. Keith bought one thousand two- to six-year-old cattle for his Pawnee Springs ranch, and his partner Guy Barton purchased another thousand for their joint venture. Mahlon Brown purchased five hundred, and the rest were sold off to various smaller outfits in the Platte Valley. When Jack paid his men, they mounted up and once again headed back to Texas, but this time without Jack Omohundro.

This time, Texas Jack was staying in Nebraska.[17]

CHAPTER FOUR

Holding Down the Fort

FORT MCPHERSON STOOD AT A FORDING POINT OF THE NORTH PLATTE River on the Oregon Trail just southeast of the city of North Platte, Nebraska. Previously known as Cantonment McKean, in 1866 it was renamed for fallen Union general James B. McPherson. The fort guarded the confluence of the North and South Platte rivers, replacing Charles McDonald's ranch at the mouth of the Cottonwood Canyon near a natural spring that had once supplied freshwater to the Plains Indians as they crossed the prairie.

Arriving in North Platte in the fall of 1869, Texas Jack first met his future friend and business partner, William Frederick Cody. Cody served as a scout under General Eugene Carr during several encounters with the southern Cheyenne, but was serving as chief herder of Fort McPherson's livestock when the vastly more experienced cowboy arrived with four thousand head of cattle.[1] Though Cody and Omohundro had served on opposite sides of what Jack called "the recent unpleasantness," they immediately bonded over a shared love for horses, gambling, whiskey, and hunting. Within weeks, the two were inseparable, Jack sharing meals with Cody and his wife at their home and helping his new friend in the management of government stock. The pair were soon partnering together on scouts, with Omohundro happy to hunt with his friend to provide meat for the troops they were escorting. Initially, Omohundro found work in Nebraska keeping bar at a local saloon owned by Cody's friend and local rancher, Lew Baker. As he had in Florida, Jack found additional work as a schoolteacher, supplementing his salary by hunting to supply the fort with meat and returning wayward cattle to thankful ranchers.

Malvern Omohundro wrote that on one of his many hunts, Jack was "surprised by the appearance of sixty hostile Indians. Instead of running for the fort like most men would have done, alone, he met the Indians, single handed, and with his repeating rifle he turned loose on them. Four fell dead, many wounded. The Indians retreated carrying the wounded and leaving the dead. Jack took the scalps of these four into the fort. Jack and his horse were both slightly wounded by the arrows that fell thick and fast around them but they both soon recovered."[2]

The threat of attack by the various native tribes that vied for control of the prime hunting ground of Kansas and Nebraska was ever present for the scouts, soldiers, and hunters of the American frontier. Roving bands of Sioux (Očhéthi Šakówiŋ) and Cheyenne (Tsêhéstáno) Dog Soldiers roamed the northern part of Nebraska, and Pawnee used much of the area as their hunting ground. In 1862 President Lincoln had signed the Homestead Act, offering 160 acres for free to any citizen who had "never taken up arms" against the government and was willing to improve the land. Tribes who had long watched the slow encroachment of white settlers onto their lands now retaliated with strikes along the Oregon Trail. The Battle of Blue Water, the massacres at the Eubanks Homestead, Plum Creek, and Kiowa Ranch Station, and skirmishes between soldiers and members of the Sioux, Cheyenne, and Arapaho (Hinono'eino) tribes at Mud Springs and Rush Creek did little to ensure the long-term safety of white settlers on the plains. The job of scout at Fort McPherson carried with it the necessity of also being an "Indian-fighter."

On another hunting expedition, a large band of warriors overtook Jack, who, according to letters he sent home, "began to think maybe his time had come. The fort had even sent out the word that he had been gone for nearly seven days and had been given up for dead." After seven days, Jack feared that he would soon starve and resolved to fight for his life. Having trained his horse to lie down on the ground and remain there while he fired his rifle over the animal, Jack "turned loose his murderous fire from over the horse with his repeating rifle . . . and having a nerve of steel, took dead aim and brought down a redskin every fire.

They fell so thick and fast they soon retreated. By this time those that formed the ring in his rear, hearing the shooting, had advanced on him. He pulled his horse around and lay down behind him as before, and as soon as the rear forces were close enough he turned loose on them with the same results as the first. As soon as they had retreated out of sight Jack and his horse got up and went back to the fort without a scratch, killing a buck on his return."The buck was cooked and served that night at dinner, where Bill Cody celebrated, and officers took note of the cowboy who had single-handedly fought off a band of Sioux after a week of starvation.[3]

It was also at Fort McPherson that Jack was introduced to Major Frank North, a native Manhattanite who had come to Nebraska at the age of sixteen to work as a transporter. During one of his many trips between Omaha and Fort Kearny, North came into contact with the Pawnee (Chaticks si Chaticks) and learned their language. He was impressed with Jack's ability to treat and trade with the Pawnee, who were notorious for their well-earned mistrust of white men. Jack, having spent his cattle-driving years trading and interacting with various groups of Comanche (Nʉmʉnʉʉ), Kiowa (Ka'igwu), Sauk (oθaakiiwaki), Fox (Meskwaki), and other tribes, had learned some of their languages and much of their signs. The Pawnee of Nebraska would come to regard Omohundro, as they had Frank North, as an honorary "White Chief," trusting him in their communications with their assigned Indian Agents as well as with the army. More commonly, they called Jack "Whirling Rope" (*ruukiraahak awikiickawarik*) because of his proficiency and dexterity with a lasso, skills he would soon demonstrate on stages throughout the East.

Frank North had parlayed his relationship with the natives into the organization and command of a band of Pawnee scouts, initially as first lieutenant, and later, as captain. Together, North and the Pawnee scouts fought in the Battles of Powder River, Tongue River, and Susannah (later known as Summit) Springs. The latter battle saw the defeat of Tall Bull and subsequent competing claims from Frank North's brother Luther and Bill Cody as to which man had made the fatal shot on the Cheyenne chief and leader of the Dog Soldiers. According to scholar Jeff Broome, it is much more likely that a shot from a soldier named Danny McGrath felled the chief, as he was significantly closer to Tall Bull at the moment he was killed. Other scholars have posited that perhaps Cody killed another Cheyenne riding Tall Bull's famous white horse, mistakenly believing that the warrior he shot was the horse's owner.

While no reports definitively place Texas Jack at the fight at Summit Springs, a newspaper report shortly thereafter details that Texas Jack "was riding his celebrated horse, 'Tall Bull,' when a fierce buffalo bull attacked both rider and horse, badly goring the latter. Texas Jack, his horse, and the buffalo all fell into Beaver River, from which they soon after emerged, and the fight continued, the result of which was the capture of the buffalo, and the probable death of the horse." The report goes on to clarify that "Tall Bull is one of the most celebrated horses in this country, having been captured in a fight from old Tall Bull, a noted Indian chief, who was defeated and killed. The horse is the swiftest and longest-winded animal on the plains, having never yet been beaten in a race, although having had hundreds of contests of speed."[4]

This horse, named after his late owner, was the subject of comment in the writings of Cody, his wife, Louisa, and Luther North. In Cody's account of the battle, he recalls that "the horse this chief was riding was extremely fleet. I determined to capture him if possible, but I was afraid to fire at the rider lest I kill the horse."[5] Cody devotes several pages in his autobiography to recount races won with "Tall Bull," but wrote that he was forced to sell the horse to buy furniture to honor a promise to his wife. His notes say that this sale was to a Lieutenant Mason, but it is possible that either Cody misremembered the sale or that Omohundro somehow convinced Mason to sell him the animal. Another possibility is that Cody, devotedly generous with those closest to him, gave the magnificent animal to his cowboy friend.

Spending time with Frank North, Texas Jack soon became well acquainted with the Pawnee scouts and their tribe. The Pawnee living in closest proximity to Fort McPherson had a reputation for ignoring the fundamental privacy that white settlers took for granted. Though their intentions weren't malicious, the cultural divide could lead to some awkward situations. Cody's wife, Louisa, remembered that "They were the ones who peered through the windows, or who more than once simply stalked into the house, bobbed their heads and grinned, said 'How kola' and proceeded to make a grab for anything eatable in sight."[6]

Mrs. Cody was particularly upset when, having spent a day preparing a meal for an arriving aristocrat and the throng of generals traveling with him, she left her kitchen to greet her husband, his friend Texas Jack, and the other guests at the door before returning to retrieve the feast, only to "open the kitchen door to stand for a moment aghast, then to rush forward in white anger, seize the big coffee pot and slosh the whole contents of it across the room. For where the dinner had been was now only a mass of messy, mussed over dishes! The kitchen was full of Pawnees! And the Pawnees were full of the dinner that had been cooked for royalty!"[7]

That the Pawnee were anywhere near Louisa Cody's kitchen belies the fact that the tribe was an ever-present part of life for the denizens of frontier Nebraska, but that their presence was seldom construed as a threat. Mrs. Cody commented that the "Pawnee rarely frightened me, for they were a friendly, good humored lot as a rule, grinning and foolish and thieving, and it was nothing to run them away."[8] It wasn't the Pawnee but their enemies, the Sioux, that worried the inhabitants of Fort McPherson.

One afternoon, Mrs. Cody recalled being roused from a book by the slamming of her door and the sound of moccasined footsteps in the next room. The frustrated woman, likely worried about the disappearance of another meal, put down her reading and rushed to accost the invading Pawnee. Her shouted commands for the men to get out of her kitchen went unheeded, as the house-crashing Pawnee had been chased in by pursuing Sioux. The quick-thinking Louisa opened a window at the back of the house and sent daughter Orra toward the fort for her father.

The Sioux soon barged into the house, informing Mrs. Cody that they were there to fight the Pawnee. The brief but tense standoff ended when Mrs. Cody heard "two men on horseback approaching. One was Will, my husband. The other was Texas Jack." The Sioux poured back out of the front door and were "faced with the revolvers of Texas Jack and my husband."[9] Buffalo Bill stayed to reprimand the Pawnee for endangering his wife while Omohundro escorted the offending Sioux north and away from the fort. The attempts of the two scouts to separate the rival tribesmen and avoid a confrontation proved ultimately unsuccessful, for according to Louisa, a wounded Pawnee returned to camp later that night after an encounter between his group and the Sioux, desperately asking the soldiers for assistance. When Cody and Omohundro arrived at the scene, having immediately headed toward where the Pawnee had told them the fight occurred, they discovered every member of the Pawnee band dead or wounded and the Sioux having dispersed.

Texas Jack's relationship with the natives was a complicated one. Jack often told friends and later reporters that he considered his Native American ancestry crucial to his success as a scout, cowboy, and frontiersman. Jack was not alone in attributing to native genetics a predisposition to and affinity for nature. Louis Warren points out that "popular beliefs maintained that tracking was the province of dark-skinned people, who were closest to nature."[10] British physician Dr. George Kingsley, one of Texas Jack's hunting companions, remarked that "Jack, being a southern man, thinks it necessary to suppose that he has Indian blood in his veins, a very popular idea in those parts." Kingsley noted that if it was true that Jack's ancestors did indeed descend from America's indigenous population, "he is rather rough on his relatives, for he is deadly on Indians. Indian hunting is, in fact, the real profession of both Jack and Bill, they being retained as trackers, aye, and as fighters too, in the case of horses being run from the neighborhood of the fort; though, from time to time, they are put in charge of a band to see that it does not exceed the limits of its reservation, and to lead it out to the hunt as a shepherd leadeth his flock to the pasture."[11]

Texas Jack and Buffalo Bill were dwellers in a world rife with suspicion and mistrust of misogyny and the mixing of race, especially in concert with the dangerous work of scouting. "The mixed-blood scout—light-skinned, fluent in English and the enemy language, too," Louis Warren tells us, "could as easily be a renegade spy."[12] Regardless of consequence, Jack long maintained that his family and their unique surname were of Powhatan (Wahunsenacawh) descent, the tribe most associated with Jack's home country in Virginia, as well as with the story of Pocahontas (Amonute)—viewed as a heroine to the early settlers of the Old Dominion. Later, friend, fellow actor, and press agent John M.

Burke said that the cowboy often repeated the claim that the Omohundro name came from an Algonquian word meaning "where salt and fresh waters meet."

When asked about the intelligence of the various Native American tribes he had come into contact with, Jack responded that "some tribes are very clever and sharp. All Indians have marked peculiarities, which are interesting. Nearly all of them are great physiognomists, and can determine your character by your face, and this with surprising ease. I inherit this." According to a reporter for the *Spirit of the Times*, Jack backed up this claim with a demonstration. "Texas Jack then told to us each our characters, in so surprisingly truthful a manner, that it seemed supernatural," reported the amazed newspaperman. Noting the man's shock, Jack explained that "[This] is an Indian gift, and a very necessary one to us who have to roam the plains amongst all kinds of dangerous men. Think of the life I've led! I am a link between civilization and the other thing. I have to endure hardships, live amongst renegades and savages, and this is the kind of life my ancestors led for countless generations before me. Do you wonder if I possess, by inheritance and habit, some peculiar gifts indispensable to a man in my position?"[13]

The Fourth Earl of Dunraven, who spent a considerable portion of his time in America hunting with both Omohundro and Cody, posited that "Buffalo Bill and Texas Jack have the same feeling for Indians that the true sportsman has for game, 'they love them, and they slay them.' They admit that in many respects they resemble human beings, but hold that they are badly finished, their faces looking as if they had been chopped out of red-wood blocks with a hatchet, and say that they must never be trusted, friendly or unfriendly, and that they must be shot if they will steal horses."[14]

Texas Jack seems to have accepted the necessity of protecting the advancement of white culture while still sympathizing with the plight of the Native Americans displaced and killed by the machine of that advancement. "Though on the warpath [Omohundro and Cody] would no more hesitate to shoot down an Indian off his Reservation than they would hesitate to throw a stone at a felonious chipmunk," wrote Dr. Kingsley, "they have a sympathy and a tenderness toward them infinitely greater than you will find among the greedy, pushing settlers, who regard them as mere vermin who must be destroyed for the sake of the ground on which depends their very existence. But these men know the Indian and his almost incredible wrongs, and the causes which have turned him into the ruthless savage that he is, and often have I heard men of their class say that, before God, the Indian was in the right, and was only doing what any American citizen would do in his place."[15]

One newspaper reporter said, "Texas Jack states that the trouble between the palefaces and red skins in the Western States was caused by the thieving propensities of the former more than the shortcomings of the latter. White men steal their ponies and 'Poor Lo'[Alexander Pope's 1734 poem "An Essay on Man" contained the line "Lo, the poor Indian! whose untutor'd mind / Sees God in clouds, or hears him in the wind." Lo became a slang term for all Native Americans.] was never able to get justice. Added to this was the deception practiced amongst them generally by Indian Commissioners."[16]

As Jack hunted with Bill Cody, tended bar, taught school, and grew in his understanding of the Pawnee, his expertise as the best cowboy in the region was often in demand. Called upon for advice by the ranchers who had purchased the stock he brought to the region months earlier, Omohundro was inevitably recruited to pursue the cattle rustlers and horse thieves targeting their herds. Jack was enlisted by a group of men to help track down a pair of horse thieves that had rustled thirteen horses from a local rancher. Omohundro and a local cattleman named Bill Dile came along to help apprehend the men and return the horses to their rightful owners. In his book about the settlement of the Nebraska frontier, *Building a New Empire*, Nathaniel Ayers writes:

Information had been gained that two men had stolen the horses and the same two men were driving the horses out of the country. They were finally located in a canyon, and a part of the horses were captured, but a desperate chase followed across the level prairies, and the pursuers seemed to have the best horses, and after miles of running they were gaining on the horse thieves, and coming nearer and nearer all the time, the pursuers were ordered to halt. But of course this order was disregarded, but the thieves were ordered to surrender, which command was answered with lead from Winchester rifles, and one of the fiercest battles ever fought on the Western plains was now inevitable. The men with the stolen horses were desperate characters, and would "die with their boots on" rather than surrender or be captured alive. The pursuers [were] under the leadership of a Western sheriff, with the laws of the State in his favor. Some of his party were very poorly armed, but himself and his two new recruits were as well armed as the thieves themselves and had plenty of ammunition. The sheriff dismounted and ordered his helpers to do the same, and then ordered two of his men to take all the horses out of range of the rifles, and ordered all his men who had long range guns to stoop low, keep cool, and shoot to kill.

Bullets went and come thick and fast, and each volley seemed to come closer. "Texas Jack" was the first man in the sheriff's party struck. A .44 Winchester ball had passed through the muscles of the thigh, but Jack never whimpered or complained.[17]

Omohundro took careful aim and sent a bullet through the heart of the man that had injured him. Another volley from his companions injured the other man, who threw up his hands and surrendered his arms. The remaining horses had stampeded when the gunfire began, and Jack helped the men round them up before taking the injured man with him to the nearest physician. The man died of his wounds a few days later, after giving a statement to the local sheriff about the affair.

Omohundro spent a few days recovering from his wound before he could ride again. He carried the scar—along with wounds he had received on the battlefields of Virginia and would receive in the future in various encounters with buffalo, bear, and Native American warrior—with him for the rest of his life.

CHAPTER FIVE

Ned Buntline

THE STORY OF TEXAS JACK'S SHOOT-OUT WITH THE HORSE THIEVES AND encounters with hostile Sioux (Očhéthi Šakówiŋ) may have been among the stories he and Bill Cody told the New York writer who approached them one night at Lew Baker's saloon where Jack tended bar between hunts and pursuing cattle rustlers across the Nebraska prairie. That man was Ned Buntline, an author whose stories of brave pioneers and adventurous pirates were voraciously consumed by dime-novel readers across the country. Buntline was both one of America's most-read authors and perhaps its most successful provocateur, having incited deadly riots at Astor Place in New York City in 1849 and three years later during an election in St. Louis. Buntline had come to Nebraska on the way back East from a temperance lecture tour through California, always on the lookout for new characters and stories to fill his pages. On or around July 16, 1869, this pursuit brought him to North Platte, Nebraska.

The name "Ned Buntline" was as much an invention as the stories the man spun under that moniker, often more affectation than substance. Perhaps the writer assumed his stories wouldn't sound as authentic with his given name, Edward Zane Carroll Judson, as the byline. Ned Buntline, according to historian Julia Bricklin, was "the human embodiment of contradictions. He delivered fiery temperance lectures and drank ambitiously. He proclaimed the virtues of public peace, but in addition to causing the Astor Place Riot, he stirred up another one in St. Louis, which killed at least three men. He despaired of social injustice but only reluctantly spoke or wrote against slavery. He admired strong and independent women but held suffragists in nearly satiric contempt. He professed a sanctimonious devotion to the institutions of chastity and marriage—but married at least nine women, sometimes two, even three at a time. He was apparently areligious but treated the faithful (including Indians and their 'pagan beliefs') with respect, and once considered embracing Spiritualism."[1] And even more than this role of America's foremost walking contradiction, Buntline was America's most prodigious and successful creator of dime-novel fiction.

Several contradictory stories have been posited concerning exactly which heroic Western man Buntline was trying to turn into reams of paper and thousands of dollars when he ended up at Lew Baker's place there in North Platte. Ned had recently embarked on a series of paid lectures on the benefits of temperance, drinking heavily the entire way. He would often stop in a town, hit the local saloon, and then set up in a theater or hall in the same town to warn patrons against the excesses brought upon by the evil drink. Buntline had lectured extensively in California, with stops in Salt Lake City, Denver, and Cheyenne during the return trip east that brought him into the vicinity of North Platte, Nebraska.

Buntline biographer Jay Monaghan and Cody biographer Don Russell hold that Buntline was in Nebraska to interview Frank North, commander of the Pawnee (Chaticks si Chaticks) scouts and supposed killer of Tall Bull, the leader of the Cheyenne (Tsêhéstáno) Dog Soldiers, at the Battle of Summit Springs mere days earlier. Joseph G. Rosa, the writer of multiple books on Wild Bill, maintains that Buntline was in town looking for Mr. Hickok. Bill Cody himself remembered that Buntline was in town to deliver a temperance lecture, but canceled the event to accompany Cody and soldiers on a scouting expedition under the command of Major W. H. Brown.

If Buntline was indeed looking for Frank North, he was ahead of his time. Though North led the Pawnee scouts, he was not a nationally prominent figure, and newspapers reporting on the Summit Springs battle had not mentioned the man in their coverage of the event before Ned's arrival. If he did hear about Frank, it was certainly from North Platte locals and not newspaper coverage, and by all accounts, North was not an accommodating interviewee. "If you want a man to fit that bill," he reportedly told Buntline after being approached to model as the hero of popular literature, "he's over there under the wagon." According to Monaghan, "Unsteadily [Buntline] poked beneath the wagon. A young giant, with sleepy eyes and straw in his long hair, looked up at the gnome whose stories would soon make him the fabulous Buffalo Bill."[2]

Bill Cody remembered meeting Buntline not by being awoken from his peaceful and straw-haired slumber beneath a wagon, but by being informed by his commanding officer that a writer of some note would be joining their next scout. "By the way," Major Brown told Cody as they prepared to leave Fort McPherson, "we are going to have quite an important character with us as a guest on this scout. It's old Ned Buntline, the novelist."[3] As Cody and the writer chatted, this version of events holds, Buntline decided that this tall and handsome scout—already a local frontier celebrity with an endearing charm and distinctive cognomen—would be the perfect subject of his next novella.

The third explanation of Buntline's presence in North Platte—that he was there seeking the famous cowtown lawman Wild Bill Hickok—is entirely plausible. If Buntline sought Frank North because he was enamored with stories of the Battle of Summit Springs, the capture of two white women by Cheyenne Dog Soldiers, and the defeat of Chief Tall Bull, why is the story he produced largely a retelling of Hickok's encounter with Dave McCanles—Jake M'Kandlas in Buntline's story—over a decade earlier? If Buntline decided that Cody was the perfect face of dime-novel fiction in his own right, why does James Butler Hickok—Wild Bill Hitchcock, as written by Buntline—feature so prominently in *Buffalo Bill: The King of Border Men*, released in installments starting later that year in Street & Smith's *New York Weekly*?

George Ward Nichols's stories about Wild Bill Hickok in *Harper's New Monthly Magazine*, printed in February 1867, piqued the curiosity of Eastern readers, and Buntline was certainly aware of the notable lawman and the success of Nichols's interview with him. If Buntline heard that Hickok was nearby, it certainly seems likely that the writer sought to interrogate and report on the now-famous gunslinger for himself. According to the version of events in which Buntline was looking for Wild Bill, it was at one of his temperance lecture stops, near either Fort

Sedgwick or Fort McPherson, that Buntline learned that the lawman was gambling nearby. Arriving late in the day, Buntline made his customary stop at the local saloon, where he found Hickok.

"There's my man!" started Buntline, moving toward Hickok's table. "I want you!"

Notoriously averse to surprise, Hickok's reaction indicated his wariness. His hand went immediately to one of his guns, carried with its twin in a sash on his side.

"What do you mean?" he spat back.

"I mean that I want you; that you are my man!"

In one quick motion, Hickok was on his feet, both of his ivory-handled revolvers bearing down on Buntline.

"Well, if you can take me," started Bill, using his thumbs to draw back the hammers on his pair of pistols, "all right."

It was at this point, with the twin barrels of the deadliest gunman in the world challenging him to a staring contest, that Buntline seems to have recognized his tactical error.

"I am representing Street and Smith . . . of the *New York Weekly*," Buntline sputtered, empty hands thrust into the air to show he wasn't attempting to challenge the man. "I'm in search of a real, live Indian-fighting hero. Seeing you, while my thoughts were on this subject, I recognized you as my ideal of such a character."

Despite legend to the contrary, Wild Bill Hickok might not have been the fastest gun in the West. "Whenever you get into a row," he once cautioned a reporter, "be sure not to shoot too quick. Take time. I've known many a feller to slip up for shootin' in a hurry." He was, though, perhaps the fastest decision-maker in the West. Had he deemed Buntline a threat, Buntline would have been on the floor with two smoking .36 caliber holes in his skull. Instead, Hickok sized up Ned Buntline and determined that the writer was no threat to his life.

In the short term, Hickok was right. Buntline wanted a story, not a fight. Long term, though, it was stories about "Wild Bill" by authors like George Ward Nichols and Ned Buntline that would make him a target for anyone who wanted to prove that they were the best gunslinger in the West, able to get the jump on the "Prince of Pistoleers."

"That right?" Bill questioned, decocking his guns. "That's pretty good talk, but let me tell you, friend, I'll give you just twenty-four hours to leave this community. I don't care what your business is, but I don't like your looks nohow."

Given little reason to doubt Hickok's sincerity, Buntline sought libations elsewhere, this search eventually landing him at the bar of Lew Baker's saloon, where Texas Jack Omohundro was pouring whiskey. Unable to convince Hickok to put his six-shooters away long enough to sit for an interview, Buntline determined that his best option was to ask the locals if they knew Wild Bill. As Ned's luck would have it, Texas Jack was a voracious reader and knew of Buntline's stories of pirates and murderers and heroes. He also knew Hickok and had another good friend who knew him even better. Texas Jack pointed Buntline across the room to this friend. The man, dressed in fringed leather and with long hair, was Bill Cody. The world did not yet know "Buffalo Bill."

When Buntline asked Cody for an interview, Cody agreed on the condition that Buntline kept the whiskey flowing. One can imagine the quick-thinking Buntline turning to Jack and making the two men a promise.

"If you two gentlemen supply the whiskey and the stories," he might have told his new friends, "I'll make both of you heroes."

For once in his life, Ned Buntline was true to his word.[4]

CHAPTER SIX

The Grand Duke

AN UNSEASONABLY WARM NEBRASKA WINTER BROUGHT WELCOME NEWS to Cody and Omohundro. Russia's Grand Duke Alexis, the fourth son of Tsar Alexander II, was on his way to Nebraska to hunt. General Joe Palmer, a pioneer and former superintendent of Indian Affairs in the Oregon Territory, exhaustively planned the trip. Two other generals, Philip Sheridan and Edward Ord, would accompany Alexis on the trek. Sheridan, the general in charge of the Union troops matched against Jeb Stuart's men, Texas Jack included, when Stuart fell for the final time at Yellow Tavern, was appointed to command the Military Division of the Missouri by President Ulysses S. Grant. Another soldier who had fought alongside Sheridan, and against Omohundro, during the Wilderness Campaign was chosen as grand marshal of the ducal hunt and its festivities: Lieutenant Colonel George Armstrong Custer.

The size and prestige of the hunting party necessitated a special Pullman train car, provided for the group by the Pennsylvania Railroad Company. On the government's orders, stationmasters along the appointed route cleared train schedules, ensuring that there would be no other trains on the tracks to delay His Imperial Highness. The Grand Duke was Russian royalty, and royal visits from any country to the United States were rare. From lavish hotel ballrooms to culinary feasts, no expense was to be spared by his American hosts to ensure that Alexis enjoyed his visit to America.

The relationship between the two countries had been redefined since the turn of the nineteenth century, when Russia had acted as mediator between the United States and Great Britain at the conclusion of the War of 1812. America's moral support of Russia during the Crimean War against Great Britain directly led to an increase in trade between the two countries. More recently, Russia had bolstered its relationship with Washington by vocally and internationally siding with the Union during the Civil War. This allegiance served Russian interests well, as it was widely believed that a strong United States would act as a counter to the European powers of France and England, both supporters of the Confederacy. Fearing that a future war with Great Britain would threaten its holdings in the New World, Russia sold the Department of Alaska to the United States in 1867, further solidifying the relationship between the two governments.

The Grand Duke's delegation anchored in New York on November 21, 1871. Admiral Samuel Phillips Lee greeted it on the USS *Severn*, as did Vice Admiral Stephen Clegg Rowan on the USS *Congress*, along with the USS *Iroquois*, the USS *Kansas*, and a host of dignitaries including William Henry Aspinwall, Moses H. Grinnell, General John Adams Dix, and Theodore Roosevelt Sr. In New York, the Grand Duke spent the evening catching a performance of the ballet, where he was enchanted by world-renowned dancer Giuseppina Morlacchi in *The Devil's Auction*. More dignitaries greeted him on his arrival by railcar in Washington, DC, where he met with President Grant, Grant's wife, Julia, daughter Nellie, and members of Grant's Cabinet.

After a tour of the East Coast and a brief detour to Canada for stops in Montreal, Ottawa, and Toronto, the Grand Duke spent Christmas in Buffalo, New York, before heading west to hunt that city's namesake. Making stops in Detroit, Cleveland, Chicago, Milwaukee, St. Louis, Kansas City, and Omaha, Alexis cut a dashing figure. At six feet, two inches tall, he towered over most of the men around him. Both his bearing and his royal jewelry marked him as something that most Americans he encountered had never before seen—aristocracy. The handsome Russian caught the eye of many young ladies along the route, leading George Custer's wife, Libbie, to remark that Alexis seemed more fascinated by "pretty girls and music" than by the country through which his menagerie was passing.[1]

Albert Bierstadt, the German-born landscape painter whose Hudson River School landscapes of Yosemite had earned him invitations to every subsequent important expedition of the West, wrote to General Sherman in July, months in advance of the Grand Duke's arrival on the plains:

> *You are doubtless aware that the Grand Duke Alexis of Russia is to be here in October, and I have learned that he is quite desirous of witnessing a Buffalo Hunt. As his visit partakes of a somewhat national character, would it not be well to give him one on a grand scale, with Indians included, as a rare piece of American hospitality?*
>
> *If a large body of Indians could be brought together at that time, say the latter part of October, the performance of some of their dances and other ceremonials would be most interesting to our Russian guests. This would probably be the only way to give them a correct idea of Red America. Some of the best Indian hunters might go with the party on the buffalo hunt, to show the aboriginal style of "going for large game." The herd could be driven up at the proper time within searching distance of the railroad.*
>
> *It would add very much to the happiness and well-being of our guests if you could find time to accompany them in person. In default of that it might accord with your views to delegate some officer of rank, as Sheridan for instance, in your place. This visit of the Grand Duke should be made a matter of no ordinary attention, as it has clearly a more important meaning than the mere pleasure trip of a Prince.*[2]

Sherman and Grant together selected General Sheridan to arrange such an event, and Sheridan and Custer left the details of the hunt to trusted scout and hunter Buffalo Bill Cody. Cody, in turn, enlisted the aid of his friend and hunting partner, Texas Jack Omohundro. "When the whole party was mounted, they started south," Cody wrote of the Grand Duke's party in his autobiography, "Texas Jack acting as their guide until I could overtake them."[3] Here rode the Confederate scout turned cowboy, heading out of the fort and toward a Sioux encampment, leading onto the prairie generals Sheridan and Custer along with some of the same soldiers he had spied on and fought against on the bloody battlefields of

Virginia seven years earlier. Cody, who had been forced to send a personal request to the Secretary of War to gain permission to enlist the former Confederate as a scout, must have felt no small amount of satisfaction as he watched his friend lead the procession away from the fort.

Arriving at "Camp Alexis," fifty miles south on Red Willow Creek, Jack and the ducal group found not the hundred Indians they had expected, but rather a thousand warriors dressed and painted for battle. Chiefs War Bonnet, Red Leaf (Waȟpé Ššapa), Black Hat, Pawnee Killer, Whistler (Jolowážna), and Spotted Tail (Siŋté Gleška), the latter dressed in an ill-fitting suit he had brought back from Washington and an army belt worn upside down, greeted Alexis and the American military officers. The American military presence included an overabundance of top brass, with six generals to only two cavalry and two infantry companies. One soldier estimated that he did more saluting during those two days than he did for the rest of his enlistment.[4]

The establishment of the camp took almost a month of labor, with most of the work completed by black infantrymen. The grounds included two big hospital tents for parties and dinners; six big-wall tents, half of them covered and floored in plush red carpets for the duke, his party, and the American officers; thirty "A" tents; and 265 Sioux lodges stretching toward the horizon.

Spotted Tail's warriors put on a display of their horsemanship for the impressed Alexis, with a staged battle designed to allow the Sioux (Očhéthi Šakówiŋ) to show off their warfare techniques and proficiency with their bows. As the sun dipped behind the rolling hills, the Sioux warriors began their ceremonial war dance. The Sioux noticed the Grand Duke lavishing his attention on one attractive young maiden, the daughter of Spotted Tail. Alexis's fondness for and attention to the women he encountered along his American visit was so oft-noted that he felt compelled to write a letter to his mother, the Empress Maria Alexandrovna, stating that "Regarding my success with American ladies about which so much is written in the newspapers, I can openly say that this is complete nonsense. They looked on me from the beginning as they would look on a wild animal, as on a crocodile or other unusual beast."[5]

Despite his offhand dismissal of such encounters, a dispute broke out between the natives and the Russian party. The dispute ended when Alexis presented gifts of red and green blankets, several ivory-handled hunting knives, and a large bag brimming with silver dollars to the defenders of the young maiden. A formal council then took place in General Sheridan's tent, where Spotted Tail smoked and passed around the ceremonial pipe.

The rising sun of the next morning brought with it the awaited buffalo hunt. Miguel Antonio Otero, who would later become the governor of New Mexico Territory, was along for the hunt and wrote that "General Custer rode up, accompanied by Buffalo Bill and Texas Jack, to take the Grand Duke on the hunt. They brought along for the latter's use the best trained buffalo horse they could find, and the Grand Duke, after taking his brace of pistols, bowie knife and rifle, mounted and started off with them. The four rode toward the east, over a slight rise in the prairie. . . . [B]uffalo were grazing just behind the rise in a beautiful little valley."[6]

Cody, Alexis, Omohundro, and Custer rode together at the lead. The Grand Duke, accustomed to the European style of hunting, sent his first shot wide of its mark. Having listened to opinions on the best methods of buffalo hunting for weeks, the duke now remarked, "You have drilled me so hard, I have a blank mind." Cody told Alexis it was best to let his horse do the hunting, riding alongside the buffalo. Alexis attempted this, but all six of his revolver shots missed the bull as well. Seeing that the duke was becoming flustered at having missed in front of his American hosts, Cody offered him his favorite rifle, the Springfield .50 caliber trapdoor needle gun he had christened "Lucretia Borgia," named for the character in Victor Hugo's famous play. The Grand Duke raised the rifle, took a shot, and, as he went to reload, looked back up to find that his first shot had been a killer. He pulled back on the reins of his mount, leaped to the ground, and ran toward the fallen bull with his knife in hand. Cutting off the animal's tail, "he let go with a series of howls and gurgles like the death song of all the fog horns and calliopes ever born," remembered Cody.

The duke went on to kill two more buffalo, after which Otero reports that "General Custer immediately sent Texas Jack back to the camp for some hunters, who quickly removed the heads and skins of the three buffalo the Grand Duke had killed and took them to camp." Omohundro soon arrived with the ambulance wagons and what one of the soldiers called "enough champagne to float the Russian Navy," and generous toasts to the duke, to Sheridan, to Cody, and to each other were poured by the Duke's servants. Freed by Alexis's success to do some hunting of their own, the larger party split into smaller groups, with Jack leading a group of the duke's comrades. Two of them managed kills, and when the hunt ended two hours later, some thirty dark carcasses dotted the prairie.

The Grand Duke personally supervised the skinning out of the head of the first animal he had killed, but it was somehow misplaced before the party returned to camp. "The head of the buffalo which the Duke Alexis killed . . . was lost by his party," Jack wrote to Ned Buntline shortly after. Returning to the hunting ground alone, Jack found the misplaced trophy and sent it to Professor Ward of Rochester, New York.[7] The professor shipped the skull to Russia, where it would soon adorn the lavishly gilded walls of the Alexander Palace in St. Petersburg.

Having missed his initial pistol shots, the Grand Duke commented that he could not believe that Sioux and Pawnee (Chaticks si Chaticks) could hunt the animals with bow and arrow alone. Cody and Omohundro talked to the Sioux and arranged a demonstration for the next day. A Sioux archer impressed Alexis when the brave notched his arrow to his bow, took careful aim, and brought down an enormous bull buffalo, his arrow traveling through the buffalo and lodging into the ground. The Grand Duke kept the arrow for the rest of his life as a memento of the trip.

With the hunt over, Grand Duke Alexis, his party, and the throng of American statesmen bid farewell to Buffalo Bill and Texas Jack, with the Russians traveling toward Memphis, Tennessee, and then on to New Orleans in time for Mardi Gras. In the Crescent City, Alexis was the guest of honor at the inaugural Rex parade. The lyrics to the popular song "If Ever I Cease to Love" were changed to suit the city's honored guest, with locals singing, "May the Grand Duke Alexis / Ride a Buffalo in Texas / If I Ever Cease to Love."[8]

CHAPTER SEVEN

The Grand Buffalo Hunt

As MARDI GRAS REVELERS IN NEW ORLEANS SANG SONGS ABOUT RID-
ing buffalo in Texas, a new family was building a house on Medicine
Creek, just south of Fort McPherson and Cottonwood Springs. The
Palmers and their daughter came west like many families, escaping desperate situations at home back East. For some of the new arrivals on the
prairie, this was economic hardship and financial ruin. For others, like
William Herbert Palmer, it was an escape from the drastic consequences
of violent actions.

Herbert had been implicated in the murder of a local doctor named
Hilliard H. Harley in Savannah after the doctor, briefly engaged to
Herbert's sister, made some unbecoming accusations about that lady's
character when she called off the marriage. The tight-knit Savannah
community believed that Herbert had pulled the trigger, but a trial was
avoided when Herbert Palmer's clothing was discovered on the banks of
the Savannah River. Police determined that Palmer must have drowned
after jumping in, committing suicide rather than facing a jury of his peers
and inevitable justice. William Herbert Palmer was never seen again, but
soon a man with an uncannily similar description named William Herbert Miles staked a claim on Medicine Creek on the Nebraska frontier.
William's parents and his sister Ena—the maiden accused by the doctor
of improper dalliances—remained for two years in Savannah, bearing the
constant accusatory looks and judgmental whispers of their neighbors
before deciding that they too would pack their belongings and make for
the prairie.

Herbert, who earned the nickname Paddy when he arrived in Nebraska, was introduced to the local scouts and spent time hunting with Texas Jack, Bill Cody, and their associates. He was more than happy to introduce his friends to his sister shortly after she stepped off the train at North Platte in the spring of 1872. Ena, whose real name was Annie— she got the nickname from Paddy, who spelled her name backward, Einna—was a true Southern belle and, to the benefit of historians, a prodigious journal keeper, whose diary entries paint a vivid picture of life on the frontier in the 1870s. At some point, either through a brief marriage or perhaps simple romantic idealism, she had taken to calling herself Ena Raymonde, though there was certainly no Mr. Raymonde in the picture when her brother introduced her to Texas Jack Omohundro on the day of one of his more widely reported exploits during his time in Nebraska.

Newspaper readers around the country were now familiar with Texas Jack, "the Hero of the Loup Fork," from reports on the Sioux skirmish that earned Bill Cody his Medal of Honor. In early June of 1872, one of those readers, Colonel Sidney Barnett, arrived at Fort McPherson seeking Texas Jack. Sidney Barnett's father, Thomas, was a British-born Canadian who founded the Niagara Falls Museum on the Canadian side of the Niagara River in 1827. The museum's displays, initially consisting only of Thomas's personal collection of taxidermied animals, rapidly expanded to include over five thousand animals, shells, minerals, and Native American artifacts. Over the course of multiple international adventures, Sidney added to his family's menagerie four Egyptian mummies—including the mummy of Ramesses I, which was returned to Egypt in 2003, after 140 years in Niagara Falls—as well as artifacts, ancient coins, and the forty-foot skeleton of a humpback whale. The father and son believed that they could attract visitors to Niagara Falls and the museum by arranging a live buffalo hunt at the Falls.

The Barnetts were not the originators of the idea of an East Coast buffalo hunt. Circus magnate Phineas T. Barnum purchased fifteen of the animals in 1843 to exhibit in Hoboken, New Jersey. Twenty-four thousand people turned out for that "Grand Buffalo Hunt" only to find the animals weak and malnourished from extended captivity. The buffalo proceeded to escape their caged pen and make for a nearby swamp, injuring several spectators. One man died after falling from his perch in a tree during the excitement.[1]

To provide the buffalo for his Exhibition, Colonel Barnett contacted Professor Henry A. Ward, who suggested Barnett contact his "Buffalo Man," Bill Cody.[2] A naturalist and geologist from Rochester, New York, Professor Ward met Cody and Omohundro on an initial trip to the Nebraska frontier in 1869. In 1872, Ward was invited to attend the hunt with Grand Duke Alexis in his capacity as the founder of Ward's Natural Science—a still-extant business that gathers specimens from around the world, preserves them, and sells them to colleges and museums. Unfortunately, his invitation failed to arrive on time, and he appeared on the Nebraska prairie too late to join the hunt.

Not to be dissuaded, the professor hired Cody and Omohundro to help him gather specimens for preservation and display. On the professor's advice, Barnett reached out to Cody to spearhead the hunt and to gather as many as a hundred Potawatomi (Bodéwadmi) tribesmen to add to the spectacle. In response to the colonel's request, dated March 29, 1869, Cody wrote:

> Dear Sir,
>
> I have just met Mr. Omohundro and am now on my way to Spotted Tail's Indian Village with horses and rations for his people. Will return as soon as I deliver them to him. Mr. Omohundro and myself will catch you the buffalo and put them in the cars in good condition for you at this place or some other station close by if you will pay enough for the trouble. It is a big job, but it can be done.
>
> Money will do anything. [Omohundro] will write you what [he] will get them for. And he will come on with them if he is well paid. I am in Government employ and cannot leave—Let him know immediately. It will take a wagon for each buffalo to haul him to the road and we have to send a good way for more good ropes. You make the arrangements with him. You will have to forward money. It will look more like business if we of course are both strangers. The same as when Professor Ward and I commenced business, but I think we can do it on the square. If anything should happen that we could not get

the buffalo, although if we commence to do the thing it will be done, but should such a thing happen as we could not get them I assure you the money will be returned if sent to our order.

Yours respectfully,

W. F. Cody Buffalo Bill[3]

It made complete sense for Cody to turn over such a feat of cowboy prowess to Texas Jack. Over the past two years spent together, Jack had proven himself equal to any task put before him, and the assistance he provided to Cody while that man managed the government's livestock at Fort McPherson must have been invaluable. By now, Cody had seen Jack's proficiency with his lasso and experienced firsthand his resolute coolness under fire. If anyone was capable of lassoing and capturing live buffalo, Bill Cody knew, that man was Texas Jack.

Barnett ran into problems when the Union Pacific Railroad Company advised him that his plan to load buffalo onto their trains and bring them east was "not only hazardous but very expensive."[4] It was estimated by the railroad that the cost to capture the animals would be $1,000 a head, plus $300 for each carload for transportation. Neither the Pawnee nor the Potawatomi would be allowed on the train without an order from Washington, as both tribes were confined to their reservations and not free to travel. It was more than two years before Cody and Omohundro could fully arrange for the capture of the animals, as attested to by a letter Colonel Barnett received from Texas Jack:

Dear Sir,

I received your dispatch several days ago. Should have given you an answer but did not know positively what to say as my pardner W. F. Cody was not here. He returned yesterday. Just after I had read your letter we had a talk together and decided that we could capture those buffalo and deliver them here or some station near for the sum of $500.00 per head and that you are to take whatever number we get from two to six head, all we ask is that you deposit $1,000.00 in the First National Bank Omaha subject to our order. This might not be necessary, only that we need aid from parties that would not work

Texas Jack in hunting gear. (COWAN'S AUCTIONS)

unless on a certainty, you can have what reference you wish in regard to your deposit.

We will expect the balance of the pay as soon as the buffaloes are safely delivered aboard the train. If you accept this offer, which I think is as well as you can do, let us know at once by telegraph and we will proceed to business. You can prepare your part, give out your

59

advertisements, and make all other necessary arrangements. The buf-falo will be there between the first and fifteenth.

I would much have preferred your offer as a pardner in this proj-ect, as I am sure it will be a perfect success, only for the objection of certain parties which I could not possibly perform the capture without. I would accept your offer; however, as you have given me some induce-ments, I have made up my mind to come through with the buffaloes, to take care of them over the road, and to play any part in the hunt that you may wish me [to] after we are once together.

Perhaps I will join you in the Exhibition that you spoke of. I will send you a sketch of my life in a few days that you may use it in your publications if necessary. We have written to the Indian Reservation to know if we can get the Indians required and will let you know as soon as we get an answer. I have a good rig here of bows and arrows that I have captured from the Indians, and also nice Lassoes that I will bring along so as I can play Indian or white man as you may wish.

I have always intended to go into something of this kind but have never had the capital to commence with. You know it requires money to do anything out here. I was speaking to my old friend Professor Ward about it last winter; he recommends the idea, and I am sure that you and whatever parties you may have with you will make big money out of what you have undertaken. What business we transact from this point on must be through telegraph, as our time will be limited. You may feel perfectly safe in regard to our success, and make your arrangements accordingly, as we seldom undertake a thing that we do not carry out.

No more at present from your most obedient,
J. B. Omohundro
Texas Jack⁵

Omohundro's interest in joining the Exhibition, as well as his willing-ness to provide information about himself for publication in the event's advertising literature, suggests that Jack considered pursuing entertain-ment opportunities well before his theatrical endeavors with Buffalo Bill.

Jack set about the task of capturing the requested buffalo with characteristic flair. Days after Barnett's arrival at Fort McPherson, the *Omaha Weekly Herald* published a letter from a correspondent detailing the proceedings:

> *A novel undertaking is on foot here, and is of gigantic proportions. Colonel Sidney Barnett, of Niagara Falls, is getting up a grand Buffalo hunt at Niagara Falls, from the 1st to the 4th of July. He is now here for the purpose of completing arrangements and superintending the starting of the enterprise, and shipping the buffaloes East.*
>
> *He has secured the services of the celebrated scout and hunter, Mr. J. B. Omohundro, better known as "Texas Jack," the hero of the Loup Fork. "Texas Jack" is a partner of "Buffalo Bill," and nothing that skill and foresight can accomplish will be spared to make this hunt a perfect success.*
>
> *Through the kindness of Major North, the commander of the Pawnee scouts, arrangements are being made for a party of Pawnee Indians—the deadly and bitter enemies of the Sioux—to go to Niagara with their fleet ponies and lodges, and full war and hunting equipment.*
>
> *The buffaloes will pass through Omaha the latter part of this, or early part of next month. We think this is a grand affair, and believe there can be no question of success from the reputation of the parties engaged in it. The spectacle that will present itself to the scores of thousands who will be spectators at Niagara will be the most novel and thrilling ever seen east of the great plains, and will give our eastern friends an idea of what buffalo hunting is in Nebraska.*[6]

It was at this moment, just as Texas Jack set out to accomplish the never-before-attempted feat of lassoing buffalo from the back of the white stallion captured from Dog Soldier and Cheyenne chief Tall Bull, that Paddy Miles introduced him to his sister Ena, newly arrived on the prairie. Jack could hardly have designed a more flattering scenario. Ena's diary entry dated June 7, 1872, makes plain the impact the dashing cowboy had on the refined Southern belle: "I have been introduced to 'Texas Jack,' one of our 'Western Heroes,' and a fine picture of handsome, dashing, manly manhood he is," she confided in her journal. "Certainly one of my beau-ideals of a hunter or a 'Scout.' Hope I shall see more of him and that I like his character as well as his face. But enough of this hero for the present, only that he now heads a party out on about as wild an adventure as even my wild brain could devise—viz.: lassoing buffalo, full grown ones for the purpose of shipping them, alive on the train. Some say it is dangerous work; some prophecy not only broken arms and legs and crippled horses, but dead men as well as dead horses!"[7]

A correspondent from the *Lincoln Daily State Journal* shared some of Ms. Palmer's enthusiasm. "I will relate an incident heretofore unheard of in Buffalo Hunting," began his account. "Texas Jack, and a man by the name of Barrett [*sic*] . . . started from Red Willow early Sunday morning, 9th June, crossed the Republican, and proceeded to Beaver Creek, 15 miles away, and before noon the eight bulls were prisoners, and loaded on wagons."

It took three men to capture a single buffalo—one to lasso the bull, and a second to chase the now-lassoed and angry animal in an attempt to rope one of its feet. The roping accomplished, the third man tied the other feet, and the trio loaded the captured buffalo onto a waiting wagon before proceeding on to the next target.

"After Texas Jack had lassoed an uncommon large ugly old bull, and before anyone could secure his leg," the reporter continued, "he turned short, and charged, caught the horse, and pitched both into a gully." Here Jack's grit and the hard-earned experience of Texas cattle drives were made apparent. "His well-trained horse waited for its rider, and my informant stated that the rope was not even dropped, but man and horse were together, again following the buffalo, until he was finally captured. To read of such things is all very well; but to do them is quite a different thing. . . . For my part," concluded the suitably impressed reporter, "I believe rather than be one to capture one of those fellows, I had rather go through the Battle of Chickamauga again."[8]

While Jack was lassoing buffalo and impressing reporters and newly arrived Southern belles alike, Ned Buntline was busy publishing stories about Buffalo Bill and Texas Jack, each new installment bearing an addendum warning readers not to miss the full-length story about Texas Jack that Buntline promised would soon follow. To tide over his voracious readers, Buntline published letters received from his friends on the plains, preparing audiences for tales of the dashing cowboy. One such letter, printed in the August 26 edition of Street & Smith's *New York Weekly* and dated July 1, 1872, is addressed to "Friend Ned."

I received your kind letter several days ago. Am very sorry I cannot accept your invitation to visit you at your camp. I am sure we would have a nice time. Our buffalo hunt was a perfect success. We succeeded in capturing seven living bison in one day; but owing to the hot weather most of them died during the transportation. It was one of the most exciting chases that I have ever witnessed. I was to take a party of Indians with me from the Pawnee tribe. When I got as far as Omaha, I learned that the commissioners at Washington had refused to let the parties at Niagara have the use of the Indians; consequently, I have returned to the Fort.

I suppose you have seen all the particulars in Eastern papers. Am very sorry that the affair has turned out so badly, as I was somewhat connected to it; however, my portion of the work here was carried out all right—that was to capture the buffalo. In doing that, I had my favorite horse, Tall Bull, badly wounded in several places, and narrowly escaped being hurt myself by a young buffalo bull. I had thrown my lasso over him, but he was too strong for my horse; and as none of the boys were near to help me, the bull had his own way. I followed him to the Beaver River and tried to entangle him in the timber. While thus engaged, he faced me several times, gored my horse badly, and once pushed us both into the river, jumping in after, and came near crushing the life out of both. Eventually I succeeded in making him fast to a tree, and you can bet I was glad of it, for old Jack was getting mighty tired of that sort of fun.

We had a dispatch from Buffalo Bill several days ago; he was at Fort Randall on the 27th of June, and will be home at the latter part of the month.

Indians are prowling round in considerable numbers in these parts. We are likely to have some trouble with them soon. I expect to be put under pay as scout again in a few days.

I have been offered the place as commander of the Pawnee tribe this summer on their buffalo hunt. Am not certain yet what I will do. I am on the war-path this summer—bigger than a wolf. The Sioux cannot come down here any too fast to suit me. However, I will try to be a little civilized by the time you get out to see us this fall.

I had a rousing time in Omaha for a couple of days. Had an invitation to go up in a balloon from there on the 4th of July. Would have gone up had I been there. Would like a trip of that kind.

If anything of importance happens I will let you know. All quiet at the fort.

As ever, yours most respectfully,

J. B. Omohundro, ("Texas Jack")[9]

With tales of Jack's lassoing feats appearing in both dime-novel publications such as the *New York Weekly* and newspapers from New Orleans to Nova Scotia, the image of the cowboy turned scout perched upon his horse, lasso whirling in the air above his head, was cemented well before Jack took to the stage to demonstrate such skills in person.

When asked later if lassoing a buffalo was more difficult than lassoing a steer, Jack turned the talk to another beast entirely. At some point in his adventures as a cowboy, Jack told a reporter, his outfit happened upon a large cinnamon bear. "We all proposed to leave him alone," said Jack, likely having encountered many bears while protecting the herds in his charge, "but there was one fellow, who didn't know as much bear as the rest, who proposed to capture him with his lasso. We told him he had better let out the job, but he was determined, and, sure enough, he made a good throw, and got the loop around the bear's neck."

The problem with lassoing a bear, as opposed to a longhorn or bison bull, said Jack, is that a bear didn't behave like a bovine when a lariat lands on its neck. "When old Cinnamon felt it get tight, what do you think he did?" asked the cowboy. "He just sat up on his haunches, felt of the rope with one paw, and then began pulling it in, hand over hand. There was a horse and a man fast to the other end of the rope, but they had to come, both of them. As for the man, he jumped off, and got away, but the bear drew the pony right up to him, and let his bowels out with one blow of his paw. We killed him, afterwards, but that chap never tried lassoing any more cinnamons. No, they're poor hunting, are bears. There are about twenty varieties of them, and the hog-backed grizzly is the worst, but they're all cross."[10]

As Jack mentioned in his letter to Buntline, the successful capture of the buffalo themselves did not spell success for Sidney Barnett's Grand Buffalo Hunt. As soon as they loaded the animals onto their wagons, Omohundro dedicated himself to procuring the buffalo hunting warriors that Barnett had requested. Newspapers announced the forthcoming hunt, noting with excitement, "The hunt will be managed entirely by Texas Jack, who will take with him Captain Matthews . . . a Pawnee lasso man, and several Pawnee Indians. They will take with them their entire equipments—horses, weapons, and Indian costumes."[11]

Jack wrote to Jacob M. Troth, the assigned Pawnee Indian Agent at Genoa, Nebraska, on the Pawnee Reservation. In his response to Jack, Troth advised that Barclay White, superintendent of Indian Affairs in Omaha, had decided that the Pawnee would not be allowed to leave the reservation due to a Department of Indian Affairs prohibition. While multiple excuses were offered, the sticking point seems to be that the hunt would occur on the Canadian side of the Falls, and granting permission for the Pawnee and Potawatomi to venture out of the country was not to be considered.

The delay led to the deaths of most of the buffalo captured by Omohundro and his party. Jack and Frank North both backed out of the venture, ostensibly deferring to the decree of Agent Troth, though North wrote to Barnett that he could "find Pawnees in Omaha that will testify that they have not been on the Reserve for six months and perhaps a year." The truth of the matter, claimed North, was that "the Quaker Agent wants to show his authority and make out that their policy is the only safe one with Indians and so help me God I never as long as I have known those Indians, I never knew so corrupt a set of Officers over them as now."[12]

A series of escalating letters displaying Barnett's discontent were mailed first to Superintendent of Indian Affairs Francis A. Walker and eventually to President Grant himself. This correspondence failed to yield results in the colonel's favor. Grant agreed that allowing the Pawnee to travel to Canada with Texas Jack to participate in Barnett's event would no doubt be beneficial, but ultimately conceded that the Office of Indian Affairs believed otherwise.

Unable to proceed with the event on the Fourth of July as he had planned, Barnett delayed the buffalo hunt to look for some Native American buffalo hunters and someone to manage the hunt. Frank North suggested that, as the Union Pacific Railroad was no longer obliging in regard to transporting additional animals, perhaps the Kansas Pacific would be a better route to pursue. The Kansas Pacific was no more excited about the idea of managing a full car of live buffalo than the Union Pacific had been, but a suggestion from Texas Jack and Frank North for Barnett to seek out the services of Wild Bill Hickok proved a valuable one.

Traveling to Kansas to determine if a group of Sauk and Fox (Meskwaki) Indians could travel to Niagara Falls in place of the unavailable Pawnee, Barnett met Hickok, recently relieved of his duties as marshal of Abilene. Several citizens of Abilene had recently complained to their marshal about an advertisement for the Bull's Head Tavern. The tavern's enterprising owners, Phil Coe and Ben Thompson, had decided that the best way to drum up business for their new establishment was to paint a picture of a large bull with a fully erect penis on the side of the building. Marshal Hickok asked the two men to alter the picture so as not to offend the ladies of the town, but the owners refused. Hickok, not remembered to history as a renowned painter, altered the image himself, angering the partners. Thompson reportedly attempted to incite his friend John Wesley Hardin into shooting Hickok, but the savvy Hardin refused, asking Thompson, "If Bill needs killin' why don't you kill him yourself?"[13] Coe told Hickok that he would do the deed himself, stating that he could kill a crow on the wing. Hickok coolly asked, "Did the crow have a pistol? Was he shootin' back? I will be."[14]

Afterward, a street brawl broke out, and Phil Coe fired two shots. Hickok ordered Coe arrested for illegally discharging a pistol within city limits. While offering the excuse that he had been shooting at a wild dog, Coe turned his pistol on Hickok. Wild Bill drew and shot first, killing Coe. Seeing another man running toward him with a gun and fearing that it was Ben Thompson or perhaps Hardin, Hickok fired and killed Mike Williams, the Abilene special deputy who was rushing to his aid. Hickok carried regret for the death of his deputy with him when he left Abilene, and his career as a lawman, behind him forever.

Wild Bill's immediate aversion to the idea of involving himself with an entertainment venture was likely tempered by the knowledge that his old friend Happy Jack Omohundro was involved. With Hickok signed on to manage the hunt and with native hunters that were free to travel to the event, Barnett was finally able to stage his hunt at the end of August, 1872. Advertisements, like this one in the *Niagara Falls Gazette*, promised that

> *[t]his novel and most exciting affair will positively take place on the days mentioned and will be under the management and direction of "Wild Bill" (Mr. William Hickok), the most celebrated Scout and Hunter of the Plains. No expense has been spared to make it the most interesting, the most exciting, and the most thrilling spectacle ever witnessed east of the Missouri River.*
>
> *The Grand Buffalo Hunt over the river opens today at 3 o'clock p.m. Sidney Barnett has spared neither pains nor expense to make the undertaking a perfect success, and the most novel and exciting time may confidently be expected. Seats have been prepared to accommodate 50,000 spectators. The hunt will be under the direction of the celebrated William Hickok, or "Wild Bill," as he is familiarly called. A number of the Sac and Fox Tribes of Indians will appear in full war costume, mounted on fleet ponies brought from the plains. A Mexican Vaquero Troupe will also participate.*
>
> *Altogether there will be over fifty Indians and mounted men taking part in the chase. The second day of the hunt will be equally interesting and exciting. Excursion trains are being run on all the principal railroads, and it is expected that a large concourse of people will witness the hunt.*[15]

Despite these lofty promises, the assembled patrons of the event were disappointed. The lengthy wait between Omohundro's capture of the buffalo in June and the staging of the hunt in August meant most of the original set of buffalo had died, and those that remained were not inclined to run for the delight of spectators. The *Toronto Globe*'s correspondent was particularly withering in his review, which carried the telling headline "The Buffalo Hunt—The Whole Thing a Farce":

The buffalo hunt to-day was a failure. The animals turned out had been caged up for some years past, and did not appear to manifest any disposition to run. "Wild Bill," mounted on a low-sized mustang, careened about after a small-sized ox, and, finally, by the aid of some of his satellites, managed to secure a cow, which required to be goaded to desperation before it would run at all. The throwing of the lasso, or lariat, was a mere sham, inasmuch as many of the Indian chiefs had de facto to take the bull by the horns to make him run. The chase after the Texan cattle was also a farce, as the Indians, disguised in the traditional war paint, wandered about on ponies after a cow that had evidently been roaming about for the last two years in the pastures of some peaceful agriculturist in the neighborhood of the Falls. The whole affair is to be repeated on Friday next, and if no better fun is to be offered to those who patronize the entertainment, the exhibition will be but poorly attended.[16]

Friday's version of the hunt fared no better. The Grand Buffalo Hunt left the Barnett family financially devastated, forced to sell their museum several years later. It also left Wild Bill Hickok with a bad taste in his mouth about show business and making what took skill and courage on the prairie into a farce for Eastern audiences. Texas Jack, having been featured prominently in press coverage for capturing the buffaloes, as well as in advertisements in anticipation of his presumed involvement in the hunt, was becoming a household name across the country. Depictions in Ned Buntline's stories bolstered this awareness, placing the cowboy in a position of prominence among others of his old profession in the imaginations of American consumers of newspapers and dime novels alike.

CHAPTER EIGHT

Indians and Cowboys

As spring gave way to summer on the Nebraska prairie, Texas Jack was presented with a nickel-plated Smith & Wesson Model Number 3, bearing the inscription "Texas Jack, Cottonwood Spring 1872," in recognition of his services as a scout. Bill Cody later claimed that a letter he penned to the Secretary of War opened the proverbial door for Omohundro to officially become a civilian scout with the army. The Fifth Cavalry under General Carr received orders to report down to the Department of Arizona, and companies B, L, and G of the Third Cavalry arrived at Fort McPherson. Jack was hired as a scout for the Third Cavalry, under the command of Colonel J. J. Reynolds, at the rate of $5 a day.[1]

While Hickok was in Niagara Falls with Colonel Barnett's buffalo, Texas Jack spent the height of the summer in Nebraska growing closer to Ena Palmer. The pair met again after the buffalo-lassoing adventure at the home of her brother Paddy, who had assisted Jack with the capture of the animals for Barnett's exhibition. Discussing the spectacle and the anticipated event at Niagara Falls, Jack teasingly challenged Ena to a shooting contest. Omohundro had already achieved notoriety in the area as a crack shot and, while he may have been joking with Ena, she was quick to take him up on this and any other offer that would allow them to spend time together.

He arrived the following day to escort her to shoot. Ena wrote in her diary that Jack "made a very graceful presentation in the way of a handsome toy-bag of China-work—its original purpose I do not know; but he used it for cartridges, and so shall I—i.e., if I keep it; for it is but the souvenir of a challenge to shoot; and after having the bravado to take up the gauntlet thus thrown down, if he does beat me (and I expect it will be 'even so!'), I shall not have the courage to retain such a memento of my defeat, but give it back, with my pistol to boot!"[2]

On another night, with Cody out with the army on a scouting expedition of several weeks, Jack camped out in an extra room at the Cody house to protect Louisa and the Cody children from any threat that might arise. Ms. Palmer, a bit under the weather, was staying in the house as well. Her journal records the events of that night:

> *I am still wretchedly unwell, but I have not given up. Went to ride with Texas Jack this afternoon and had a good ride of it, only my Injun pony, Falcon, got* de mal en pis, *and I don't know if I can ride him again, tho' I have made an engagement to ride tomorrow afternoon. I've spent one night with Mrs. Cody. She took me in out of charity because I have to get up so early over here, with the promise that I might sleep just so late as I pleased. But I did not sleep late—I was delirious all night—talked or rather raved in my usual crazy style. Hope I said nothing* mal a propos, *as Mr. Omohundro slept in the adjoining room.*

Writing about Ena in her book *Medicine Creek Journals*, D. Jean Smith posits that "Sleeping in the room next to Texas Jack was not conducive to sleeping soundly. If being ill and feverish didn't cause her to ramble wildly in her sleep talk, just knowing that Texas Jack was in the next room would have, for the man did have a disconcerting effect on her. If she did say something *mal a propos*, Texas Jack was a gentleman and did not embarrass her, for the subject never came up when they went horseback riding that afternoon."[3]

A subsequent entry in Ena's journal belies her growing affection for the handsome cowboy. "At noon I was over to Mrs. Cody's and I saw a windstorm for the first time. Such clouds of dust whirring and rushing like mad everywhere! After it, we had a rain, which, while it rendered everything very muddy, still did away with the dust and made riding possible. Mr. 'Texas' had quite a time lassoing my little rascal of a pony!

We found it pleasant after getting out on the prairie and my (I mean our!) Western Hero made himself just as pleasant as possible, delicate, yet kind and manly in his attentions." Jack warned Ena that it was dangerous to attempt to ride the animal, but despite these warnings, Ena was more than happy to brave the pony's back again if it resulted in more time spent with the scout. She was dismayed the next afternoon when Texas Jack arrived not to ride with her or lasso her belligerent animal, but to bid her good-bye.

Earlier in the summer of 1872, the Pawnee (Chaticks si Chaticks) had requested the government's permission to go on their annual buffalo hunt. Hunting for the Pawnee meant long periods on the plains, killing deer, bear, elk, beaver, otter, and other animals, but especially bison. A full-grown buffalo could provide enough meat to feed a man through the long Nebraska winter. Pawnee hunts ranged up to nine hundred miles, and what couldn't be eaten fresh was cut and dried in the sun to make jerky or placed in buffalo-skin hides with marrow fat to make pemmican.

Illness rendering Frank North unable to assist the Pawnee, generals Sheridan and Ord turned to the cowboy who'd led the expedition out of Fort McPherson during the ducal hunt. White agents were assigned to the Pawnee hunts at all times, tasked with the prevention of "picnics," as the scouts called skirmishes between the Pawnee and their rivals, the Sioux (Očhéthi Šakówiŋ). In addition to ensuring that the Pawnee didn't fight with the Sioux, Omohundro was charged with preventing white settlers from harassing the Pawnee hunters. White hunters were known to fire their guns in the air to scare herds away from the approaching Pawnee, only to return later and slaughter the animals for their hides, leaving the meat to rot in the summer sun.

Ena recorded her disappointment when Jack, who she often in her journals refers to affectionately as "TJ," was appointed trail agent for the Pawnee, as that assignment would take him hundreds of miles from Fort McPherson. Before he left for the hunt with a Pawnee translator named Baptiste Bayhylle, Jack stopped at the home where Ena was staying to bid her farewell. As he left, the homeowner's wife threw an old shoe and broom after him, meant to foretell his chances at a safe return. When the broom landed "turned toward the house," the woman informed Ena that this meant that Jack would indeed make it back safely after the hunt. Ena wrote that "We all laughed and had a noisy time of it. The broom and shoe business was in fine keeping with the chivalric appearance of our hero. That made the fun."[4]

The hunt was certainly a memorable experience for Texas Jack, who wrote about pursuing buffalo with the Pawnee for the *Spirit of the Times* magazine. Just as Omohundro's descriptions of trail riding and stampedes printed in Wild West programs served as a primer on the cowboy, his words about pursuing buffalo with the Pawnee were included as an accurate description of native hunting practices on the Western frontier. Reading Jack's words one senses the penchant for Southern colloquialism and easy charm that endeared so many to the Texas cowboy. "I'll try and give you an idea of one of the most exciting scenes I ever saw or read of, not excepting my school-boy impression of Andy Jackson's hoo-doo at New Orleans," began Jack. "I thought I had seen fun in a Texas cattle stampede, been astonished in a mustang chase; but it wasn't a marker, and it made me believe that Methuselah was right when he suggested that the oldest could 'live and learn.' It is a pity the old man didn't stick it out. He could have enjoyed this lesson."

Jack recounts a journey across the rolling Nebraska prairie, with "scenes and incidents of wild Indian camp life," including "the magnificent sight of a moving village of 'nature's children,' looking like a long rainbow in the bright colors of their blankets, beads, feathers, [and] war paint" as the Pawnee completed an eleven-day march from their reservation to Plum Creek, a tributary of the North Platte River. As the Pawnee set about making camp on the twelfth day, translator Bayhylle informed Omohundro that "the blanket is up three times," signifying that the hunt would begin in earnest in the morning, with "fun and fresh meat" to follow.

"There was a great powwowing that night, and all the warriors were to turn out for the grand 'buffalo surround,' leaving the squaws and papooses in the village," wrote Jack. Just before daybreak, Jack prepared for the hunt in the dark. Unable to view the preparations made by the warriors around him, he admits that his thoughts were "of the grand sight soon to be witnessed . . . wondering how I would 'pan out' in the view of my 'red brothers.'" As the hunters set out, and with the first blue streaks of dawn just appearing over the horizon, Jack took note of several peculiarities that he immediately recognized "placed at a disadvantage, the 'white brother.'"

Jack had followed the custom he had established on the cattle trails of Texas. His mount was fully equipped with bridle, saddle, lariat, rifle, pistol belt, and other gear. The Pawnee wore "as near nothing in garments as Adam and Eve, only breechcloth and moccasins, no saddle, no blanket, not even a bridle, only a small mouth rope, light bow and a few arrows in hand—in fact, not an ounce of weight more than necessary, and, unlike myself, all scudding along at a marvelous rate, leading their fiery ponies, so as to reserve every energy for the grand event in prospect." Comparing the sight of his fully laden bronco to a government pack mule, Jack dismounted, and "mentally gave up the intention of paralyzing my light-rigged side pards in the coming contest." As the Pawnee dismounted, walking along and leading their steeds, Jack assumed that one of them had signaled that the buffalo were quite near. "But what was my surprise," he wrote, "as mile after mile was scored, that I gradually found myself dropping slowly but surely behind, and, so as not to get left, compelled every now and then to mount and lope to the front, there to perceive from the twinkling eyes of friend 'Lo' a smile that his otherwise stolid face gave no evidence of. How deep an Indian can think and it not be surface plain," Jack confided to his readers, "I believe has never been thoroughly measured. Just imagine this 'lick,' kept up with apparent ease by them for ten or twelve miles, and you may get a partial idea of your friend Jack's tribulations. Fortunately, I kept up, but at what an expense of muscle, verging on a complete 'funk,' you can only appreciate by a similar spin."

Just as the combination of pace and distance became too much for Jack, the Pawnee stopped, and three scouts rode back toward the group. A brief council preceded the passing of the pipe. Each warrior walked a short distance before remounting his "now almost frantic steed, each eagerly seeking to edge his way without observation to the front." The Pawnee formed three crude lines, nearly two hundred standing abreast in front, one hundred and fifty just behind them, and another hundred behind that. "The chiefs [were] in front gesticulating, pantomiming, and, with slashing whips, keeping back the excited mass, whose plunging, panting ponies, as impatient as their masters, fretted, frothed and foamed—both seemed molded into one being, with only one thought, one feeling, one ambition, as with flashing eye they waited for the signal, 'Go' to let their pent-up feelings speed on to the honors of the chase."

Spotting a herd of buffalo grazing in a low, flat valley, Pitaresaru, head chief of all four bands of the Pawnee, signaled to the warriors that the buffalo were just below. When he dropped his blanket, the men sped toward the waiting herd. "Whew! Wheez! Thunder and lightning! Talk of tornadoes, whirlwinds, avalanches, water-spouts, prairie fires, Niagara, Mount Vesuvius (and I have seen them all except old Vesuv.); boil them all together, mix them well, and serve on one plate, and you will have a limited idea of the charge of this 'light brigade.' In an instant," wrote Texas Jack, "nothing is visible but a mingled mass of flying arrows, horses' heels, buffaloes' tails, Indian heads, half of ponies, half of men, half of buffalo."

The best of the Pawnee hunters drove the single buffalo of their choice away from the herd, just as a cowboy might cut a bull from a group of cattle. "The clouds of dust gradually rise as if a curtain was lifted, horses stop as buffaloes drop, until there is a clear panoramic view of a busy scene all quiet, everything still (save a few fleet ones in the distance); horses riderless, browsing proudly conscious of success; the prairie dotted here, there, everywhere with dead bison; and happy, hungry hunters skinning, cutting, slashing the late proud monarch of the plains." In his fascination as he observed the Pawnee demonstration of hunting prowess, Jack had failed to kill any buffalo of his own. With Pawnee hunters beginning to grin at his failure, Jack wrote that "a lucky long-range shot (the only one fired during the day) at a stray heifer saved my reputation." If anything, the shot bolstered his reputation, leaving the Pawnee warriors who had questioned his reputation as a hunter mere moments ago now suitably impressed by his skills as a marksman.

As the Pawnee prepared their kills for transport, it became apparent to Jack that the gear that had slowed him down on the walkout from the camp would similarly hinder his ability to ride his kill back to camp. Removing the buffalo's tenderloin, Jack gave the rest of the animal to a Pawnee warrior, much to the apparent amusement of Pitaresaru, who rode up to tell Texas Jack that he could certainly fit more meat on his pony. "He laughed at my objections," wrote Jack, "but as he had loaned me the pony I had to submit. He even directed the gait, and kept up a continual jabbering of 'Wisgoots, ugh! De goinartsonse stak-ees, ugh,' which I afterward learned meant 'Hurry up; I am tired, hungry, and dry—how!'"[5]

Indian Agent Troth, the same man who had denied permission for the Pawnee to travel to Niagara Falls, spent the hunt worrying about the possible outcomes of a Pawnee encounter with either hostile Sioux or white settlers encroaching on the hunting grounds. Receiving a reassuring letter from Omohundro, Troth wrote to the Pawnee in response:

> *Dear friends,*
>
> *I received a letter from Jack, and have also heard . . . of your progress and success which is very satisfactory, and I hope you will succeed in getting a large amount of buffalo meat. You can say to the Pawnee their crops look fine. They will have the largest crops they have ever had since I have been with them. Baptiste's corn opposite my place is very fine indeed. Tell the Pawnees I often think of them, and pray to God that they may succeed on their summer hunt and not do any wrong thing to anybody whilst they are away from me.*
>
> *I was glad to hear you had recovered the horses that were stolen from the Indians. Let me hear from you every opportunity, as it is a great satisfaction to hear from you.*[6]

The return of the stolen horses mentioned in the above letter is no small matter. Most of the white trail agents viewed their assignments and the Indians in their care as inferior in all ways to the interests of the white settlers encroaching on their lands. Most wouldn't have pursued stolen Pawnee steeds with the vehemence of Texas Jack. Omohundro took his job seriously and viewed the interests of the tribe as his priority. In pursuing

Texas Jack, 1873. (HARVARD THEATRE COLLECTION, HOUGHTON LIBRARY, HARVARD UNIVERSITY)

the horse thieves and returning the animals to the Pawnee, Jack was preventing hostility between the settlers and the tribe while at the same time demonstrating to the braves in his care that he viewed their rights and ownership as equal to that of the whites. It grants some insight into Jack's character that he would pursue white horse thieves stealing from the Pawnee with the same zeal he had demonstrated in pursuit of Miniconjou Sioux fleeing with stolen horses from the army a few months earlier.

In the middle of the hunt, we see more evidence of the burgeoning romance between Texas Jack and Ena Palmer. In her journal entry dated July 24, 1872, Ena records that

I, very unexpectedly, received a call from Texas Jack, evening before last, I believe it was. He remained in but a short time; had a few Pawnees with him. I do not think them as fine looking, not so erect as the Sioux; but they say they are better "braves" than the latter. When asking one of the Pawnees if he was not afraid to venture so far on the hunting ground of the Sioux, it was fine to see the expression of unutterable scorn that lighted up for a moment, the stolidity of his face; then instantly relapsing into the grim Stoic, he quietly crossed his throat, giving the sign of the Sioux, and said they were "heap squaws." Mr. Omohundro said that the Indians were in fine spirits; plenty of buffalo, and the papooses all fat.

Jack's willingness to come into town with Pawnee in his care during the hunt without prior authorization from Indian Agent Troth illustrates his fondness for the Southern belle. While Jack spent the summer tracking buffalo with his new Pawnee friends, Ena met another new arrival to North Platte—a dentist named Dr. William Frank Carver. As Ena and Carver spent time together, she showed him some of the same shooting tricks that Texas Jack had demonstrated to her earlier that year. In some ways, Carver might have been considered a competitor for the romantic interest of Ms. Palmer, but for the fact that she made it so readily apparent that she was enamored with the handsome cowboy, even in the company of the erstwhile dentist. In her diary, Ena Palmer recalls one tense moment when Omohundro was passing through town and noticed Ena and Dr. Carver walking together. Leaving Carver without an introduction in her rush to speak to Texas Jack, Ena wrote of her embarrassment that the sight of Omohundro had so distracted her from the attentions of the dentist.

As Texas Jack and the Pawnee hunters entered the final weeks of their summer trek, they were joined by several military officers from Fort McPherson, along with Major North's brother Luther and naturalist George Bird Grinnell. Grinnell, whose later writings would do much to persuade Americans of the necessity of preserving both the Native American way of life and the dwindling buffalo population, was fundamentally affected by his exposure to the Pawnee under the care of Texas Jack. Throughout a career tirelessly dedicated to the conservation of native peoples and the animals that provided their source of sustenance, Grinnell worked with many of the men most prominent in shaping the common perception of the American West, including Owen Wister and Theodore Roosevelt, who wrote that "George Bird Grinnell has [especially] portrayed [the Pawnee] with a master hand; it is hard to see how his work can be bettered."[7] Later instrumental in the establishment of Montana's Glacier National Park, Grinnell included accounts of Texas Jack hunting in the region in the *Forest & Stream* magazine he edited from 1876 to 1911.

Consumers of dime novels and newspapers alike were kept apprised of the adventures of the cowboy hunting alongside Pawnee on the Nebraska prairie. Ned Buntline made sure of that. This letter to the writer from Jack was published in the August 26, 1872, issue of the *New York Weekly*:

Friend Ned,

    I have just returned from one of the longest and hardest trips of my life across the plains. I have been in charge of three thousand Indians on their summer hunt. The game was very much scattered, consequently we had to go a great ways. I was three months away from the settlements. We met with a great many other parties of Indians, some war parties, some friends. Had some little fighting, but no general engagements. We killed some two or three thousand buffalo, packed our animals with dried meat, and reached the Indian Reserve some six days ago.

    I shall be at leisure for the next six weeks. I wish you could contrive to pay us a visit during that time and go out on a hunt. Bill left here yesterday for a hunt in company with Judge Cronnes, of Omaha, and others. Will be gone several days. There is prospects of fresh war with the Sioux. Will be lots of chances for Indian pie before spring. I can take my tribe, the Pawnees, and clean them out two to one if the government will allow it.

    Will write more when I have leisure.

    Yours, as ever,

    J. B. Omohundro

    Texas Jack[8]

For his "services in accompanying a hunting party of Pawnee Indians," Jack was paid $216.66.[9] The Pawnee had grown to trust Texas Jack, who would often refer to the tribe, as he did here, as "my tribe." It was no coincidence that the dime novel Ned Buntline wrote to showcase his friend to the reading world would bear the title *Texas Jack; or, The White King of the Pawnees.*

If the Pawnee people left an impression on Omohundro, the cowboy equally impressed the Pawnee. Though Texas Jack was reportedly honored with the name "Whirling Rope" by tribesmen impressed by his skill with the lasso, his own name would enter the Skidi Pawnee lexicon. For the Pawnee, a cowboy or any man who works with cattle is simply known as *téksis.*

CHAPTER NINE

The Earl of Dunraven

As reports of Grand Duke Alexis and his Nebraska buffalo hunt spread through newspapers across the globe, intrepid sportsmen with the means to reach the American frontier headed west, tempted to try their luck at deer, elk, and moose, but especially bison. Often these trips began with a letter of introduction to an official in the American government, who would find an army officer or scout willing to escort the esteemed gentlemen toward the waiting herds and a significant payday. In the fall of 1872, the Fourth Earl of Dunraven, an English aristocrat, arrived with one of these letters from General Phil Sheridan, requesting that Bill Cody lead him and his friends on an elk hunt.

Windham Thomas Wyndham-Quin, the thirty-one-year-old earl of Dunraven and Mount-Earl, was an Oxford-educated lord who had served as a lieutenant in the 1st Life Guards cavalry regiment. After his service ended, Lord Dunraven covered the Abyssinian War between the British Empire and the Ethiopian forces of Tewodros II as a war correspondent for London's *Daily Telegraph*. In this capacity, he met and shared a tent with *New York Herald* correspondent Henry Stanley, still several years removed from his famously apocryphal greeting of missionary Dr. David Livingstone.

In their discussions, the two journalists compared notes. Dunraven told Stanley about his service with the Life Guards while Stanley described for the earl his time in the Union Army and his travels throughout the American West. Stanley was especially adulatory in his praise of Wild Bill Hickok, whom he had met while working as a special correspondent for the *Weekly Missouri Democrat*. Stanley told the earl about what he called "that particular class, known as Frontiersmen, rangers, hunters, and Indian scouts," and urged the other man to seek out such men if he ever made it to the West.[1] This was the kind of man Dunraven sought in Buffalo Bill Cody as he traveled west in 1872, and the kind of man he found in Texas Jack Omohundro.

Cody was happy to lead the earl and his party, until a second request from General Sheridan intervened. Sheridan now asked Cody to lead a group of personal friends from Chicago, including wealthy Chicago merchant William Milligan. Cody suggested to the earl that his friend Texas Jack Omohundro, fresh off of his long buffalo hunt with the Pawnee, was as capable a scout and hunter as Buffalo Bill himself. "The Earl seemed to be somewhat offended at this, and I don't think he has ever forgiven me for 'going back on him,'" wrote Cody in his first autobiography. "Let that be as it may, he found Texas Jack a splendid hunter and guide, and Jack has been his guide on several hunts since."[2]

Whatever his trepidation may have been in being handed off by Cody, the earl seems to have been immediately taken by the sight of the cowboy, who had altered his hunting outfit after a summer spent chasing buffalo and pursuing Pawnee under the unforgiving Nebraska sun:

> He wore moccasins and had his lower limbs encased in a pair of comfortably greasy deerskin trousers, ornamented with a fringe along the seams. Round his waist was a belt supporting a revolver, two butcher-knives, and a steel, and in his hand he carried his trusty rifle, the "Widow." Jack, tall and lithe, with light brown close-cropped hair, clear laughing honest blue eyes, and a soft winning smile, might have sat as a model for a typical modern Anglo-Saxon.[3]

Accompanying the earl on his travels was Dr. George Henry Kingsley, of the British Kingsley family of writers. Throughout a lifetime of travel not only to America, but to Spain, Polynesia, Canada, Japan, New Zealand, and Australia, Kingsley was a fastidious writer whose missives to his wife were later collected and published by his daughter. One such letter includes this rapt portrait of Texas Jack:

*Come forth! O Texas Jack, known in the "sorf south" before the war as
J. Omahundro [sic], Esquire; and would that a better hand than mine
were here to paint your portrait! If Buffalo Bill belongs to the school
of Charles I, pale, large eyed, and dreamy, Jack, all life, and blood,
and fire, blazing with suppressed poetry, is Elizabethan to the back
bone! He too, is an eminently handsome man, and the sight of him
in his fringed hunting buckskins, short hunting shirt decorated with
patches of red and blue stained leather, pair of delicate white moccasins
embroidered by the hand of some aesthetic and loving squaw, with his
short, bright brown curls covered by a velvet cap with a broad gold
band around it, would play the very mischief with many an Eastern
girl's heart. He, however, has his love and his longings out here, the
pale maiden who lives down on the [Medicine] River, who rides
like a chipney, writes poetry by the yard, shoots pistols as well as Jack
himself—and he is the best shot in the territory . . .*[4]

This pale maiden could only be Ena Palmer, recently moved with
her family from North Platte to nearby Medicine Creek. A summer of
separation served only to fan the flames of her desire, and she'd soon
spurned the advances of Doc Carver, who had followed the Palmer family to Medicine Creek to be closer to Ena. As Jack led the earl and Dr.
Kingsley after buffalo, he stopped to introduce the pair to Ms. Palmer,
who was much impressed by the appearance of her cowboy friend and
his aristocratic charges.

The hunt proved to be a successful one. "[Jack] started for me my
first bison," wrote Dunraven, "a solitary savage old bull, down on one of
the tributaries of the Republican, and under his auspices I slew my first
elk also, and, though it was not a very large one, I thought it the most
magnificent animal the world had ever produced. Together we once made
the most successful run at elk that I have ever heard of, and enjoyed a
day's sport such as I shall never see again."[5] One set of elk horns from
a bull that Jack shot during the hunt was sent to General Sheridan, the
general who had commanded the Union cavalry that fought against Jeb
Stuart's Confederates during the Overland Campaign, and who had
suggested Cody and Omohundro as guides for Dunraven. "The horns are

the largest and handsomest I ever saw," wrote Sheridan in reply. "Please accept my thanks for your attention."[6]

While Jack was busy hunting with both English aristocracy and Pawnee braves, Bill Cody was far from his usual prairie haunts, being introduced to the people and customs of Lower Manhattan. The men that Cody had abandoned the hunt with the Earl of Dunraven for were well connected in New York, and it wasn't long before Cody could no longer politely decline their multiple invitations. Cody's initial reluctance was tempered by the urging of both Professor Ward and Ned Buntline to accept the offer. An embarrassed Cody conceded that he would come as soon as his wife could sew him an appropriate suit of clothes. Arriving in New York, he was hammered with questions about Indians and buffalo, and Ward urged him to set up a public appearance so that he could earn money answering these questions and telling eager listeners about life in the West. Bill declined, telling the professor that he felt it would be questionable to profit when others had so generously brought him East.

The scout was staying at Ward's home when he was convinced by Buntline to accompany him to the theater to see the scout's own life portrayed onstage. Buntline's dime novel *Buffalo Bill, King of the Border-men* had been hugely successful, and an enterprising playwright named Fred Maeder had turned the story into a stage play. Actor J. B. Studley portrayed the scout in the play, and Buntline urged Cody to come see the performance. After watching appreciatively as the actor imitated him before a sold-out house, Cody was invited onto the stage by cheering patrons who had learned that the subject of the drama was in the house.

A nervous Bill Cody stammered before the crowd, mostly unintelligible as he muttered quietly. Nonetheless, the crowd applauded voraciously and the theater owner offered Cody $500 a week if the scout would portray himself onstage. Ned Buntline urged Cody to accept, but the scout declined, fearful that his brief sojourn before the stage lights would be indicative of his dramatic future. "I told him that it would be useless for me to attempt anything of the kind," wrote Cody, "for I never could talk to a crowd of people like that, even if it was to save my neck, and that he might as well try to make an actor out of a government mule. I thanked him for the generous offer, which I had to decline owing to a lack of confidence in myself; or as some people might express it, I didn't have the requisite cheek to undertake a thing of that sort."[7]

At least, not alone. As winter fell on the Nebraska prairie, Jack's "pale maiden" Ena Palmer lamented to her diary that "I have seen Texas Jack *once* since my return to the Medicine. He made a dash call one evening while out here with the Earl of Dunraven. Jack was guide, etc., for the Lord and his party. He told me that he and Buffalo Bill expected to go east on quite a tour. They have been gone for some time now. Of course the papers are full of their sayings and doings."[8]

The two friends had boarded a train bound for Chicago, where they would make history.

ACT II

We had rattling houses, and did a business that was simply immense, and since then we have done well. My summers, you know, I spend on the plains, and winters I strut and fret my time away before the footlights. So I have the solitude of the country and the excitement of the city in mine.

—Texas Jack

CHAPTER TEN

The Scouts of the Prairie

THERE ARE VARIOUS ACCOUNTS OF WHICH MAN CONVINCED THE OTHER to leave the prairie and step on the stage in Chicago. In his first autobiography, Cody says that he had already decided to accept Buntline's offer to act onstage, and that while he was in the process of selling his horses in preparation for the venture, "one of my brother scouts, Texas Jack, said that he would like to accompany me. Now as Jack had also appeared as the hero in one of Ned Buntline's stories, I thought that he would make as good a 'star' as myself, and it was accordingly arranged that Jack should go with me."[1] Cody was likely misremembering, as Buntline's first dime novel about Jack wouldn't be published until three months after the December 1872 debut of *The Scouts of the Prairie*.

Buntline maintained correspondence with both Cody and Omohundro following his departure from Fort McPherson after their initial meeting. According to Louisa Cody, each letter that her husband received was "more pressing than the other and telling of the fortune that could be made if Will would only come back East and be an actor." But Bill's brief sojourn on the stage in New York had shaken him far more than any encounter with hostile Sioux on the plains ever had. Now that Buntline had extended an offer and the promise of wealth, it might be tempting, but to her husband, "the task appeared more difficult than ever." The letters kept coming, and Mrs. Cody admitted that the promise of stardom and thousands of dollars was tempting, but Bill remained scared of the prospect of stepping on the stage again alone.

"Mamma," he confided to his wife, "I'd be awful scared. I'd get out there and just get glassy-eyed from looking at those lights. I couldn't do it. I'd just naturally be tongue-tied." Louisa, who was equally unsure that her husband would manage to retain some measure of dignity if he ventured into acting, tried to show her confidence in Cody, but couldn't keep herself from asking, "Is play-acting just the right thing?"[2]

Despite his self-doubt, Bill couldn't dismiss the words of Ned Buntline promising that hundreds of thousands of people were waiting to see him star in some kind of border drama, and that thousands of dollars were waiting to flow into the Cody family coffers. The opportunity to provide his children and his wife with a lifestyle that was strictly unavailable at Fort McPherson was almost enough to convince Cody that acting was worth the risk. Then, according to Louisa Cody, "When Texas Jack roamed down to the house, he heard that Will was seriously considering the Buntline proposition and immediately decided that he would like to go on the stage himself. Will, wavering, was strengthened." He immediately sat down and wrote a letter to Buntline, telling him that Buffalo Bill and Texas Jack would be on the train to Chicago.[3]

The idea that Texas Jack decided to go East and act only because the offer had been extended to Cody seems dubious at best. Omohundro maintained correspondence with Ned Buntline as well and was likely being lured with the same promises of fame and fortune. In addition to mentioning in his letters to Barnett that he had "always intended to go into something of this kind," Jack later told a New York critic that "he had always, from his earliest infancy, determined to have a natural talent for acting, and now he has it. He had never failed in anything he undertook, and he would not fail in this."[4] Louisa Cody noted that though her husband still had misgivings as he and his cowboy friend prepared for their journey to Chicago, "As for Texas Jack, never was a person happier, for Texas Jack had absorbed the stage fever; he wanted to be an actor, and, what was more, he was going to be an actor whether the audiences said he could act or not."

In addition to his letters to Ned Buntline, Jack also maintained correspondence with Professor Ward, who urged him to come East and give talks—informal lectures simply telling people about the Sioux (Očhéthi

Šakówiŋ) and Pawnee (Chaticks si Chaticks) and the buffalo hunts that occupied the life of a scout. During Ward's artifact-collecting exhibition following the ducal buffalo hunt, Jack asked the professor why he was out West collecting "buffalo hides, Indian garments, and relics." The professor answered that "the people of the East rush in crowds to view these relics and curiosities."

"Thinks I to myself all night," recounted Omohundro, "if the Eastern folks will go see dead buffalo and stuffed Indians, and pay their money for it, what would they not give to see live buffalo and shake hands with live Indians?"[5] Jack asked Professor Ward if he would manage such an operation, but was informed that Ward's duties as professor of geology at Rochester University left little time for theatrical management. It was Ward who had then suggested Texas Jack to Sidney Barnett at the Niagara Falls Museum. Jack's agreement to manage the Grand Buffalo Hunt indicates his understanding that long-term success meant returning to the East, at least long enough to show the eager city folks what life was like on the plains.

It is likely that both Buffalo Bill and Texas Jack assumed that, as Louisa Cody wrote, this was all that acting entailed—standing in front of the audience and talking to them just as you would talk to a group of eager children waiting at the fort when you got back from a hunt or an encounter with the Sioux. By all accounts, the two men arrived in Chicago woefully unprepared for the realities of acting in a written drama. Louisa worried that "neither of them ever had seen more than a dozen stage plays in their lives. They had no idea of how to make an entrance or an exit, they did not know a cue from a footlight, and they believed that plays just happened. The fact that they would have to study and memorize parts never entered their heads."[6]

The pair of scouts were met at the train station by Ned Buntline, who immediately scolded them for not bringing the dozen Sioux and Pawnee chiefs he had promised the local newspapers, but likely had failed to mention to either of the scouts. Shaking off his disappointment, Buntline slapped his stars on the back.

"All right, boys! We'll do a little quick work now and have this play on by Monday night."

The boys were stunned.

"Monday night?" asked Jack, "Ain't . . . ain't that rushing things just a little?"

Buntline smiled reassuringly and admitted, "It is going a little fast, but you fellows ought to be accustomed to that. Come on now. We'll go over and fix up for the theater."

Texas Jack scratched his head.

"I thought that'd all be arranged for."

"Nothing of the kind!" Buntline said knowingly. "The owner's got to see his stars first. So come on."

The trio jumped in a carriage bound for Nixon's Amphitheatre, for the first time discussing the practicalities of a full-fledged dramatic stage show.

"So, who all's going to be with us in this rig-out?" asked Cody, now concerned.

"The company?" asked a nonplussed Buntline. "Oh, I haven't given that a thought. But there are plenty of actors around town. Don't worry a minute about them."[7]

The writer's cavalier attitude covered what was likely a great deal of concern on his part. In truth, Buntline had arrived in Chicago mere hours before his stars. Whether he was worried that his scout and his cowboy would be a failure or that they would fail to show up at all is a matter of conjecture. According to Jay Monahan in his wonderfully titled biography *The Great Rascal: The Life and Adventures of Ned Buntline*, Ned hedged his bets by accepting a contract to travel to Chicago as a fire insurance agent, a promising gig in a city that only a year prior had been devastated by the massive blaze popularly attributed to Mrs. O'Leary's cow. Though it had killed up to three hundred people and left over one hundred thousand Chicagoans homeless, the larger-than-three-square-mile swath of destruction had spared the city's theater district. Buntline may have been all but destitute when he arrived, spending the money he had procured to peddle insurance to rent the theater.

Buntline took Cody and Omohundro to meet theater manager Jim Nixon at his Amphitheatre, a crudely constructed canvas-topped building shaped like a circus tent with board walls. It was erected over the course of two weeks in May, and audiences had been flocking there ever since. Despite its humble beginnings, the *Chicago Tribune* described it as "[a] really elegant and comfortable place of entertainment" boasting an "exterior presenting a brilliant and attractive appearance with its hundreds of flaming gas jets and transparencies, while the interior scene, with the tasteful adornments and blaze of light, was no less attractive."[8] Nixon came out to meet the stars of the new show and asked if they were prepared for their dramatic debut. They responded they might be ready if they had ever seen the thing.

"Where are the Indians you had me advertise?" asked the now-concerned Nixon. The partnership Buntline had initiated with the theater manager was to be a sixty/forty split in Buntline's favor, with Nixon providing the theater, advertising, and orchestra, and Buntline providing the company, the drama, and pictures to hand out at the shows. The writer lied that at the last second, the Pawnee warriors had gone on the warpath and couldn't make the trek.

Jim Nixon was furious. "We advertised Indians! People will demand to see Indians!"

Buntline pointed to the scouts' fringed shirts and beaded leggings.

"We can hire twenty or so actors to play the Indians. Why, they'll be better in my play than the real Indians would!"

Noting the obvious fact that the company was not currently present, Nixon moved on to ask Ned when the company planned to rehearse.

"Tomorrow," answered the writer, almost casually.

"Why wait until tomorrow? There's no one on the stage this afternoon and time's getting short. This is Wednesday, and if you're going to open next Monday, you'll have to do a lot of practicing. So I'd suggest a rehearsal just as soon as you can get out the parts and—"

"Well," Buntline interrupted him, "that's just it. You see, I haven't actually written the play yet."

At this point, theater manager Nixon, Buffalo Bill Cody, and Texas Jack Omohundro each had the same incredulous look on their faces. According to Mrs. Cody, each audibly gasped. The manager recovered enough to inform Buntline that he was not willing to sign a contract on a play that hadn't been written for two "stars" that had never acted in a debut performance scheduled for four days hence.

Not to be dissuaded, Buntline casually asked, "What's the rent on this theater for a week?"

"Six hundred dollars," replied Nixon.

Buntline pulled a wad of money, presumably his advance to sell fire insurance, from his pocket and counted out $300, slapping it on the table.

"Taken—here's three hundred in advance." He asked the stunned Jim Nixon for a receipt and motioned for his actors to come with him.

Returning to the hotel, Buntline retired to his room to produce the play. As he furiously wrote, his stars realized that their expectations were as far from reality as they were from their familiar haunts on the Western prairie. Louisa Cody wrote:

> They had shot Indians on the plains, they had ridden Pony Express, they had lain for days and nights when they did not know whether the next sun would see them crumpled in death, and they had managed to assimilate it all. But here was something new, something different. All the way from the wild, free West had they come, to be hustled and bustled about in a big city, there to learn that they were stars in something that had not even become permanent enough to be placed on paper.[9]

The play that Buntline indelibly placed on paper over the course of the next four hours was titled *The Scouts of the Prairie; and Red Deviltry as It Is!* It was less a new story than an amalgamation, in almost every important detail, of several earlier stories by Ned Buntline. The first was Fred Maeder's play that Cody had seen in New York, itself a dramatization of Buntline's dime novel *Buffalo Bill, the King of the Border Men*, which he based on the stories he'd heard from Cody and Omohundro—about Wild Bill Hickok. The second was *Buffalo Bill's Last Victory; or, Dove Eye the Lodge Queen*, which included the characters of Texas Jack and the Indian maiden Dove Eye. The third was *Hazel Eye, the Girl Trapper*, which included a character Buntline would assume in his new play, a trapper named Cale Durg. Buntline filled out most of his dramatic lines by reciting pieces of his extant temperance speeches. Asked to describe his style of writing, Buntline said, "I never lay out plots in advance. First,

I invent a title; when I hit a good one I consider the story about half finished. . . . After, I begin to push ahead as fast as I can write, never blotting out anything I have once written and never making a correction or modification."[10]

When Buntline rushed into the room four hours later, he shouted to his would-be actors, "Hurrah! Hurrah for the Scouts of the Prairie!"

Texas Jack stood up and looked around the room suspiciously.

"Who are they?"

"They're you! You're the Scouts of the Prairie! That's the name of the play. Now, all that you have to do is memorize these parts."

Script now in hand, Buntline called a bellboy and demanded that he bring every spare hotel employee, along with every pencil, pen, and bit of paper available to Buntline's room. Clerks, maids, and other hotel staff were tasked with copying the hastily written drama while Ned went to hire the additional actors he would need to fill the rest of the parts. He needed warriors for the scouts to repeatedly fight, as well as a stereotypical Mormon antagonist (Mormon Ben), a stereotypical Irish comical character (Phelim O'Laugherty), and a stereotypical Indian maiden with a weakness for the brave scouts (Dove Eye). Cody and Omohundro set to rehearsing, though both were dismayed by the prospect of memorizing Buntline's words, especially given that they had now only three days to accomplish the task.

According to Louisa Cody, at this point the pair decided that acting was not something they were made for. She wrote that looking at the pages of dialogue, Bill reached for his hat and twisted it in his hands. "Jack," he said at last, "I guess we're on the wrong trail. Maybe—maybe we're better at hunting Injuns! I reckon I don't want to be an actor, after all."

Jack was only slightly more optimistic.

"We'll do our best. If I'd known all this, I'd never come on, honest I wouldn't. I thought all there was to play-acting was to just get up there and say whatever popped into your head. And we've got to learn all this?" Texas Jack asked his friend how long he thought it would take to memorize his part.

"About six months. How 'bout you?"

"It will take me that length of time to learn the first line," the cowboy replied.[11]

When Buntline reminded the pair that their reputations were on the line, Jack agreed.

"Yeah . . . and I'd rather be tied at the stake right now. But if I say I'll do a thing, I'll do 'er. Lock us up somewhere and we'll do our derndest!"[12]

Retiring to their room to study the parts, Cody decided that this was the hardest work he had ever done. "This is dry business," joked Jack in agreement, and at his friend's suggestion, rang the bell to summon a bellboy to return with liquid refreshment.

After Buffalo Bill's death in 1917, his wife wrote:

I know there were nights in Will Cody's life that were horrible night-mares from a standpoint of danger and privation. But I am just as sure that there never was such a night as the one when he tried to learn the first elements of being an actor. No one ever will know just what did happen in that room; from the outside it sounded like the mutterings of a den of wild animals. Now and then Will's voice would sound high and strident, then low and bellowing, with Texas Jack's chiming in with a rumbling base [sic]. Every few minutes, bellboys would rush up the hall with ice clinking in the pitchers, hand the refreshments through the door, then hurry away again, with a sort of dazed, non-understanding expression on their faces. And all the while, the rumbling of prairie thunder, the verbal flashes of lightning and crashing of mountainous speech torrents would continue, while guests in the adjoining rooms made uncomplimentary remarks.[13]

The limited rehearsal time was abridged further by the fact that Cody and Omohundro were well known as frontiersmen even before their stage debut. While in Chicago, interested parties would stop at their hotel to ask them questions about hunting buffalo, hunting with the Pawnee, and Texas cattle drives, or just to catch a glimpse of the King of the Border-men and the White King of the Pawnees having a drink or playing a game of billiards. Two bears had recently been released into Lincoln Park, and when the justice of the peace tasked the constable with capturing them, the officer politely declined, as he did not carry life insurance. The *Chicago Tribune* noted that the lawman stopped by the Barnes House hotel to get the advice of Buffalo Bill and Texas Jack. The next day, the three men went to the park together and removed the bears.[14]

After a few days' rehearsal, Texas Jack and Buffalo Bill had managed to memorize a fair share of their lines—as well as stage cues, entrance notes, and anything else written on the page. After Cody yelled out one stage direction at the same volume he recited his lines, Buntline informed the pair that they did not need to recite the cues. Cody yelled back, "Cue! What mischief do you mean by the cue? I never saw a cue except in a billiard room!"[15] When it was time for either of the scouts to speak, they nervously put their hands in their pockets, turned their backs to the audience seats, and shouted their lines without pausing for breath. Buntline and Nixon patiently showed the men where they were supposed to stand and how they were supposed to enter, and then watched as they failed to follow his directions when action was called.

Several hours of intense practice later, Nixon's Amphitheatre filled with Chicagoans anticipating the presence of the Western heroes of the prairies and the "savage Indians." Some of the locals that crowded the theater were well-known to Cody and Omohundro. General Sheridan was there, as was Mr. Milligan. The two scouts stood nervously offstage. After a beautiful Italian ballerina acted in an opening farce penned by Buntline, the appreciative crowd was ready for the main act. The house-lights dimmed, the footlights came up, and the curtain rose.

Neither man could remember any of their lines.

After two hours of the same dozen or so actors dressed as native warriors being lassoed, shot, thrown offstage, or stabbed multiple times by the two scouts, the play was over. Neither of the actors had recited a single line as written. Buffalo Bill failed to introduce Texas Jack by name, leading some in the audience to believe that Jack was actually playing Mr. Milligan. The audience suffered through as many as four separate temperance lectures by Buntline as Cale Durg, cheering when he finally perished at the hands of the native warriors, who then invariably met vengeance at the end of Buffalo Bill's pistol or the coil of Texas Jack's lasso. The Indians were Chicago actors that many of the theatergoers had seen in plays before. Despite all of this, the audience loved it.

The *Chicago Times* critic wrote that Texas Jack and Buffalo Bill were "the real attractions, not only as the heroes of the play, but as celebrities whose fame long antedates their appearance before the footlights."[16] The play might have been poorly written, the lines melodramatic, the plot unbelievable, the Indians fake, and the sets mediocre, but the heroes that the audience thronged to Nixon's to see were real.

Louisa Cody recorded one journalist's reaction:

> *There is a well-founded rumor that Ned Buntline, who played the part of Gale [sic] Durg in last night's performance, wrote the play in which Buffalo Bill and Texas Jack appeared, taking only four hours to complete the task. The question naturally arises: what was he doing all that time? As Gale Durg, he made some excellent speeches on temperance and was killed in the second act, it being very much regretted that he did not arrange his demise so that it could have occurred sooner. Buffalo Bill and Texas Jack are wonderful Indian killers. As an artistic success, "The Scouts of the Prairie" can hardly be called a season's event, but for downright fun, Injun killing, red fire and rough and tumble, it is a wonder.*[17]

The December 19, 1872, issue of the *Chicago Tribune* included this decidedly tongue-in-cheek review:

> *This long-neglected place of amusement has suddenly loomed up as the most largely patronized of any in the city, the audiences making up in quantity what they lack in quality. The drama entitled "Scouts of the Prairie," written in Chicago by Ned Buntline, and introducing two frontier celebrities, is the immediate occasion of the large attendance.*
>
> *It purports to be a vivid picture of life in the Western wilds, and is such to a certain extent—as much so as are the average sensational novels on the same subject, and like the latter, full of inconsistencies.*

The original plan was to concoct a play to suit the material at command, and it is apparent that the design was carried out.

"Buffalo Bill" (William F. Cody), now a member of the Nebraska Legislature, and Texas Jack, both widely known scouts, and a half-dozen genuine Pawnee Indians, having nothing in particular to do, stood ready to accept a histrionic engagement. They had never been on any but the overland stage, and the copper-colored portion of the troupe had generally been accredited with a greater capacity for robbing than ranting.

It occurred to Colonel Judson ("Ned Buntline") that here was a chance for a sensation. The "Scouts of the Prairie" was the result, and it proves to be a sensation. The Pawnees, however, failed to keep their engagement, probably on account of pressing duties with reference to a projected horse-stealing expedition, and in their places there have been substituted a collection of talented supers [supernumaries, or extras] in tan-colored frocks and cambric pantalettes.

Buffalo Bill and Texas Jack are on hand, however, completely equipped in buckskin shirts and leggings, and fairly bristling with revolvers, knives, rifles, etc. Of course, they look like "Scouts of the Prairie," but they seem to labor under a distressing uncertainty as to what they ought to do with their hands, fidgeting uneasily when silent, and when in dialogue poking out the right and then the left at regular intervals, with an evident determination to show no favor between the two.

Their elocution differs somewhat from Booth's and Barrett's, but then Edwin and Lawrence are not scouts, and cannot be expected to stand as exemplars under the circumstances. The fact that Bill and Jack speak their places after the manner of a diffident school-boy in his maiden effort must not be taken as an evidence of meagre dramatic talent or training; all this weakness of voice and nervousness of deportment is but an artful assumption, designed to show that beneath the rough exterior of the daring scouts there beats a heart as tender as a chicken's, while his reckless bravado is merely put on to conceal a delicate, shrinking nature.

The cast of *The Scouts of the Prairie*. From left, Ned Buntline as Cale Durg, Buffalo Bill Cody, Giuseppina Morlacchi as Dove Eye, and Texas Jack Omohundro. (BUFFALO BILL CENTER OF THE WEST, CODY, WYOMING)

The illusion is so complete, however, that one would be almost ready to swear that these gentlemen are not great actors. What with the aid of numerous bloody conflicts, wherein persons, who a minute before, were twenty miles away, are telegraphed back and get there just in time; the beautiful Indian maiden with an Italian accent and weakness for scouts; the lovely white girl held in captivity by the aborigines; the poetical trapper and his felicitous homilies on the beauties of nature and the superiority of water to rotgut as a beverage; the cambric-clad Pawnees from Blue Island Avenue; the inexplicable inebriate who manages to keep drunk for several days without a drop of anything; the prairie fire, the fight for life, the vengeance wreaked on the murderous redskins, and the grand tableau at the close—all these put together furnish rare entertainment for the toiling masses who patronize the show.[18]

The toiling masses might well be entertained, but Nixon and Buntline agreed that their actors couldn't improvise their way through the show every night. No matter how authentic their scout and cowboy might seem, it was in the financial interest of the enterprise that both men receive some assistance in the finer points of acting. They determined that the most experienced thespians in the troupe should give the scouts private acting lessons. Nixon took Buffalo Bill aside to begin working with him while Ned Buntline introduced Texas Jack to the dancer and actress he had hired to play Dove Eye and to dance before every show in what he called a "curtain raiser."

"Texas Jack," he said, "meet the Peerless Mademoiselle Morlacchi." According to Louisa Cody, "Texas Jack put out his hand in a hesitating, wavering way. His usually heavy, bass voice cracked and broke. There were more difficulties than ever now, for Jack had fallen in love, at sight . . . And never did a pupil work harder than Texas Jack from that moment!"[19]

CHAPTER 11

The Peerless Morlacchi

IN HIS AUTOBIOGRAPHY, BILL CODY NOTES THAT ON HIS FIRST TRIP TO
New York to see the play about himself, he "occasionally passed an evening at Niblo's Garden, viewing the many beauties of *The Black Crook*,
which was then having its long run." *The Black Crook*—considered by
theater historians to be the first modern musical—opened in 1866 and
ran for a record-setting 474 performances, despite each show being in the
neighborhood of five and a half hours.

John Banvard, a panorama painter turned museum and theater
impresario, demanded a play for his theater to compete with *The Black
Crook* at Niblo's. Banvard's business manager brought him a play with a
trapeze, ballerinas, magic, a live donkey, and jugglers titled *The Devil's
Auction*. The play's author, Spanish playwright Arthur Armengol, convinced Banvard that if he wanted to pack the house each night, he needed
exotic foreign ballerinas. Banvard agreed, and at a cast dinner at Lorenzo
Delmonico's New York restaurant a few months later, he introduced his
star, a dancer and actress imported from Europe specifically to compete
with the cadre of dancing beauties in *The Black Crook*. Her name was
Giuseppa (Giuseppina) Antonia Morlacchi.

Mademoiselle Morlacchi—or, as she was invariably referred to by
newspapers and in advertisements, "the Peerless Morlacchi"—was an
Italian danseuse and ballerina trained at the Imperial Academy of Dancing and Pantomime at La Scala in her hometown of Milan. Under famed
instructors Augusto Hus and Carlo Blasis, Morlacchi and the other stu-
dents at La Scala endured marathon dance classes of up to four hours.

After assisting in minor roles as a small child, at the age of ten she made her professional debut at the Teatro Carlo Felice in Genoa, dancing in Julian Perrot's ballet, *Faust*.

At the age of sixteen, an Italian aristocrat's attention—and his wife's subsequent scorn—led Morlacchi to leave her native Milan, initially for Turin, but soon to tour Europe with various ballet commitments. She eventually returned to her home country to dance in Naples, Turin, and Florence and was invited by Benjamin Lumley, director of Her Majesty's Theatre in London, to join his ballet, where she was well reviewed. She acted as Esmeralda in *The Hunchback of Notre Dame* in Germany and at the *café chantant* on the Champs-Élysées in Paris, where newspapers christened her with the nickname "The Peerless." She was dancing at the Teatro Real in Lisbon between seasons in London when Don Juan DePol convinced her to travel to America to dance in New York.

A notice in the *New York Herald* announced the arrival of "Mlle. Giuseppina Morlacchi, the acknowledged greatest Terpsichorean artiste of the day." The theater's management also posted an advertisement stating that:

> *In alluding to the debut of this great artiste, the management feel that there will at once and entirely be dismissed from the mind of the public the rumors that an artiste of so great a reputation as Mlle. Morlacchi would never come to this country; and her reputation and artistic merit being already acknowledged, the Management although not desirous of intruding their financial affairs on the public, must necessarily allude to the immense additional outlay the engagement of Mlle. Morlacchi has occasioned, and feel warranted on the evening of her debut and during Mlle. Morlacchi's limited season of thirty nights in making a slight augmentation of the prices of the Orchestra and Balcony chairs.*[1]

Ticket prices doubled to $2 each, with the caveat that prices would return to normal "on the evenings that Mlle. Morlacchi does not appear." With Giuseppina—whose name was often anglicized as Josephine— prepared to debut at Banvard's theater in New York, DePol had a clever idea to publicize the appearance. The Academy of Music Orchestra arrived and set up under the window of her Fifth Avenue hotel room and serenaded her, drawing a sizable crowd.

According to the *Courrier des Etats-Unis* newspaper, DePol had Josephine's legs insured for the exorbitant sum of $100,000 (over $1.5 million in 2020) with Lloyd's of London. "This means," they explained to their readers, "that if the beautiful Italian girl has some accident; if she breaks a kneecap, dislocates an ankle, ruptures a shin or breaks a femur, she will receive $100,000. A lot of people would want to break their legs at this cost."[2] One reporter commented that Mademoiselle Morlacchi's legs were worth more than Kentucky, then the world's most successful racehorse.

Reviews of Morlacchi's American debut were glowing. The *New York Herald* critic was of the opinion that "Signorina Morlacchi fully justified the prestige of her European reputation. The lithe and symmetrical figure, the flashing, dark eyes, the graceful and dashing movements of this fascinating 'queen of the dance' elicited the heartiest applause." A reviewer in the *Courrier des États-Unis* wrote that:

> *Mlle. Giuseppina Morlacchi sparkles among them all, buoyant, audacious, vigorous and original, made to delight and making marvelous use of her marvelous legs. Her performance is bewitching, and she hits upon fortunate results at every moment through her gracefulness, flexibility, ease, and delicacy. In her pas de deux, that she dances with Mlle. Diani or Mlle. Blasina, her rivals, she has some of that languidness, then some of those sudden quivers, that send an involuntary shiver through the entire hall. . . . Mlle. Morlacchi isn't only a dancer with passion and elegance; she's a dancer with style, such as we haven't seen here since Fanny Elssler.[3]*

The kind of dancing that Morlacchi was doing on a nightly basis was incredibly demanding. "Your joints must be trained to do things nature never intended of them," she told an interviewer:

> *To begin with, you must put your heels together and then sit on them, spreading out your knees. Then you must raise yourself up straight.*

This you must do a hundred, a thousand times a day, until your knee-joints seem so hot that you wonder they do not melt. Oh, how they ache when you get through your day's practice. Then you put your feet as far apart as you can and try to touch the floor with your body. These are called splits. It hurts terribly, and you imagine you are going to split apart. The further down you go the worse it hurts. When you get down to within five or six inches of the floor, the teacher is apt to hurry matters by standing on your thighs. If you don't yell then, it is because you were born dumb. After that comes the toe practice. It is worse than the rack. You must learn to raise yourself up and stand on the points of your big toes, not the balls of the toes, but the ends. And you must be able to walk, run, dance, and even to jump and alight on those ends. I have had my toe-nails come lose and my shoes filled with blood over and over again doing this exercise. Then you have to take hold of a door-knob and kick as high as you can for hours at a time. These exercises have to be gone through with daily while you are dancing.[4]

When the show left New York for an extended stay in Boston, a critic for the *Boston Daily Evening Transcript* gushed that

[i]n form she is the ideal of a danseuse: slender in figure, graceful in movement, and with a bright and fascinating countenance which always expresses the poetic emotions illustrated by her artistic achievements. She is, perhaps, as nearly perfect as any danseuse who has ever visited Boston. It is seldom that the performances of any one cause, literally, continuous applause, but in Mlle. Morlacchi's case it may be said that her presence seems to have a magical influence and there is uninterrupted clapping of hands by half or two-thirds of the spectators while she is on stage.[5]

Morlacchi herself was embarrassed by this reception. After her New York debut, the appreciative audience tossed so many roses onto the stage at her feet that she had trouble walking to center stage to acknowledge the applause. One reporter recorded: "Again and again she was recalled, and in the acknowledgment of applause only, can we discern flecks which diminish the luster of our new star. She is entirely too self-conscious."

Another dancer with the company, Augusta Sohlke, received a great deal of press and attention for her "Hungarian Polka" dance, and not to be outdone, Morlacchi decided to introduce her specialty. When the show's choreographer became ill and returned to New York, Giuseppina stepped into the role to provide choreography of her own. At the Theatre Comique in Boston, on December 23, 1867, she introduced America to a style of dance they had never seen—the cancan.

The cancan is a dance consisting of several main constituent movements. The first is the *port d'armes*, wherein the dancer turns on one leg, grasping the other leg by the ankle and holding it above their head. Next is the *grand écart*, which are jumping splits, and the *rond de jambe*, a fast circular motion of the dancer's lower leg with her knee raised and her skirt held up. The final movement is the *battement*, the high kick still performed by the Rockettes at their Radio City Music Hall show every night. The dance remains closely associated with the piece of music Morlacchi most often paired it with, Jacques Offenbach's "Infernal Galop" from his *Orpheus in the Underworld* operetta.

The cancan is incredibly physically demanding, and the flashes of leg and lifted skirt were as scandalous to the audiences in America in the 1860s as the pelvic gyrations of Elvis Presley and the mop-top haircuts of the Beatles would be a century later. Dancers wore black stockings and colored undergarments to be even more provocative. One common move in the cancan dancer's repertoire was to approach a man and wager that she could remove his hat without using her hands. When he invariably accepted the bet, she would high-kick his hat off, exciting him with a glimpse of her pantaloons while simultaneously cautioning him with the threat of a second kick, this time to his face.

According to some accounts, scandalized ladies of Boston soon refused to see the show. An article in Boston's *Christian Register* newspaper warned readers that "The plays now put upon the stage at the Theatre Comique are such as no lady willingly sees. The ballet itself is a legitimate and pretty entertainment . . . the prostitution of the ballet to the demands of the lowest appetites is an evil."[6] The *Daily Advertiser* went further, saying:

Giuseppina Morlacchi, 1867. (FROM THE COLLECTION OF TONY SAPIENZA DMD, RIDGE-
WOOD, NEW JERSEY)

An exhibition, call it what you will, in which women as nearly naked as flesh-colored tights fitting closely to the whole form can make them, dance and posture and with kisses and motion offer to the eye every lascivious suggestion that can be acquired by sight, is nightly attended in Boston—pianoforte-leg-covering Boston—by church members, lawyers, doctors, indeed the promiment examples of the city, and these too with wives and daughters accompanying. The young ladies are—allowed, shall I say? No, let me rather say obliged—to sit beside young gentlemen of their acquaintance and look upon what I have attempted to describe, while every new posture elicits shouts of delight and applause from their possible partners of the last or the following evening. . . . One of the worst features in this case is the fact that in M'lle Morlacchi the managers had an "artiste" such as had rarely, if ever, been seen in America, and it is the misfortune of this young woman to have encountered managers and a public taste that obliged her to appear in such an exhibition.[7]

The scandal does not seem to have proved as effective a deterrent for the city's male populace, as the night after Morlacchi debuted the cancan, the Theatre Comique grossed $1,500, the most it had ever earned for a single performance. Local comics joked that the fire brigade Barnicoat Engine Company's Steamer No. 4 had been permanently stationed outside the theater to douse the arduous heat theatergoers could expect to experience.[8]

Among Morlacchi's many admirers was Jim Fisk, New York robber baron and business partner of Jay Gould. Fisk—who owned the Grand Opera House, where Giuseppina was performing—earned his riches as a stockbroker after a rocky start in life. At the age of fifteen he ran away from home to join a circus before becoming a waiter, a shoe peddler, and eventually a salesman in Boston. During the Civil War he sourced cotton smuggled from the South to fulfill his textile contract with the federal government. His attempt, with Gould, to corner the market on gold would result in the famous Black Friday market scare of 1869.

As Morlacchi waited backstage at the theater one evening, Fisk walked into the room and placed a diamond ring on her finger. Without

Advertising for Morlacchi's cancan, which premiered to American audiences in December 1867, at Boston Theatre Comique. (HARVARD THEATRE COLLECTION, HOUGHTON LIBRARY, HARVARD UNIVERSITY)

time to respond, she was rushed to the stage to dance. Returning to her room after the show, she found Fisk waiting. She removed the ring from her finger and handed it back to Fisk.

"My dear young lady, it's real," he promised. "I don't think you quite understand the value of that little stone. It's of the first order and worth at least $5,000!"

Giuseppina shrugged and showed Mr. Fisk the door. "Bah! I can make that with one of my toes."

As he left the theatre, Fisk commented to an associate, "There is a good woman that a bad man could fight for."[9] Bad man Fisk was eventually murdered after a failed extortion attempt by a business associate who had fallen in love with Fisk's mistress.

Touring taught Morlacchi a great deal, and as she observed management and dealt with rapid turnover in the cast, she developed an understanding of the financial problems that managers faced. Gradually she assumed the role of spokesman for the dancers, defending them against managerial injustice. In July 1868, DePol's *corps de ballet* was stranded in St. Louis when the manager went bankrupt. Morlacchi came to the rescue, offering her services at a benefit for the dancers and finding a theater manager willing to let her use his venue.[10]

Giuseppina was an advocate and vocal champion of those she believed were being wronged. This was demonstrated especially when the disadvantaged party was a female who, unlike Giuseppina, lacked the position and power to stand up for themselves. Preparing for one performance, she watched as the theater's property manager carelessly broke a helmet belonging to one of the ballerinas in the company. When management demanded that the girl pay the requisite two dollars to replace it, the indignant Morlacchi stormed into the office and explained that she herself had seen the property manager, not the girl, break the helmet. When the manager refused to refund the two dollars, Giuseppina grabbed the girl's hand and left the theater, refusing to complete her engagement.[11]

She was also a perfectionist, demanding the best from herself and from the other dancers and musicians on tour. At one performance in New York, a critic noted that there seemed to be some disconnection in the timing between the musicians and the dancers during the first act. As Act II began, this dissonance continued, and twice Giuseppina glared at the orchestra leader and shook her head. The critic noted that the orchestra leader visibly trembled the second time this happened. "The Hungarian Parlor Quadrille," a number in the show, had just begun when suddenly Morlacchi,

> [w]ith flashing eyes and frowning face, stepped forward to the orchestra, and, looking down upon the nervous leader, petulantly exclaimed, "Once more!" The leader rapped with the bow of his fiddle upon his music stand, and the musicians, in obedience, ceased their blowing and their scraping, while the troupe of sylphic beauties, somewhat confused, withdrew. Again the music started, and in came the dancers, and, at about the same point at which the ballet had first ceased dancing, Morlacchi flashed into anger, and her little feet pattered into rapid motion, and away she went, leaving the stage in utter disgust.[12]

In 1869 she toured with her own Morlacchi Grand Ballet Troupe under the management of veteran actor John M. Burke, and they appeared in a well-reviewed version of Shakespeare's *The Tempest* at New York's Grand Opera House. The following year she purchased a farm in Billerica, Massachusetts, and in April returned to Europe to retrieve her father. When she arrived again in America a few months later, the seventy-two-year-old Antonio joined Giuseppina and her sister Angelina on the farm. They would remain at Giuseppina's Billerica farm while she toured with her company.

Giuseppina found that she enjoyed the quiet life on her farm with her family, and theater managers who wanted to book her production company were obliged to travel to Billerica to find her. A writer in the *Boston Post* noted that when two Boston theater owners traveled to her farm to secure her services at that city's Adelphi Theatre, a servant informed them that she was not in the house, but somewhere on the farm. A quick survey revealed Morlacchi in a field, digging potatoes for dinner. Morlacchi insisted that the gentlemen stay for dinner, of which the potatoes she had dug served a humble part.[13]

As Morlacchi toured, reviewers continued to praise both her beauty and her skill as a dancer. A *New York Times* review of a performance of *Undine* at the National Theatre gushed that "Morlacchi's dancing is a song without words. It is delicate, intricate and fanciful, yet so thoughtful, earnest and intelligible as to make one really feel magnetically all that her bewitching movements are designed to express." The *Chicago Thespian* reported that "of her dancing there is but one voice and one judgment—she is peerless—her graceful movements and postures are the poetry of motion—exquisitely beautiful and not vulgar—graceful, without offense to the most refined, one can only think of a light-limbed fairy, performing the most difficult evolutions with a masterly grace and finish as wonderful as beautiful."[14]

John M. Burke—later billed as Arizona John when he toured with Texas Jack, and then as Major Burke while serving as marketing mastermind for Bill Cody's Wild West shows—likely met Morlacchi when he was playing a minor role in a production of *The Devil's Auction*. By all accounts, Burke became smitten with the beautiful dancer the moment he met her. When Morlacchi left *The Devil's Auction*, Burke offered himself to her as a business manager, and in that capacity was hugely devoted to the danseuse, encouraging her to continue to explore choreography and eventually to seek and accept her first speaking role onstage.

In 1870, Giuseppina was well established with her sister Angelina and her father Antonio at their little farm in Billerica, Massachusetts. That year's census record also shows John M. Burk [*sic*] of New York living at the farm, listed as a domestic servant.[15] At the end of the year, Morlacchi's troupe traveled to San Francisco for an extended engagement at the new California Theatre. According to Burke, as they returned east in the spring of 1871, "happening to stay over at North Platte, Nebraska, with the company, I accidentally met and was introduced to W. F. Cody (Buffalo Bill) and John B. Omahundra [*sic*] (Texas Jack)."[16] The scouts were invited by Burke to see Morlacchi's next performance in Omaha.

According to Jeff Lyon of the *Chicago Tribune*, by 1872, "a kind of balletomania seized Chicago. The Nixon [Amphitheatre], Rice's Theater and the McVickers Theater imported a series of La Scala–trained ballerinas, including the redoubtable Giuseppina Morlacchi."[17] Morlacchi was featured at Nixon's Amphitheatre beginning in mid-November, and her run was coming to an end when Buntline, Cody, and Omohundro arrived in town. John Burke was likely approached by Ned to hire Giuseppina. Initially, her acquisition by Buntline was meant to ensure crowds by opening proceedings with a pantomime dance number, but short of actors and assured by Burke of her dramatic abilities, Buntline extended an offer to Morlacchi to play the lead female part of Dove Eye.

According to Burke, "So soon as [Buntline] saw M'dmlle play Narra-mattah in *The Wept of Wish-Ton-Wish*, a standard character in those days, founded on the story of the romance of *The Last of the Mohicans*, then he conceived the idea of writing a play in which M'dmlle should be the central figure, and which should also intro-duce his two great western celebrities, Buffalo Bill and Texas Jack. When the proposition was made to M'dmlle Morlacchi it, for some reason, pleased her greatly, and Buntline got to work and wrote the play."[18]

As actors, Buffalo Bill Cody and Texas Jack Omohundro were far from a sure thing. Though the audi-ence in New York had been happy to see Cody onstage after watching a professional actor portray him for a few hours, Ned Buntline was well aware that his stars might have only ever seen a dozen plays between them, and that neither had ever acted before. He needed a way to guaran-tee ticket sales, and Morlacchi was that guarantee. She had never failed to attract an audience, and Buntline hoped that people would be willing to pay to see her, even if his scouts got off to a rough start.

Giuseppina Antonia Morlacchi, as she appeared in 1869. The management of Boston's Atheneum Theatre pre-sented the medal to her in apprecia-tion for her record-setting ticket sales. (HARVARD THEATRE COLLECTION, HOUGH-TON LIBRARY, HARVARD UNIVERSITY)

Morlacchi's role as the production's lone trained actor is noted in an article in Street & Smith's *New York Weekly*, the same publication that showcased Ned Buntline's dime-novel stories about Buffalo Bill and Texas Jack. The article may have been submitted by Buntline himself:

*Originality ever begets popularity. And this, perhaps, added to his own genius, is the great secret of the literary success of our contributor, "NED BUNTLINE." His tales are wonderful in their originality, for he never has been charged with copying a thought or description from another, though his stories run up into the hun-*dreds *in number.*

But his last wonderful success deserves a special notice. In four hours in Chicago, on December 15, 1872, he wrote the drama, Scouts of the Prairie—*with five rehearsals in two days, with a new company, he placed before an audience of 2,500 people, a perfect success.*

His heroes were "Buffalo Bill," "Texas Jack," and himself as Cale Durg, all in person.

The rest were Indians, squaws, actors, etc., with but one star, the far-famed and peerless Morlacchi as DOVE EYE, a character which the great danseuse fills to perfection.[19]

It is worth noting that Morlacchi, the Italian ballerina billed under the French title Mademoiselle, dancing on the toes of her moccasined feet while adorned in a tribal headdress and decoration, served as another connection between civilization and savagery, the theme of the show. Morlacchi's character Dove Eye neatly parallels Pocahontas, the native maiden ensuring the safety of a white man while forsaking her own, contextually inferior, people and culture. That the Dove Eye character eschews her own people for the love of a white scout purposefully demonstrated the inevitable victory of white Anglo-Saxon culture over Native American tradition. The contrast between Dove Eye, the maiden who joins the white men out of love, and the warriors who dared to oppose Cody and Omohundro only to meet their ends at the hands of those heroes, shows the choice that Buntline sought to make clear. Andrea Harris points out that *[w]hen read intertextually with the narrative of the ballet-girl in popular literature, the spectre of a European "other" who gestured Eastward to the class and cultural reorganization of the metropolis emerges in* The Scouts of the Prairie, *the earliest prototype of the* Wild West *spectacles. In addition to affirming Dove Eye's civilized side, Morlacchi's ballet-dancing body pointed to social and economic worries about class, gender, and race in capitalist civilization.*[20]

Morlacchi in her stage costume as Dove Eye, "the beautiful Indian maiden with an Italian accent and weakness for scouts." (HARVARD THEATRE COLLECTION, HOUGHTON LIBRARY, HARVARD UNIVERSITY)

That the first depiction of what would eventually become the modern Western included a diminutive Italian ballerina dancing on the tips of her toes while dressed in a headdress that would realistically have been worn only by male members of the plains tribes, and then only for ceremonial purposes, does not stand out as a glaring inaccuracy. The reason for this is simple: It set a precedent that continues to permeate Western myth.

Though Morlacchi would be the first, Latin people would go on to portray Native Americans in theater, film, and television for years to come. And the "good Indian woman," however inaccurately dressed, falling in love with the white cowboy exists in countless pieces of Western literature. This trope remains firmly enshrined in the Western to this day, with native love interests appearing in movies such as *The Bronze Bride, Broken Arrow, The Indian Fighter*, and a slightly altered version in *Dances with Wolves.*

CHAPTER TWELVE

The Scouts on Tour

THE *SCOUTS OF THE PRAIRIE* HAD AN IMMEDIATE IMPACT ON THE THEAT-rical world. By December 29, 1872, while the troupe moved from Chicago to St. Louis and then to Cincinnati, the Myers' Opera House in Chicago was preparing for its forthcoming season by announcing, "A complete change of programme . . . for New Year's Week . . . *Chicago in 1873*, introducing Billy Rice as *Buffalo Bill*, Cotton as *Texas Jack*."[1] This copy of Buntline's play, like the many competing border dramas that sprang up in the wake of the *Scouts* success, owed its existence to what Sandra K. Sagala calls "drama pirates . . . Men who sat in the audience, took shorthand notes, and later transcribed them into dialogue. If the bootlegger could prove in court that he had only witnessed a play, then memorized it, he had the right to present it as original. In the days before ubiquitous photographs, too, anyone calling himself 'Buffalo Bill' could easily pull off the deception."[2]

Imitators and competitors were something Cody and Omohundro would have to deal with for the rest of their lives. The two threatened some of the more-obvious copies with lawsuits and other legal action, most often when those shows played in the same city as Buffalo Bill and Texas Jack. Despite this, neither man was ever able to completely stop other men from appearing as "the original heroes" onstage, and trading on their hard-earned fame for personal gain.

These imitations came because of the play's commercial success and despite its critical failure. The first critics to write about Buntline's drama were harsh, though they occasionally lavished their sparse praise on the real-life heroes portraying themselves onstage or on the production's leading lady. When the tour reached its fifth stop in Indianapolis in January, readers of the local *Indianapolis News* were informed that:

> *"Scouts of the Prairie," a merciless reflection upon the intellect of any person that willingly witnesses it, drew another crowded house last night, though what there is to see beyond three men who have been made notorious by sickly weeklies and thinly written Indian stories, is a matter of curiosity. The play is no play, neither drama, comedy, farce, or common tragedy, but is a conglomeration of the most aggravated incongruities. The same party of Indians are scalped and rescalped— two of the Red Skin race are represented as fighting against their own tribe; Cale Durg, very untrapper-like, coolly walks into the midst of a band of his enemies, is captured by two renegade whites who walk up from behind, and shot. He falls, dies, revives, stands up, shoots one more Injun and then dies for good. Buffalo Bill and Texas Jack revenge his death by attacking the same old squad and reslaying some of them for the third or fourth time. There should be less killing or more Injuns.*[3]

Though no night after the first would prove to be quite so disjointed and far removed from the script Ned Buntline had jotted down in his Chicago hotel room, *The Scouts of the Prairie* was different almost every show. After the false start of the initial performance, manager Nixon attempted to avoid a repeat by advising Texas Jack to greet Buffalo Bill onstage "just as though you had not seen him in several years." As the two men walked onto the stage for the sophomore show, Jack yelled out, "Jesus Christ! How are you, Bill?" As the audience erupted in laughter, Cody responded in kind, asking, "Jack, ya damned fool! Don't you know you are before an audience?" Texas Jack then told the audience about an elk hunt and the hundreds of pounds of meat he had brought to market, and the show proceeded from there.[4]

On December 21, the troupe's final night in Chicago, they were joined onstage by a young man named Carlos Montezuma, playing the role of Azteka, a young Apache captive. Carlos, a Yavapai-Apache (Yavapé/Na'isha) whose birth name was Wassaja, was kidnapped by

Pima (Akimel O'odham) raiders as a child to be sold or bartered. He was purchased by an Italian photographer named Carlo Gentile for thirty silver dollars, as Gentile was worried that someone with less than wholesome intentions would buy the boy. Gentile raised the boy as his son, and the pair were in Chicago when Gentile's old friend Giuseppina Morlacchi introduced them to Ned Buntline. Gentile was contracted to take pictures of the scouts to be used as promotional material, and Montezuma was taught to act for his brief appearance in the play's third act. As Azteka, he attacked Phelim O'Laugherty, the drunken Irish character in the play, until Buntline's Cale Durg came to the rescue, launching into one of his impassioned temperance speeches.

Carlos Montezuma would go on to become the first Native American student at the University of Illinois. After graduation, he studied medicine at Northwestern University, becoming the first Native American man to earn a medical degree from an American university. He worked as a doctor for the Bureau of Indian Affairs for a time before founding the Society of American Indians in 1911 and dedicating himself to supporting the rights of his own Yavapai and other Native American people.

By the time *The Scouts of the Prairie* appeared on Broadway at Niblo's Garden on the last day of March 1873, the play had been refined quite a bit. After their run in Chicago, the troupe moved to St. Louis, Louisa Cody's hometown. Here, Bill Cody's extended family was present to watch him in his new venture. At one point during the show, Bill leaned over the footlights to ask his wife, "Honest, Mama, does this look as awful out there as it feels up here?" Louisa was mortified when the audience laughed at her husband and applauded for her, demanding that she join her husband onstage. For the rest of the tour, she insisted on sitting either in a private box or at the back of the theater.

Before arriving on Broadway, the troupe made twenty-seven stops in various cities, including Cincinnati, Pittsburgh, Rochester, Louisville, Hartford, Boston, and Lowell, Massachusetts, near Morlacchi's Billerica farmhouse, where her father and sister attended a performance.

Josephine also invited Jack to accompany her to an opera performance in Hartford, Connecticut. Approached by reporters, Omohundro instinctively cultivated a kind of folk persona, affecting a backward Southern charm as part of his stage character. Theater patrons and dime-novel readers were shown a former Rebel turned cowboy and frontier scout but were not privy to the former schoolteacher and voracious reader, prone to quote Shakespeare, Milton, and Mark Twain. According to a reporter for the local paper, Jack "expressed the opinion that it would have been a pretty good show if the singing had been omitted."[5]

By the time *The Scouts of the Prairie* hit Broadway, the principal actors knew their lines, reciting them without including a single stage cue. They were well received in the city and praised for their authenticity. Had Cody and Omohundro been proper actors, they might have been criticized for their elocution or lack of stage presence. Representing themselves, however, they came across as truly genuine—something even the finest New York stage actors could not achieve.

A reporter in one New York paper was quite taken with the scout's demeanor when he described his first encounter with Texas Jack:

Jack is never without a gun—swears he could not breathe without one; and in his recent walk up and down Broadway always carried his rifle with him. He carries a brace of elegantly mounted pistols in his pockets, and a bowie knife is a conspicuous feature of the furniture of his apartment at the Metropolitan Hotel. In spite of his exposures and adventures, J. B. Omohundro, or Texas Jack, is very fresh-faced—almost boyish looking. In fact, he says that his youthful appearance has always been against him in one branch of his business—when guiding immigrants across the Plains—for travelers have often preferred trusting themselves with older guides, simply because these latter were older, and consequently, they reasoned, must be more experienced. But, as Jack says, "a man don't always carry all he knows in his wrinkles."

In his demeanor Texas Jack is very unassuming. There is no "swagger" or "bounce" about him, and, as he phrases it, he "hates a quarrel worse than a snake," though he had killed over a score of men in his time, when, as he expresses it, he "got mad on principle"—that is to say, when the quarrel was forced upon him. He dresses in plain stuffs, though he affects heavy watch-chains and diamond jewelry, smokes all the time, never walks save when he cannot help it, and then could walk a hundred miles if necessary; prefers whisky to any other known liquid, though he seldom drinks to excess, and is free and easy in his social discourse.[6]

During the months of working together between shows to refine his acting chops, Texas Jack and Giuseppina Morlacchi grew increasingly close, often meeting privately for meals after the show finished. Jack initially continued to send letters to Ena Palmer, including clippings of reviews from newspapers in the cities they had visited, but these ceased as his relationship with Josephine deepened. Ena followed the progress of Omohundro and Cody from Medicine Creek but wondered in her diary if this business venture was as doomed to fail as the buffalo wrangling for the Niagara Falls hunt had been.

As the show moved from city to city, the touring company incorporated the parts of the Chicago run that had worked, and the show now began with Buntline's Cale Durg, a frontier trapper, staring into the imaginary sun and asking what could be taking his scout friends so long. After fretting about their whereabouts for a few moments, while slipping in briefer versions of his temperance messages whenever possible, Buntline is interrupted when Buffalo Bill and Texas Jack make their triumphant arrival. The pair then regale Buntline and the audience with tales about the hunt they had just finished. In some cities, friends of Cody and Omohundro were mentioned, just as Milligan had been in Chicago. Omohundro often used his portion of the tale-telling to try to crack his friend Cody's dashing stage demeanor, as Cody was always amused by Jack's frequent Southern colloquialisms and turns of phrase. Eventually, Morlacchi, as the Indian maiden Dove Eye, dances onto the stage to warn the scouts that there are "dangerous Indians" about, and that their chief Wolf Slayer is searching for the trio with ill intent. With a rousing speech about wiping out the warriors, the scouts set off on the trail.

The villain of the piece, Mormon Ben, is dissatisfied with his fifty wives and seeks to add to their number a maiden named Hazel Eye, an orphan girl that Cale Durg has taken in as a ward. Mormon Ben discusses this with a trio of racial pastiches in the form of Dutchman Carl

Pretzel, Italian Sly Mike, and Irish Phelim O'Laugherty. Mormon Ben has allied these non–Anglo Saxons with the "savage Indians." He sends Wolf Slayer to capture Hazel Eye as she tells Buntline's character at length how wonderful she thinks he is for providing for her now that her parents have tragically died.

The Indians rush in and seize Hazel Eye and Cale Durg, tying them to a stake before proceeding to imitate a ceremonial war dance, flashing both tomahawks and foreboding glances at members of the audience. While Buntline remonstrates the native warriors for being drunks and cowards, Morlacchi's Dove Eye lithely dances in and cuts the ropes that hold Hazel Eye and Durg. As the Indians attempt to recapture the escapees, Texas Jack and Buffalo Bill appear. They restate their intentions to wipe out the native braves and proceed to shoot and kill—sometimes multiple times over—the warriors that Louisa Cody described as "Chicago Indians from Clark Street and Dearborn and Madison, Indians who never had seen the land beyond the borders of Illinois, Indians painted and devilish and ready to be killed."[7]

While the villainous Mormon Ben and his associates collaborate with the "bloodthirsty" Indians, Buffalo Bill and Texas Jack fall in love with Dove Eye and Hazel Eye, not always in that order. Buntline seizes the opportunity to launch into another temperance lecture. The warriors attack again after the lengthy diatribe against the evils of alcohol, and once more the scouts arrive just in time to shoot down most of them, with Texas Jack demonstrating his skills with the lariat by lassoing the last pair of escaping braves. A retreating Wolf Slayer manages to shoot and kill Carl Durg on his way out. Buntline's death scene sometimes stretched out for up to fifteen minutes, invariably greeted with some of the show's most raucous applause.

Texas Jack and Buffalo Bill swear to get revenge on the warriors that have murdered their friend but are forced by a surprise attack to fight to the death sooner than expected. The white villains start a prairie fire to keep the scouts from escaping, but the pair manage to make their way out of danger just before the fire would consume them. The maiden Dove Eye shoots Wolf Slayer, the civilizing influence of the white scouts having prevailed over her "savage" nature. As the bad guys retreat, the handsome plainsmen are at last able to declare their love to the pair of beautiful ladies, signaling the end of the play.

Critics reporting on the drama in Eastern papers were often more accustomed to viewing Edwin Booth in Shakespeare than John Omohundro and William Cody in a melodrama. In this context, reviews could be scathing. A critic for the *New York Herald* wrote:

> *Mr. Judson (otherwise Buntline) represents the part as badly as it is possible for any human being to represent it and the part is as bad as it was possible to make it. The Hon. William F. Cody, otherwise "Buffalo Bill" and occasionally called by the refined people of the Eastern cities "Bison William," is a good-looking fellow, tall and straight as an arrow, but ridiculous as an actor. Texas Jack, whose real name, we believe, is Omohundro, is not quite so good-looking, not so tall, not so straight, and not so ridiculous. Mlle. Morlacchi, as Dove Eye, is only an insipid forest maiden, but the worst actor of the lot is Senorita Carfana, the representative of Hazel Eye, a young white woman who is very tall, very straight, and very virtuous. She is worse, even, than Ned Buntline, and he is simply maundering imbecility. Her first appearance is ludicrous beyond the power of description, more ludicrous even, than Ned Buntline's temperance address in the forest. To describe the play and its reception is alike impossible . . . everything was so wonderfully bad that it was almost good. The whole performance was so far outside of human experience, so wonderful in its daring feebleness that no ordinary intellect is capable of comprehending it—that no ordinary mortal can discuss it at any length with good taste and good temper . . . The entertainment began with a farce by Buntline called "The Broken Bank," probably the worst ever written, and certainly the worst-acted atrocity ever seen on any stage.*[8]

When an Omaha newspaper described the Italian ballerina Giuseppina Morlacchi as, "a mulatto dancer from Chicago,"[9] Buffalo Bill penned a letter to the editor reproaching him for his "allusion to an estimable lady, of irreproachable public and private character, whose skin is as white, and blood as pure as your own—if not purer—[as] simply contemptible."[10]

Not swayed by rumors of the actors' heritage or questions of their dramatic skills, audiences packed theaters everywhere *The Scouts* appeared. On the first night in Chicago, the company brought in $2,800 in ticket sales. Typical ticket prices were 75 cents for seating on the floor or in a booth and 25 cents for a spot in the gallery. Often the galleries were crowded with children who had saved each cent they could to see the heroes whose adventures they had so recently followed in their dime novels.

Publicity went beyond newspaper advertisements and the occasional shooting demonstrations by Cody and Omohundro, such as the exhibition of their pistol skills during a tour of the Samuel Colt factory when they played Hartford. In St. Louis, the tour's second stop, Ned Buntline announced to reporters that his scouts had subscribed to *Temperance Monthly*. On the day after Christmas 1872, the scouts were laughing at the announcement of their sobriety while sharing a drink in the lobby of the Southern Hotel at two o'clock in the afternoon. Buntline was in his room preparing advanced publicity for their next stop in Cincinnati. When a telegram arrived at his door, Ned protested that he had no change and had to go to the hotel lobby to break a bill. At the foot of the stairs, he found a large group of men waiting for him. One of the men slapped him on the back and said, "Mr. Buntline, I want you."

The man introduced himself as Deputy County Marshal Reinstadtler and told Buntline that he should consider himself a prisoner. Buntline asked what he was being arrested for, glancing toward Cody and Omohundro, sitting at a table and sharing a drink with some of the other actors in the show. One of the Chicago actors pulled a revolver from his belt. Omohundro put his hand over the barrel of the man's gun and shook his head.

"If we were on the plain we might have something to say," he told the actor. "Here in the city, that's no use. We must take what comes."

The deputy explained to Buntline that he was under arrest for jumping bail after inciting an anti-German riot in the city some twenty years earlier. After a friend fronted the money to have the author released on a $5,000 bond, Omohundro and Cody heard a rumor that Buntline had precipitated the arrest by sending an anonymous letter to the city's attorney in order to gain more newspaper coverage for their opening night in the city. If true, Buntline's promotional efforts greatly exceeded his advertising in Chicago, where he had offered every lady who attended the play a photographic portrait of himself with Cody and Omohundro. In leaving St. Louis to travel to the next stop in Cincinnati, Buntline jumped bail once again.

Often newspaper advertisements consisted merely of the names of the actors and the theater they would be performing at, but occasionally there were more-extended pieces, including a biographical sketch of Texas Jack that initially appeared in the *Springfield Republican* newspaper:

J. B. Omohundro was born of French parentage, in Virginia, in 1846, and is now in his twenty-seventh year. His early life was a succession of adventures, divided between sea and land, all over the western continent, finally locating in Texas. Very early in his life the peculiar qualities marking his manhood were developed, and at the breaking out of the rebellion he gave his sympathies and energies to the Confederate cause, though it is only justice to say that he was long ago thoroughly reconstructed. He entered the service in the First Texas regiment, but soon found his proper situation as a favorite scout and guide of Stuart's famous cavalry force. After the close of the war his peculiar qualities were further developed, and his rare skill as a rider, and in managing and driving vast herds of cattle, gave him the familiar cognomen of "Texas Jack," and finally brought him in charge of the Government cattle on the western plains, where he met Buffalo Bill and Ned Buntline. . . . [T]here is not a young lady of romantic disposition who ever got a view of his face but will pronounce him a downright good-looking young fellow, and the best of it is that he is not yet a "married man."[11]

It wasn't Jack's skill as a cowboy or Bill's reputation as a buffalo hunter that most interested theater patrons, dime-novel afficionados, or newspaper readers. News of an ongoing conflict in California between the US Army and Modoc tribesmen under Kintpuash, known as Captain Jack, was beginning to reach newspaper readers on the East Coast.

A standoff led to increased fears that further encouraged theater patrons to flock to see the famous Indian fighters now gracing the New York stage.

Two hundred Modoc departed from the Klamath reservation after the federal agent assigned to the area failed to prevent the theft of Modoc lumber by Klamath tribesmen, with the fleeing Modoc returning to their former homes on the Lost River. While they were confined to the reservation, settlers had moved into Modoc lands, and the settlers' new homes were now raided by the returning Modoc. When the Modoc hid out in caves in the lava beds on the south shore of Tule Lake, a lengthy standoff ensued. The Modoc eventually killed members of a federal peace commission, including General Edward Richard Sprigg Canby, believing that the deaths of the Americans would discourage the government from attempting to remove the Modoc.

Quite naturally, the deaths of federal agents had the opposite effect on the willingness of President Grant to tolerate the native resistance. Additional troops were dispatched, capturing Captain Jack and his fellow tribesmen. The federal troops were assisted by fourteen scouts from the Warm Springs tribe under the leadership of Donald McKay, who turned his involvement into frontier celebrity and later a theatrical career of his own. Captain Jack and five of his fellow Modoc were tried and sentenced to death, with two more committed to life sentences on Alcatraz. The remaining members of the tribe were sent to the Quapaw Agency in Indian Territory, present-day Oklahoma.

When a newspaper reporter asked Cody for his assessment of the situation as an Indian fighter, he responded, "Give me old 'Nancy Ann,' my breech-loader there, and let Jack have a lasso and scalping knife, and I'll bet every cent I own we can clean out every bloody red son-of-a-corkscrew of 'em inside of thirty days, and do our own scouting and cooking too!" When their theatrical season finished, Cody said, he and Omohundro were planning on heading out to California to take care of the situation. "We'll see if we can't get enough hair to stuff a rocking chair for the old woman . . . if clean 'em out is the order, we won't leave a papoose a week old. It's harder work to kill and drag off twenty Indians on the stage every night than to perform the same job in real earnest."[12]

It is unlikely that either man had any intention of following through on Cody's threats. Still, they understood that a certain amount of trepidation regarding the natives was a boon for business. In Baltimore, the actors playing the Indians in the show walked the streets in full costume and war paint, much to the shock of the well-heeled Easterners of the city's theater district.

Back on the Nebraska prairie, Ena Palmer wrote in her diary that she had at last heard from the cowboy turned showman. "The papers speak of Jack as a fine good-natured fellow who the public really learns to like," she wrote. "He may be wild and reckless, but I believe he has a manly generous heart that must win him friends among honest honorable people despite his many alleged faults." These faults were certainly not listed or even alluded to in the papers. Likely they were the product of Dr. Carver, jealously reading the same reports in his North Platte dentist office and now living with the Palmer family on Medicine Creek.

When the touring company played Washington, DC, during the first week of May 1873, it was without Giuseppina Morlacchi. The ballerina had returned to Broadway to fulfill a previously booked engagement at the Olympic Theatre. To say that Morlacchi was missed by the company when it debuted with actress Bessie Sudlow in her place was an understatement, as the play opened to a half-full house for the first night in DC without her guaranteed draw. It was only after a volley of pistol shots caught the attention of locals that the theater filled up. As much as audiences missed her, Texas Jack missed her more.

Josephine's father Antonio passed away on June 7, and a few days between shows provided Texas Jack the opportunity to travel to the funeral and console his former costar, making it back to Elmira, New York, just in time for the next show. Josephine gave Jack a tour of her farm. Here, John Omohundro was a Southern gentleman, not a trail-riding cowboy, frontier scout, or fierce Indian fighter. He didn't come in the guise of hero but as a friend, which perhaps served to render him both to Josephine Morlacchi.

That the first dramatic tour by Buffalo Bill and Texas Jack captured America's imagination despite their limitations as thespians is perhaps no surprise. The people packing the theaters to see the dashing hunter and the famous cowboy were not there for a well-written line of dialogue or a subtle bit of character development; they were there for Cody and Omohundro, the real heroes of the West. In newspaper advertisements for *The Scouts of the Prairie*, both characters were listed as being portrayed "by the original hero." In his book *John Wayne's America*, Garry Wills wrote that "our basic myth is that of the frontier. Our hero is the frontiersman. To become urban is to break the spirit of man. Freedom is out on the plains, under endless sky. A pent-in American ceases to be an American."[13] The audiences that filled the floors and balconies of theaters to see the scouts felt increasingly pent-in and urban. Their frustrations found release in the same idealized version of manhood that would later be acted out on-screen by John Wayne, Gary Cooper, and Ronald Reagan. From the end of 1872 and throughout 1873, the production would play more than 170 shows in 58 cities across Illinois, Missouri, Ohio, Kentucky, Indiana, Pennsylvania, New York, Rhode Island, Connecticut, Massachusetts, New Hampshire, New Jersey, Maryland, Delaware, and Virginia.

Critical reception soon beat a steady retreat from the negativity that greeted the earliest performances. Still, the show found its greatest success not in the writers, reviewers, and newspaper critics but in the theatergoers venturing to a range of venues, many for the very first time. A New York critic said the appearance of Cody and Omohundro on the stage at Niblo's

> [h]ad the effect of thronging the gallery of that classic edifice with an audience altogether representative of the polite patrons of what, for the want of a better name, is known as popular fiction done up in ten-cent packages. The youths and maidens who revel in frontier sketches, who dream of war whoops and scalp hunts, whose waking fancy teams with hatchets, scalping knives, tomahawks, and firearms, whose high conceptions of life have been reared upon the deeds of the stoical Lo and his gentle adversary, the dauntless peddler of moccasins and bear skins, occupied all the front seats and made themselves pardonably conspicuous by the frequency and heartiness of their applause.[14]

Another reporter wrote that the scouts' appearance on Broadway left the more-populist Bowery Theatre across town deserted. The little boys of the East, who had until this point romanticized the scout and cowboy in no greater measure than they had criminals like Jack Sheppard or pirates like Bluebeard, now wholly devoted both their imaginations and their play to hunting imaginary buffalo and lassoing imaginary Indians. After the Civil War, and with citizens leaving farms and fields for factories, fears raged that the American man would become too feminine. The people of the large East Coast cities felt far removed from their childhood heroes like Davy Crockett and Daniel Boone, men of a frontier that no longer existed who had once personified masculinity in the popular imagination. In Buffalo Bill Cody and Texas Jack Omohundro, these childhood heroes were reborn and set on the new frontier audiences were told still separated savagery and civilization. And these heroes were now appearing live on the stage of a local theater rather than only on the yellow pages of dime-novel stories.

One critic seemingly understood that Cody and Omohundro appearing as themselves onstage was not just different from what had come before, but was the start of a new genre of entertainment altogether. Writing for the *Cincinnati Daily Gazette*, the critic commented that

> *[t]he play is beyond all precedent in the annals of stage lore . . . it has in it all the thrilling romance, treachery, love, revenge, and hate of a dozen of the richest dime novels ever written. The play bids fair to have a most wonderful run, for its novelty is so striking, and its subject is such a popular one with so many readers of thrilling border tales, that the temptation to see the real actors in those tragedies cannot be resisted.*[15]

These were the first reality stars, portraying stylized versions of themselves. Their failings as actors could be brushed aside in favor of their authenticity, and their dramatic inabilities served to bolster this assumption. As to their pretensions about being great actors, the scouts were tongue in cheek. Buffalo Bill told one reporter:

> *My idea is to go to New York next winter, and show the play-goers what real acting is. I propose to run Booth and Fechter into New*

Texas Jack in his stage costume for *The Scouts of the Prairie*, late 1872 or early 1873. (HARVARD THEATRE COLLECTION, HOUGHTON LIBRARY, HARVARD UNIVERSITY)

Jersey by playing Shakespeare right through, from beginning to end, with Ned Buntline and Texas Jack there to support me. I shall do Hamlet in a buckskin suit, and when my father's ghost appears, "doomed for a certain time," I shall say to Jack, "Rope the cuss in, Jack!" and unless the lasso breaks, the ghost will have to come.[16]

Both men knew that it wasn't their ability to deliver a line that brought in the crowds; it was that by virtue of the lives they led offstage, they had proven themselves genuine and therefore reliable. People weren't coming to see great actors; they were coming to see real heroes. With the season done and the scouts preparing to head to familiar Western haunts to hunt together with some men they had met in New York, Cody summed up the new reality when he spoke to a reporter in Omaha.

"I'm no damn scout now," he told the man. "I'm a first-class star."[17]

CHAPTER THIRTEEN

End of the Pawnee Lifeway

THEIR PRESENCE ON THE STAGES OF THE EAST MEANT THAT TEXAS JACK and Buffalo Bill, for the first time since they had met at Fort McPherson, were not scouting, hunting, and working on the frontier. In early October of 1872, well before Omohundro and Cody left Nebraska in pursuit of theatrical fame, Jack wrote to Agent Troth requesting a repeat appointment as trail agent for the Pawnee. Troth was inclined to believe that the lack of complications on Jack's previous hunt with the Pawnee was not entirely due to Omohundro's skill as trail agent, and he determined that the tribe could be allowed to hunt without an escort. By the time Troth had changed his mind, Omohundro was standing on a New York stage, and the Pawnee's summer hunt was entrusted to an untested trail agent named John Williamson.

Troth's belief that the historical animosity between the Sioux (Očhéthi Šakówiŋ) and Pawnee (Chaticks si Chaticks) peoples had been overcome is made clear in a letter he sent to the Bureau of Indian Affairs in Washington. "The prospects of a permanent peace between them is very promising," he wrote, perhaps unaware that Pawnee Pitahawirata chief Terrecowah was informed by a group of Sioux he encountered while hunting the previous summer with Texas Jack that the Sioux could not make peace at that time because some of their chiefs were in Washington.

Pitaresaru, the chief of the Chaui band of Pawnee who had hunted with Omohundro the previous season, pressed Agent Troth to ensure that the peace he believed in be formalized. Martha Royce Blaine, in her book *Pawnee Passage*, writes that "Pitaresaru, maintaining pressure for a formalized peace with the Throat Cutters, asked the agent in October to write to J. B. Omohundro, who knew and had contacts with the Sioux and who had accompanied the Pawnees on their last winter's hunt. He wanted him to seek out Whistler, a chief of the Brulés, and ask him if he would consent to make peace with the Pawnees."[1] Omohundro volunteered for exactly this duty, but Troth believed formalizing the peace was unnecessary. Troth delayed, and by the time a letter belatedly reached Omohundro, he was treading the boards on his theatrical tour with Buffalo Bill and Ned Buntline.

As the Pawnee trekked west with some Otoe (Jiwére) tribesmen along the Republican River in Nebraska, a band of more than a thousand Oglala and Brulé Sioux was moving east from Colorado along the same river. After a month of hunting on Beaver and Prairie Dog creeks, the Pawnee were returning to their reservation when a group of white buffalo hunters warned them that a significant number of Sioux were traveling through the region. Accustomed to being harassed by white hunters, the Pawnee believed the warning was a scheme designed to convince them to leave the area without hunting buffalo nearby.

The hunters had spoken the truth. The combined force of Oglala and Brulé Sioux that was approaching from the west comprised the largest group of Native Americans that would ever be seen again in the Republican Valley. Spotted Tail and his band had left the Fort Laramie region without a trail agent in April and were joined by Pawnee Killer's group as they traveled east. When Secretary of War Belknap delayed in responding to a request to provide rations for the Brulé, a band of seven hundred hungry and angry members of that tribe set off to hunt with Chief Two Strike. This group soon joined Pawnee Killer and Spotted Tail's combined group. When six Oglala warriors returned to the combined camp reporting that Pawnee hunters were spotted west of their current hunting grounds, neither agent assigned to the Sioux, Antoine Janis or Stephen F. Estes, was able to convince the warriors not to attack. Janis reported that when an Oglala Sioux chief named Little Wound asked him if he had express orders to keep the Sioux from attacking the Pawnee off their reservation and with no danger to white settlers, he had to confirm that he had received no such orders. When the rest of the Brulé heard of this, trail agent Estes was unable to offer an excuse as to "why one band of Sioux should be prohibited from going to war and not another."[2]

Williamson, the young first-time trail agent who had joined the Pawnee on their hunt, wrote that when the white buffalo hunters warned the Pawnee of the immense band of Sioux:

> *I took [them] to Sky Chief who was in command that day for a conference. Sky Chief said the men were liars; that they wanted to scare the Pawnees away from the hunting grounds so that white men could kill buffalo for hides. He told me I was a "squaw" and a coward. I took exception to his remarks and retorted: "I will go as far as you dare go. Don't forget that."[3]*

In his account of the forthcoming battle, Paul D. Riley wrote:

> *At that point Williamson failed as trail agent. In a conflict between boyish egotism and his empowered duty, egotism won. His letters of instruction from Agent Burgess had been clear. If the possibility of trouble with other Indians arose, Williamson had the authority as well as the orders to use this authority to compel the Pawnee to do as he saw fit. Unfortunately, the young greenhorn cared more about his own masculine image than he did his legal wards. The freedom of the hunt and the buffalo range after months of Quaker dictation caused Sky Chief to act rashly, and unfortunately Williamson did not have the maturity to withstand the chief's harangue.[4]*

The chief, convinced that the white hunters were lying to keep the Pawnee away from the herds of buffalo, refused to send out scouts. When buffalo were sighted, Sky Chief (Tirawahut Lesharo) and the Pawnee men scattered to hunt, one of them borrowing Williamson's rifle and leaving him unarmed. Williamson followed the Pawnee hunters along with the women and children. Soon he noticed that the hunters had halted, stopping the hunt. A group of three chiefs was conferring. A boy of about sixteen rode back to Williamson, tied a piece of red flannel to the bridle of his horse, and told him that the Sioux were coming. They had already killed several of the hunters, as well as Sky Chief, who had dismounted to skin a buffalo he had taken down.

The Pawnee women, children, and packhorses rushed to the safety of a nearby canyon as Williamson urged the braves to retreat to a more-defensible position. Fighting Bear (Coruxtapuk) demanded that the Pawnee make their stand where they were, and Williamson was unable to convince him to move to safety. As the Sioux pressed in, it became clear that their force massively outnumbered the Pawnee. Williamson rode toward the Sioux, waving a white flag in an attempt to avoid a massacre. The Sioux ignored his flag and began firing, and Williamson's horse was shot out from under him as he turned back toward the safety of the canyon. The Sioux divided into two groups and took command of both sides of the low canyon entrance, firing indiscriminately down into the surrounded Pawnee.

As the Pawnee ran toward safety at the opposite end of the canyon, the Sioux decided not to pursue, mercifully avoiding more casualties. They instead gathered and burned the possessions left by the Pawnee as they fled, raping the wounded Pawnee women and killing the injured Pawnee children. The bodies of the dead Pawnee warriors were tossed into the flames. All told, as many as 156 Pawnee died that day, while the Sioux lost only between 10 and 13 warriors.

The tragic loss of life suffered by the Pawnee weighed heavily on Texas Jack Omohundro. He had grown close to Pitaresaru, whom he called Old Peter, and some of the braves while on the hunt the previous summer, both parties finding amusement in the hunting style of the other. The thought that he might have been able to prevent their deaths troubled Jack profoundly. When Jack stopped in Rochester that fall to visit Morlacchi, a reporter noted that "Texas Jack says his sympathies are with the Pawnees in their fight with the Sioux, and he hopes the government will interfere on behalf of the Pawnees, as they are the best 'Injuns' and inferior in number to the Sioux."[5]

When news of the brutal slaughter of their people at what is still called Massacre Canyon reached the rest of the Pawnee, the impact was profound. Though they had long been offered a new reservation in Indian Territory, most of the older members of the tribe were reluctant to leave their ancestral lands in Nebraska. Now, demoralized by the loss of life, the tribe decided to accept the offer and travel to their new reservation. Massacre Canyon would prove to be the last battle between the Pawnee and the Sioux, and the final encounter between disparate bands of Native Americans in Nebraska. A monument on Highway 34 in Nebraska commemorates the battle.

The Pawnee tribe that had commandeered Louisa Cody's dinners, impressed Ena Palmer with their stoicism, and hunted buffalo alongside Texas Jack departed Nebraska forever. The prairie that Texas Jack and Buffalo Bill returned to was significantly different from the place they had departed.

Chapter Fourteen

Payday

THE TWO MEN WHO WALKED AWAY FROM THE STAGE AT THE END OF A successful dramatic tour at the end of June 1873 in Auburn, New York, were far removed from the pair that had departed Fort McPherson for Chicago the preceding December. On tour, they had lived—and spent— like kings. Louisa Cody writes that her husband and his cowboy friend were making "more money than any of us had ever dreamed of before. Unheard extravagances became ours. Will . . . believed that an inexhaustible supply of wealth had become his forever." These extravagances came at a cost, however. According to Louisa, at the end of the dramatic season, her husband "looked somewhat ruefully at his bank account. Instead of the hundred thousand dollars or so he had dreamed of possessing, the balance showed something less than $6,000. And Texas Jack's bankbook had suffered far more—for Texas Jack was in love."[1]

One newspaper report claimed that Buntline cleared $30,000 (almost $640,000 in 2020) that season with Buffalo Bill and Texas Jack, and that the scouts earned $1,000 (the modern equivalent of just over $21,000) a week. "Jack has an Indian fondness for gewgaws," the reporter wrote. "He bought of Tiffany, in New York, a huge gold chain, almost the size of a ship's cable, and long enough to go around his neck, for which he paid $1,000. He also scoured the city for the biggest watch that money could buy, and he got one, they say, as large as a spittoon. He is now prepared to astonish the natives of the effete European capitals."[2]

An Omaha reporter who had been familiar with the scouts prior to their stage success spoke to them as they arrived in Omaha on the way to Fort McPherson:

> *Bill thinks [acting] more remunerative than the honor of being a Nebraska Legislator, while Texas Jack is of the opinion that financially it eclipses buffalo hunting and scouting. . . . [B]oth men are reported as looking exceedingly well, and carry considerable jewelry, especially Jack, whose shirt bosom is adorned with a $1,200 diamond pin, and diamond studs, and he wears a $1,000 chain with a magnificent watch, while his little finger on his left hand is encircled with a valuable diamond ring. During Jack's trip in the East, he was presented with a $650 breech-loading gun by the Earl of Dunraven. He also has a splendid rifle, given to him by Remington, the great manufacturer. Jack has the most beautiful six-shooter that was ever manufactured in this country, it being of the Smith & Wesson pattern, and over a foot in length. Jack claims to be the best shot with a six-shooter now living. An Omaha gentleman, in whose employ Jack was for two years driving cattle from Texas to the Plains, testifies that he has seen him shoot with a six-shooter the heads off of four quails out of five, while they were running in the grass. Jack will hunt the buffalo in a match with any man in the world for any sum from $1,000 to $5,000.*[3]

This article ends, as did several chronicling the scouts' return to the plains after the successful dramatic season, with Texas Jack and Buffalo Bill stating their intention to return to the stage in a few months in New York with a new equestrian show they would call *Alexis in America*, a dramatization of their hunt with Grand Duke Alexis.[4] They planned to premiere the new play on Broadway and then travel to the capitals of Europe to give the Europeans a taste of life on the American plains.

This may well have been the intention of the pair, but two factors changed their plans. The first was their decision to part ways with Ned Buntline. Buntline—who wrote both their play and the dime novels that preceded it—was more fiscally prudent on the road than either of

Texas Jack wearing the diamond pins and gold watch chain he purchased at Tiffany's of New York. (BUFFALO BILL CENTER OF THE WEST, CODY, WYOMING)

Seated left to right: Texas Jack Omohundro, Buffalo Bill Cody. Standing left to right: Elijah P. Greene, James Scott, Eugene Overton. (BUFFALO BILL CENTER OF THE WEST, CODY, WYOMING)

his stars, and the pair may have assumed that as tour manager, he had profited at their expense. In Cody's autobiography, he writes that at the end of the tour, "when I counted up my share of the profits, I found that I was only $6,000 ahead. I was somewhat disappointed, for, judging from our large business, I certainly had expected a greater sum."[5]

Historian Joseph G. Rosa posits that "The break-up between Cody and Buntline brought Buffalo Bill and Texas Jack closer together. Texas Jack had always sided with Cody in his arguments with Buntline, and had been the steadying influence on Buffalo Bill ever since they started. For no matter what history has made of Buffalo Bill, the fact is that he was an erratic character in all things. He drank too much, talked too much, and often lapsed into depressive moods. Several times he threatened to quit, and only Jack's quiet reasoning kept him on the stage."[6] When Cody declared that he was done with Buntline and done with the stage, Omohundro convinced him that they could make a go of it without Ned, and eventually, Bill agreed.

If the scouts felt that Buntline was unfair in his dealings with them, they did not seek any recourse to resolve the matter, aside from choosing not to continue to tour with him. In any case, Buntline maintained correspondence with both men after their business partnership was through, suggesting a lack of hard feelings on either side. One of the actors that joined the troupe for its second season remembered accompanying Buffalo Bill and Texas Jack to one of Buntline's temperance lectures in New York. There, Cody and Omohundro laughed as Buntline drank whiskey from a jug while admonishing a full room about the dangers of drinking.

It seems more likely that the decision to continue without Ned Buntline was the fallout from the second major factor, which changed the men's plan to dramatize their hunt with Alexis. They had recruited for their next tour a friend who had not been part of that venture, Wild Bill Hickok.

CHAPTER FIFTEEN

Romance for Texas Jack

TEXAS JACK WROTE LETTERS AND SENT CLIPPINGS BACK TO ENA PALMER at her home on Nebraska's Medicine Creek for a few weeks after the Chicago premier of *The Scouts of the Prairie*. But the letters soon became fewer and further between before ceasing altogether. By the time the show reached New York, Jack failed to mention the Southern belle when a reporter for the *Sunday Mercury* asked him about his romantic history:

> *Texas Jack has always been a ladies man, in his way—as the Western phrase goes, "a lucky dog with the women." He has incurred the enmity at sundry times of diverse red skins for his flirtations with their dusky squaws, while amongst the Mexican beauties he has been somewhat of a Lothario.*
>
> *Once at a fandango he was introduced by a bosom friend, or a man whom he took to be so, to a senorita with whom he danced incessantly that evening. This marked attention and the marked favor with which they were received, excited very unexpectedly the ire of the very man who introduced him, and while dancing with the lady Jack was stabbed in the shoulder from behind. The wound was serious, but Jack finally recovered, and never knew his assailant till some time afterward, when his former "bosom friend," who had by this time become his open enemy, avowed the act, and endeavored to repeat it, whereupon Texas Jack "shot him in his tricks."*
>
> *During Jack's captivity for several months among the Indians a squaw became passionately attached to him, much to the chagrin of her*

Indian suitor, and it is currently reported that Jack's ultimate escape
was facilitated by the aid of the love-sick Indian, who wished, at all
hazards, to get rid of his too handsome rival.[1]

Cody and Omohundro spent much of the summer of 1873 together
in their familiar haunts near Fort McPherson, leading a hunt for Elijah P.
Greene, a member of Cody's hunt with Mr. Milligan the previous summer. Near Fort McPherson, they hunted buffalo with Dr. Carver. The
hunting party was eventually joined by Eugene Overton and Mr. Scott, a
Chicago hatter, and still later by Wild Bill Hickok. Late at night on the
trail, the younger men regaled their friend with stories about their stage
exploits, laughed about Ned Buntline's temperance lectures while passing
the jug, and planned the next season's tour. It seems likely that Cody and
Hickok could tell that Texas Jack's mind was occupied with thoughts of
a certain dark-eyed ballerina.

A writer for the *Cincinnati Enquirer* claimed that Cody had been
unhappy at the end of the tour, "not because he drew thin houses of the
vociferous readers of wishy-washy weeklies and blood and thunder dime
novels, for the contrary was the case." Neither did his melancholy stem,
according to the reporter, "from a lack of fire-water . . . for Bill was to be
seen as of yore raising foaming breakers of most villainous stuff to his
facial orifice with an evident satisfaction and gratified look of pleasure."
No, it was that after spending his nights in the hotels of Indianapolis,
Cincinnati, Chicago, and New York, "he had grown tired of the slow
monotony of life in the gay cities and longed once more for the bracing
air and untrammeled freedom of his native plains."[2]

Both of the scouts longed for the freedom and space of the plains,
but the *Cincinnati Enquirer* writer continued that when Buffalo Bill left
for the expanse of the prairie,

Cody did not intend to fly alone. The arrow of Cupid had pierced his
heart and long association with Dove Eye, of the blood and thunder
troupe, in which Bill is a shining light, had made him a slave to her
charms. . . . Bill was in love with Dove Eye . . . he loved her with
a devotion which was only equaled by his love for red eye. Yesterday

he approached the object of his affection, and in accordance with the dime novel code of etiquette, cast a longing look at Dove Eye, and exclaimed, "Fly with me. Let us once more live on the boundless prairie, never to return to the haunts of the pale face. Toward the setting sun we will rear our dusky race, and swear them to eternal enmity to the whites in general, and constables, and other varmints in particular. My steed awaits, let us go. . . . [T]he heart of the buffalo slayer is lonely; there is no one to share his wigwam, none to cook the leathery buffalo when he returns home weary from the chase."

According to the reporter, at this point Cody tried to encircle Dove Eye's slender waist, which brought the conversation to a sudden close:

Dove Eye, the real and loving—has a temper of her own . . . she made no reply, but picked up a war club used on the stage and laid it with such gentle force and precision over the bison hunter's occiput, that he rolled to the floor.

"I'll tache yees ye long-haired spalpeen to be calling a dacent girl all them names," she said. With this sole observation she proceeded to sit down on William's manly but prostrate form with a heftiness that left him little breath for war-whoops in the evening performance. He also has a dim recollection that a few handfuls of his locks that he lost were twisted out in the fray. As soon as Dove Eye got out of breath, William left the room a sadder and a wiser man, and will at once advertise for another Indian maiden.[3]

It seems unlikely that Bill Cody, whose wife and young children accompanied him for much of the tour, would have made any such advances on Morlacchi as Dove Eye. Louisa Cody never mentions any animosity toward Giuseppina in her biography of her husband, and indeed, Morlacchi continued to appear with the troupe for the next three years. A more likely explanation is that this news was received by the article's writer second- or thirdhand, and that in the course of telling and retelling was shaped to fit the author's imagination. The article describes Morlacchi as Irish and with red hair when she was in fact Italian and brunette. The only other actress with the troupe at the time was Cuban-born Eloe Carfano, a longtime associate of Morlacchi who played Hazel Eye, and was also dark-haired. If the initial report was that one of the stars of the troupe had expressed his desire for the foreign actress playing Dove Eye, the reporter's excitement could have easily turned it tawdry.

Some reports added romantic embellishment to the relationship between Morlacchi and Omohundro, the beautiful ballerina and the rugged cowboy, claiming that they had managed to fall in love despite not sharing a language. The truth is that Morlacchi was fluent in English—she gave interviews in New York, Boston, and Chicago to reporters enchanted by her slight but charming accent—and was equally equipped in Italian, French, and Spanish. Omohundro had picked up some limited Spanish from vaqueros in Texas and recalled a little French from the private tutor his parents had hired for their children. Morlacchi may have taught her costar a few words and phrases in Italian as they spent evenings practicing parts and engaging in conversation. In each of these languages, the pair managed to forge a deep affection for each other, and both were dismayed at the prospect of parting when Josephine left the troupe to resume her career during their first season touring together.

Before the 1873 season began, Texas Jack faced a personal crossroads. He had approached acting like he had most things in his life. If you don't want to go to school, go for a hunt. When the call comes, go to war. When the war is done, take to the Chisholm Trail. If life as a cowboy becomes tedious, ride north to the prairie and give scouting a try. If the opportunity to act onstage presents itself, give it a go, knowing you can always pick up and head off again if things don't work out. The man that had not had a permanent home since he'd left his father's farm in Virginia had not had a reason to hitch his horse for any length of time, until now.

As he stepped off the train in Rochester, New York, Texas Jack must have been uncharacteristically nervous. As he walked through the city, his thoughts likely kept him from noticing the stares of the locals, unaccustomed to seeing a man in beaded buckskins and wide-brimmed Stetson sauntering their streets. Patrons were beginning to filter into the theater. They must have wondered why the tall cowboy was pacing at the back

Texas Jack Omohundro and his wife, the "Peerless" Giuseppina Morlacchi.
(BUFFALO BILL CENTER OF THE WEST, CODY, WYOMING)

door of the ballet. He had rushed to New York after telling his friends Buffalo Bill Cody and Wild Bill Hickok that he had urgent and important business. He had arrived in Rochester with a question.

The local *Democrat and Chronicle* newspaper noted his arrival, remarking that "Texas Jack, the hero of the plains, well-known to our citizens in his newly-assumed dramatic character, is in town spending a few days."⁴ That newspaper's next mention of Jack, dated September 1, 1873, sheds light on his pressing business:

Last winter fortune decreed that the charming and famous danseuse, Mlle. Morlacchi, and John B. Omohundro, known throughout the land as "Texas Jack," should meet in the city of Chicago. It proved to be a case of love at first sight. The fair actress immediately took a liking to the gallant scout of the prairies, the renowned Indian fighter and Buffalo hunter. The affection ripened, until it took the form of a declaration of love on the part of Mr. Omohundro, which resulted yesterday in a ceremony which made the twain one.

Our citizens who have been delighted for the past fortnight with the graceful acting of Mlle. Morlacchi, need no description of her personal appearance. For the benefit of outsiders, however, we may state that she is a native of Italy, and was born at Milan about twenty-five years ago. Like most of her countrywomen she is a brunette, whose personal beauty is heightened by a grace of a manner that is unsurpassed. She is a highly educated lady and such as have been fortunate enough to gain her personal acquaintance are loud in their praises of her accomplishments and character.

The man of her choice is a magnificent specimen of physical manhood. He is about six feet in height, and of the finest proportions. A native of Virginia, born in 1847, the blood of Powhatan flows in his veins, and the aquiline nose, jet black hair, erect form and piercing eye of that famed aboriginal warrior are reproduced in the gallant "Texas Jack." He arrived in this city on Saturday from New York, and took rooms at the Osborne House.

It was rumored during the day that he came on business of importance—indeed, nothing less than his marriage with Mlle. Morlacchi. A reporter of the Democrat and Chronicle called on the gentleman to learn the facts. Mr. Omohundro, with great courtesy and frankness, stated that Mlle. Morlacchi and himself were to be united in the holy bonds, but when, he was unable to state, although he believed the event would take place very soon.

The fact was that the lady, who is a rigid Catholic, insisted that the ceremony should take place under the forms of that church, and the gallant groom acquiesced willingly. He had been brought up in that faith himself, but during his life on the plains, remote from all churches and religious ministration, he was, perforce, compelled to forego some of the duties incumbent on all members of the church. This fact occasioned some delay, but suffice it, without going into further and impertinent details, that all obstacles were removed and yesterday morning the marriage took place at St. Mary's church.

With proper contempt for the vulgar display which is too often made on such occasions, the interested parties desired that the ceremony be performed with as much privacy as possible. Their wishes ever complied with. Immediately after 8 o'clock mass, at which the affianced pair attended, and after the congregation had departed, Rev. Father Stewart appeared behind the altar rail, and in a short time the vows were plighted and words were spoken which united two hearts that beat as one.

Mr. and Mrs. William McCarthy appeared as groomsman and bridesmaid, and with a few personal friends of the contracting parties were the only witnesses. After leaving the church the newly wedded pair were driven to the Osborne House, where they received the congratulations of their friends, and remained until yesterday afternoon, when they left for the west, carrying with them the best wishes of a host of friends for a long life of conjugal happiness.[5]

Chicago newspapers were quick to take credit for the marriage on account of the first meeting of the pair in their city. The *Inter Ocean* hastened to remind readers that it was in the Second City at Nixon's Amphitheatre that "the peerless danseuse became infatuated with the manly strength and stateliness of the scout, and the 'hero of a hundred fights' became bewitched by the fairy-like charms of the actress."[6]

The truth was slightly more mundane. The acting lessons that Morlacchi gave Omohundro had blossomed into friendship and respect, and often after shows, the two could be found sitting together discussing in a trio of languages how that evening's performance had gone, their histories, and their desires for the future. They quickly became inseparable, perhaps much to the chagrin and heartache of Josephine's manager, John Burke. Louisa Cody writes in her memoir that as she sat backstage one night during a performance, Burke approached her.

"Mrs. Cody," Burke said, "I have met a god and a goddess in my life. The god was Bill Cody. I came on him just at sunset one night, out on the Missouri, and the reflection of the light from the river was shining up straight into his face and lighting it up like some kind of an aura. He was on horseback, and I thought then that he was the handsomest, straightest, finest man that I ever had seen in my life. I still think so."

Burke was silent for a moment, while some rampage of Indian killing happened on the stage. Then he leaned closer.

"The goddess was Mlle. Morlacchi. But I can't have her, Mrs. Cody. I wouldn't be the man that I want to be if I tried. Jack's a better man—he's fought the West, and he's had far more hardships than I've ever seen and—and—he deserves his reward. I'll never love any other woman—but there's one thing I can do, I can turn all my affection from the goddess to the god, and so help me, I'll never fail from worshipping him!"[7]

Dexter Fellows, longtime publicity agent for the Ringling Brothers Barnum & Bailey Circus, wrote in his biography *This Way to The Big Show* that he learned the ropes of the publicity world from Major Burke. According to Fellows, Burke always wore women's rings on his fingers, and, after two years of friendship, Fellows learned why.

One evening while we were playing the city of Quebec, Burke and I dropped into a cafe. At a nearby table was a group of young women, one of whom was of a pronounced Spanish type. Burke could not take his eyes off her. After a period of silence, he went to her table and induced her to change her position so that he could observe her face and profile to the best advantage from where we sat. When he returned, there were tears in his eyes.

"She looks like the girl I was going to marry," he said.

In earlier days he was engaged to the renowned Mademoiselle Morlacchi . . . who toured with Cody in Ned Buntline's thriller Scouts of the Prairie. *Their affair had progressed to the point where he had furnished a home in Billerica, near Lowell, Massachusetts. I, too, was moved when he told of the ineffable joy he experienced in buying chairs and furniture for the first permanent home he had had since he was a child. But Burke's romance was short-lived. Mademoiselle Morlacchi met the handsome "Texas Jack" Omohundro . . . she returned the rings Burke had given her, and he wore them for all the years I had known him.*[8]

Extant pictures of Burke do not show the rings mentioned. If Burke was jealous of Morlacchi's affection for Texas Jack, he had a strange way of showing it. Burke acted as advance agent, manager, and actor with Texas Jack until the cowboy's death and spoke warmly about him to newspapers ever after. He included Jack's writings in the programs of Buffalo Bill's Wild West show and more than perhaps anyone else ensured that Texas Jack was not forgotten.

When Josephine had left the *Scouts of the Prairie* production during the preceding season to fulfill her prior contract, Texas Jack must have quickly realized that this wasn't only a loss to the company—it was a huge personal loss to him. As he and Cody returned to the open expanse of the Nebraska prairie, Omohundro was likely overwhelmed with a desire not only to be with Josephine, but also to do something he had not done since he'd left home to be a headquarters courier as a young man—to stay.

While Texas Jack toured the country with Buffalo Bill and the Peerless Morlacchi, Doc Carver invited Ena Palmer to share his home on the Medicine Creek. Though Carver was quite enamored with the Southern belle, Ena's diary entries show that she spent much of her time preoccupied with thoughts of Texas Jack. When Jack returned to Fort McPherson on the way to hunt with Cody, he and Ena met briefly. Though we can't know for certain the details of their conversation, it is evident in her writing that their relationship had reached its end. In July of 1873, a year to the day from her first ride with the handsome cowboy, she wrote:

Every day now is an anniversary to my weary life. This stormy warmth of July is so fraught with many memories. And do I alone remember? Whom do I ask? The winds? Their sympathy gives so much unto my lonely life as aught else, now! One year ago I fancied that I had found that which would make me count the hours of life jealously. Perhaps I had, but it has slipped from my grasp or has been thrown away in madness. God only knows which.[9]

The following day's entry, musing about what she had referred to as her "Western Hero's delicate, yet kind and manly attentions" as they rode across the Nebraska prairie, she wondered:

Who, besides myself, thinks of this day with strange memories tugging at their heartstrings. When just one year ago today comes back with visions of tearful sunshine, dewy plains, and shadowed hillsides? And yet the doubt that I feel is my work I fear!

Ena's journals go silent for a period of several months, an uncharacteristic ceasing of her recorded thoughts. She received no further letters from Omohundro. Folded inside the pages of her journal along with the previous entry is a hand-colored picture of the cowboy and a clipping from a Nebraska newspaper:

Texas Jack was married last Thursday, at Rochester, NY, to Mlle. Morlacchi, a lady actress, reported to be very wealthy and beautiful. Such is greatness.[10]

Ena's journal sat silent for the better part of the next two years. After rejecting a marriage proposal from Doc Carver, she became a well-known marksman and married a local cattleman named David Woulter Ballantine. After becoming a Nebraska state senator, Mr. Ballantine fell to his death while trying to board a moving train. Ena married for a second time, to a man named Washington Lafayette McClary in 1884, but her life was tragically cut short in a wagon accident later that year. Her journals serve as a lasting memorial to her life and to the people of the Nebraska frontier she adopted as home.

National newspapers from New York and Boston to Los Angeles and San Francisco reported on the marriage between Texas Jack, the cowboy turned scout from the fringes of civilization, and the Peerless Morlacchi, the La Scala–trained ballerina who had danced before the world's most sophisticated audiences. Though there was an incredible amount of public curiosity about their marriage, Josephine and Jack were always reticent to discuss their relationship and were incredibly private about their shared lives off stage.

The marriage of border scout and ballerina intrigued an American audience that sought to reconcile its own savagery and civilization. Soon after the wedding, a writer in the *Detroit Free Press* reported that "Texas Jack, who was married a few days ago, has already scalped the wash stand, shot the looking-glass, and knifed the head-board in his dreams of Pawnee warfare. His wife wants a divorce."[11] The truth was that the couple enjoyed their time offstage quietly together, each content in the company of the other.

When the couple appeared with Cody and Hickok in Chicago on the next tour, the *Chicago Daily Times* ran a long piece about Josephine— her abilities as a ballerina and her history on the stage. The article concluded with a description of the beautiful dancer and her relationship with Texas Jack:

> *It is conceded that this is a love-match purely, and although there is no doubt she might have made many a more brilliant alliance, yet from the high character universally given Jack, and the evident esteem and good feeling with which he is regarded by the troupe, and indeed all his friends, there is little doubt but that the fair little danseuse obtained for a husband a genuine diamond in the rough. Warm-hearted, frank, and courteous, everybody seems to admire him, and all speak well of him with whom he comes in contact.*[12]

Chapter Sixteen

The Scouts of the Plains

While Texas Jack and Morlacchi were getting married and enjoying a short honeymoon, Bill Cody returned to New York to play the lead in the same play he had watched from his private box on his first trip to the city. Far from the reluctant plainsman anxious at the thought of having to speak in front of an audience of theater patrons, Cody was now a self-assured success. An actor named Joseph Winter took over the Texas Jack part, establishing a pattern that Cody would maintain throughout his stage career. Even when it was Buffalo Bill's name alone on the marquee, he needed someone to be his Texas Jack, a solid figure always nearby to connect the real William F. Cody with the Buffalo Bill character he portrayed.

When Omohundro and Morlacchi returned from their brief honeymoon, John Burke returned with them. He assumed Buntline's role of public relations manager for the touring company, traveling in advance of the troupe to ensure favorable newspaper reports and advertisements to draw the readers of the dime novels to see the heroes of those works live onstage. Burke would remain in this capacity with Omohundro and Morlacchi for the remainder of Texas Jack's life. Hiram Robbins took over day-to-day tour operations. Having replaced Buntline as manager, Cody and Omohundro now awaited his replacement as actor.

Wild Bill Hickok was perhaps the only man in the West more famous than the pair who had toured as *The Scouts of the Prairie*, and convincing him to join *The Scouts of the Plains* was a major coup. Tall, handsome, and renowned for his legendary accuracy, James B. Hickok added to the cachet of the company, and both Omohundro and Cody were glad to have their friend with them for the upcoming dramatic season. In Cody's autobiography he recalls that the two friends, "thinking that Wild Bill would be quite an acquisition to the troupe, wrote to him at Springfield, Missouri, offering him a large salary if he would play with us that winter. He was doing nothing at the time, and we thought that he would like to take a trip through the States, as he had never been East."[1]

Cody was incorrect about the extent of Hickok's travels, as Wild Bill had traveled East during the buffalo hunt at Niagara Falls after Omohundro had been unable to attend. Hickok had also spent time in Boston, but was far from convinced that life back East was meant for him. He was reluctant to dandy himself up and prance about the stage, but was convinced by the success the pair of fellow scouts had experienced the prior season, as well as by the desire to spend time with his friends Buffalo Bill Cody and Happy Jack Omohundro. In his autobiography, Cody wrote:

> *Wild Bill accepted our offer and came on to New York, though he told us from the start that we could never make an actor out of him. Although he had a fine stage appearance and was a handsome fellow, and possessed a good strong voice, yet when he went upon the stage before an audience, it was almost impossible for him to utter a word. He insisted that we were making a set of fools of ourselves, and that we were the laughing-stock of the people. I replied that I did not care for that, as long as they came and bought tickets to see us.*[2]

Though he had been to Niagara and Boston, Will Bill stepped from the train from Missouri a New York City novice. Cody's letter to his friend noted that he would be staying at the Metropolitan Hotel, and that Hickok should join him there when he arrived in the city. Cody informed Hickok that he should pay two dollars for the cab ride, and when the driver demanded five, he was informed by the plainsman that he would receive no more than two. When the driver climbed down from the cab and threatened to exact his toll physically from Hickok, "Bill then handed the driver five dollars, at the same time striking him a blow in the face that sent him plowing up the settlings in the gutter. A policeman very soon came after Bill, but bail being furnished by me, he was kept out of the Tombs; but the next day I paid a fine of $10 for him. This was his first experience in New York."[3]

When Texas Jack arrived at the hotel to introduce Hickok to his bride, he found Wild Bill pacing the floor of his room, increasingly nervous about the prospect of acting in front of an audience. Hickok told his friend Happy Jack that Cody had given him so many pointers about acting that he was starting to unwind. Omohundro assumed his familiar role as the calm and collected member of the group, convincing Hickok that if Texas Jack could do it and Buffalo Bill could do it, it was worth a shot for Wild Bill Hickok.

Left with just a few days to rehearse, Hickok was given a minimal number of lines in the new play that had been written for the scouts by Fred Maeder. The play adhered closely to the format of its predecessor, *The Scouts of the Prairie*, and was named *The Scouts of the Plains*, a fact which has led to no end of confusion ever since. The troupe occasionally staged Maeder's other play, *Buffalo Bill, King of the Border Men*, which seems to have been performed on the rare occasions that Morlacchi was unavailable for a performance, but the vast majority of stops gave the audiences the chance to see this new version of *The Scouts*, ostensibly improved by the presence of legendary lawman Wild Bill Hickok and a lack of temperance lectures from Ned Buntline.

One significant problem Hickok faced was keeping a straight face while reciting the melodramatic dialogue called for by the play's script, written in a style that seemed not just inauthentic, but approaching blasphemous in comparison with the way Hickok and his friends actually spoke to each other on the plains. Agreeing with Hickok's sentiment regarding the believability of the dialogue written for her husband and Omohundro, Louisa Cody writes:

> *Many a time I heard Texas Jack call a dance. Many a time I saw him swing off his horse, tired and dusty from miles in the saddle, worn from days and nights without sleep, when perhaps the lives of hundreds depended on his nerve, his skill with the rifle, his knowledge of the prairie. But I don't believe I ever heard him say, at any of those*

Left to right: Elijah P. Greene, Wild Bill Hickok, Buffalo Bill Cody, Texas Jack Omohundro, and Eugene Overton on a hunting expedition in 1873. (BUFFALO BILL CENTER OF THE WEST, CODY, WYOMING)

times: "Yet I know not who she is." Marvels indeed were those old-time "drameys" when the East, the West, and the imagination of the Bowery dramatist, all met in the same sentence.[4]

Hickok, more than the others, chafed against these lines, struggling nightly to spit out, "Fear not, fair maid! By heavens! You are safe with Wild Bill, who is ever ready to risk his life and die, if need be, in defense of weak and defenseless womanhood!" Cody and Omohundro both joked about the quality of the lines but, unlike Hickok, committed to reciting them as written. Hickok equally disliked certain aspects of the play itself, such as the part where he ended the life of one of the piece's villains. Hickok told his partners he'd prefer it if he gave the man a warning and chance to walk away instead of just shooting him while he kidnapped one of the girls.

Even when he did manage to remember his few lines, Hickok was unpredictable onstage. The first scene of the new play took a page from Cody and Omohundro's stage debut, with the three scouts sitting around a fire and sharing stories of various hunts and Indian encounters they had participated in. Cody began, lifting a prop whiskey jug to his lips and taking a sip before telling about a buffalo hunt on the Kansas plains. Cody passed the jug to Texas Jack, who took a long draught and then told about a wild stampede during a cattle drive on the Chisholm Trail. When Jack passed the jug to Wild Bill to tell a story about law in the West, Hickok nodded to his friend and then turned the bottle up, taking a long gulp. He suddenly stopped, righted the jug, and shifted his eyes between his two friends. He turned his head and spewed the contents of his mouth at the stage lights.

"You must think I'm the worst fool east of the Rockies," Hickok yelled at his friends, "that I can't tell whisky from cold tea. This don't count, and I can't tell a story under the temptation unless I get real whisky."[5]

The audience erupted into laughter and applause as Cody tried to convince Hickok that this was the way a professional drama was staged and Texas Jack yelled at a stagehand to run next door to the saloon and fetch real whiskey. Cody was mortified that Hickok had gone off script, but Jack managed to convince him that Wild Bill had unconsciously made a big hit. The whiskey bit was incorporated into the play and continued to amuse audiences while Hickok continued to receive real whiskey.

Though Wild Bill may have been unhappy about the literary merits of the play and the fake whiskey that had been supplied as a prop, he must have been more pleased about his share of the ticket sales. A writer in the *Troy Times* newspaper reported that the average weekly take for each scout was $500 and had been as high as $800 each in some of the bigger cities. Texas Jack invested much of his earnings into a thoroughbred colt he named Yellow Chief.

In early November, the troupe arrived in Titusville, Pennsylvania, for a run of shows. As their managers went to arrange hotel accommodations, Buffalo Bill, Texas Jack, and Wild Bill walked toward the billiard room to relax. The three tall scouts attracted much attention, and the trio was greeted at the door to the establishment by its proprietor, who warned them that a group of rough men inside had seen posters for *The Scouts of the Plains* and decided that they would kill these famous men if given the chance. The scouts agreed to use a side entrance to the hotel so as to avoid an unpleasant scene, but Cody later recalled that:

While I was standing at the door of the theater taking the tickets, the landlord of the hotel came rushing up and said that Wild Bill was having a fight with the roughs in the bar-room. It seemed that Bill had not been able to resist the temptation of going to see what kind of a mob it was that wanted to test the pluck of the Buffalo Bill party; and just as he stepped into the room, one of the bruisers put his hand on his shoulder and said:

"Hello, Buffalo Bill! we have been looking for you all day."

"My name is not Buffalo Bill; you are mistaken in the man," was the reply.

"You are a liar!" said the bruiser.

Bill instantly knocked him down, and then seizing a chair he laid out four or five of the crowd on the floor, and drove the rest out of the room. All this was done in a minute or two, and by the time I got down stairs, Bill was coming out of the bar-room, whistling a lively tune.

"Well!" said he, "I have been interviewing that party who wanted to clean us out."

"I thought you promised to come into the Opera House by the private entrance?"

"I did try to follow that trail, but I got lost among the cañons, and then I ran in among the hostiles," said he; "but it is all right now. They won't bother us any more. I guess those fellows have found us." And sure enough they had. We heard no more of them after that.[6]

Between stops in Maine, while Texas Jack returned with his wife to the farm in Billerica and Cody caught a train back to his family in Rochester, Wild Bill stuck to the hotels. He had just settled into his bed one night but was kept awake by the sound of laughter and the occasional shout from the room across the hall. Putting his coat on over his dressing gown, Hickok left his room and knocked on the door across the hall to tell the occupants to quiet down, only to discover a group of local businessmen playing a friendly game of cards. When one of the men invited the stranger to join in for a hand of poker, he accepted, but insisted that the men show him the basics of card play, explaining that he had never played the game.

Though Hickok made some deliberate mistakes, when the game ended four hours later, he stood up with the men's money after cleaning each of them out. Reaching the door, he turned to the table and said, "Gentlemen, I appreciate your hospitality, and especially the good luck in which I have played tonight, therefore I will tell you a little secret, for it may prove very valuable to you hereafter; never wake up a stranger, destroy his rest, and invite him to take a hand in a game of poker with you. Good night."[7]

Before another show, Hickok told the front desk of his hotel that he would like a fire to be lit in the fireplace in his room before he returned that evening. After the curtains closed on that evening's show, he arrived to find no fire warming his chambers, so he returned to the hotel desk to remind them of his request. After midnight, guests were woken by a loud voice yelling "Fire! Fire!" As the guests poured from the hotel into the street, hotel management stood looking up to the building's top floors and trying to catch a glimpse of the flames. Soon a figure in a nightshirt was spotted leaning out of a window and screaming the "Fire! Fire!" warning from a top floor. When the hotel's clerk shouted, "Where's the fire?" Hickok yelled back, "That's what I want to know! I ordered one four hours ago, and it hasn't been built yet!"[8]

In Philadelphia, noticing the effect of the brilliant calcium light upon his friends, Hickok decided that he too deserved proper illumination. Hiram Robbins told an interviewer:

The light did not belong to the theatre but was owned by an outside man, from whom we rented it, paying him so much for every time it was turned on. It was thrown from above, and the manipulator occupied a place among the flies. One night, Wild Bill conceived the idea that Buffalo Bill and Texas Jack were receiving too much light. Suddenly sensitive of his obscure part, he was determined that more blaze should be thrown on him, so one night just before the curtain went up, he climbed the ladder leading to the calcium light manipulator, and finding that gentleman at his post, said:

"Say, does Bill and Jack pay for this extra light business?"

The manipulator, thinking that he meant the management, replied, "Yes, they pay for it."

"Yes, that's what I thought. It makes them look pretty, don't it?"

"Well, it heightens the effect."

"That's what I thought. Now when I come out tonight, I want you to throw it on me."

"I can only turn it on when I'm directed."

Bill always carried a revolver, and drawing it, he remarked, "Say, throw that stuff on me. If you don't I'll have to try you with this. I can kill you nine times out of ten from below, and if you don't throw the light on me when I appear, I'll try you one just for luck."

Bill occupied an obscure position in the scene where a cabin was being raided. Wild Bill, with a very meager part, occupied scene three. The signal for the calcium light was given, and it would have been grand, but the entire effect fell upon Bill, who, with his weak eyes, blinded by the intense light, stood for a moment and then yelled:

"Turn the blamed thing off!"

The entire act was spoiled. Bill, in explanation, said that they had put something in the light to hurt his eyes.[9]

Onstage the scouts loaded their revolvers with gunpowder blanks, and when they massacred the Indians of the troupe it was by shooting these blanks over their heads, ensuring that the hot powder didn't burn the exposed skin of the stage natives. Hickok amused himself by aiming low onstage, deliberately burning the legs of the supers hired to play the native warriors. The actors were supposed to fall down as if dead after they were shot by the scouts, but those that Hickok burned would either jump out of the way of Wild Bill's shots or roll around holding their singed legs, making it frustratingly hard to play dead. The actors complained to Cody and Omohundro, who in turn received assurances from Hickok that he wouldn't do it again, a promise kept until the next time Wild Bill got bored onstage. Cody later wrote that, "Wild Bill continued his pranks, which caused us considerable annoyance, but at the same time greatly amused us."[10]

The amusement seems to have come to an end when the company arrived in Rochester, where Cody had purchased a home and planted his family. Buffalo Bill asked Hickok to refrain from his antics, anxious to impress the crowd in his new hometown. Hickok agreed and then pulled the stunt anyway in the second act, perhaps as either a challenge to his old friends or an excuse to leave the boards he was increasingly unhappy to tread. Offstage, Cody argued with Wild Bill, who turned and walked toward his dressing room. After the scene was done, the building's carpenter told Cody and Omohundro that "the long-haired gentleman who passed out of here a few minutes ago, requested me to tell you that you could go to thunder with your old show."

Buffalo Bill and Texas Jack returned to the Osborne House, where the troupe was staying, and found Hickok waiting for them. Cody wrote that, "by this time he had recovered from his mad fit and was in as good humor as ever. He had made up his mind to leave for the West the next day. I endeavored to persuade him to remain with me 'til spring, and then we would all go together; but it was of no use. I then paid him the money due him, and Jack and myself made him a present of $1,000 besides." The two also presented Hickok with a pair of Colt revolvers. The guns he kept, but the money was quickly left by Wild Bill on gambling tables throughout New York.

Explanations other than a fight with Cody about his fun with the supers have been posited as reasons that Hickok decided to quit acting with his friends. One story suggests he got so drunk before one of the shows that Bill and Jack bought him a train ticket home and hired an actor to replace him. Another story, backed up by reporting in the *Rochester Democrat and Chronicle* at the time, says that Hickok's presence at Fort Laramie was requested by General Sheridan, and that he planned on heading to Wyoming after a brief sojourn in New York. Several newspapers reported that General Custer had requested that Cody, Omohundro, and Hickok return West to serve their country as scouts. Cody later told an interviewer that Wild Bill left the company because Phil Coe's brother and some friends had called him a coward for joining Cody and Omohundro onstage rather than face their wrath. According to Buffalo Bill, Hickok had set off to face his accusers in Abilene as soon as the rumor reached him.[11]

Hickok gambled away the money Buffalo Bill and Texas Jack had given him and then boarded a train headed west. His problems with his eyes led him to Kansas City, where a doctor diagnosed him with glaucoma and opthalmia and advised him to rest. Wild Bill stayed in Cheyenne for a time, renewing a friendship with Charlie Utter. In March of 1876, he married Agnes Thatcher Lake, the widow of a circus magnate he had met in 1871 when her circus passed through Abilene. The two had maintained a steady correspondence, and Hickok first proposed when Agnes attended a show while he was on tour with Cody and Omohundro.

Though his new wife was a wealthy woman, Hickok was determined to add to his new family's fortunes. Hearing of industrious miners striking it rich in the Dakota Territory, he left Cheyenne with Charlie Utter for the gold boomtown of Deadwood.

CHAPTER SEVENTEEN

A Season Offstage

WHILE WILD BILL HICKOK HEADED FOR CHEYENNE, TEXAS JACK AND Morlacchi remained in Rochester for several weeks with Bill and Louisa Cody. The scout and the cowboy enjoyed leisurely strolls through town and time spent with Cody's children without the pressing needs of theatrical touring. Ever fond of children, the pair spent much time interacting not only with the Cody children, but with other Rochester youth. One local child would remember fifty years later that "Texas Jack was always the life of the party. One day he got all the horses from the two livery stables . . . and turned them loose on Main Street. Then he chased the horses up and down the street to show people how they caught them with the lariat and other customs of the plains."[1]

Before leaving Rochester with his wife, Omohundro wrote to the Earl of Dunraven, inviting him to join them at their Massachusetts home. In Lowell, the aristocratic lord and the rugged cowboy were noted by citizens and the local newspaper as they strolled the streets or recounted their hunting trips and discussed American politics in the confines of local eateries. On one of their walks, they noticed a commotion near the Suffolk canal and rushed to find that a young lady had fallen in while washing her laundry. Running toward the bridge on Market Street, Omohundro tossed down his fine meerschaum pipe and dove in, still wearing his black suit and dark wide-brimmed hat, and swam the young lady back to the safety.[2] When Dunraven commented that he had never seen anything like it before, another Lowell citizen told him that he had seen Texas Jack lasso a boy who had fallen into the canal and that the cowboy had then used the lasso to pull the child out.

Two years removed from his first hunt on the Nebraska plains with Texas Jack, in 1874 Dunraven once again set his sights west, this time with a particular destination in mind. Writing later in the preface for his book, *The Great Divide: Travels in the Upper Yellowstone in the Summer of 1874*, he recalled his thinking:

> Being in the United States during the summer of 1874, and having two or three months of spare time, I determined to pay a visit in the autumn to the far-famed region of the Upper Yellowstone, and to judge for myself whether the thermal springs and geysers there situated were deserving of the superiority claimed for them. . . . Its lakes had for me a magnetic attraction which drew me towards them with an irresistible impulse; and there was an atmosphere of mystery enveloping its upper waters like a mist, which I eagerly sought to dispel.[3]

"I had, moreover," he continued, "heard the district spoken of as an excellent game-producing country; and pursuit of large game is to me a great delight: but it was less for any special design of hunting than for the satisfaction of my curiosity and the gratification of my sightseeing instincts that I really decided to attempt the trip."[4]

Lord Dunraven was not alone in his desire to "sight see" in the young Yellowstone Park. Newly established by President Grant in 1872, the park was already attracting many such curious tourists. John Colter—an early mountain man and member of the famous Lewis and Clark Expedition—had become one of the first white men to enter the area in the winter of 1807 when he explored parts of the region on a trip to establish a trade partnership with the Crow (Apsáalooke) nation. After wandering unguided for months through a region with typical nighttime temperatures around -30 degrees Fahrenheit, Colter appeared at Fort Raymond, having traveled hundreds of miles. With his descriptions of steaming geysers, bubbling mud pots, and sulphurous springs, Colter was taken as a lunatic, and contemporary reports jokingly referred to his discovery as "Colter's Hell." Modern assessments of Colter's descriptions put his travels near present-day Cody, Wyoming.

In 1856 Jim Bridger reported seeing mountains of glass and yellow rocks, boiling springs, and spouting water in the same region, but was widely ignored due to his established reputation as a foremost "spinner of yarns" and the inaccessibility of the area. The beginning of the Civil War ensured that no explorations could be mounted until 1869, when the Cook-Folsom-Peterson Expedition followed the Yellowstone River to Yellowstone Lake.

A year later, Montana's surveyor-general, Henry Washburn, along with Nathaniel P. Langford and a detachment of the US Army, spent a month collecting specimens, naming landmarks, and exploring the area. The efforts of these men, as well as geological surveys by Ferdinand V. Hayden, paintings by Thomas Moran, and photographs by William Henry Jackson, led President Grant to sign The Act of Dedication declaring the area the nation's first national park, after Congress agreed to withdraw the land from public auction.

Nathaniel "National Park" Langford was appointed as superintendent of the park, but without the benefit of funding, staff, or salary, he was left without the means to spend time there. Over the course of five years as the park's superintendent, N. P. Langford managed to visit the Yellowstone area just twice. The creation of the park had piqued the curiosity of the nation, but the lack of resources meant that the land visitors traveled to see was truly wild. There were no maps, no permanent roads, and no protection from the threats of wild animals, treacherous terrain, and hostile Indians that might be encountered within the confines of the park.

"My first act after making up my mind to undertake the trip to Geyserland," wrote Dunraven, "was to write my old friend, hunting companion and guide, Mr. John Omohundro, better known as Texas Jack, and endeavor to secure his services for the expedition. . . . I had had plenty of experience . . . of Jack and knew him to be just the man I wanted." Dunraven was initially unsure whether he could entice the now happily married Jack away from his wife and back into the saddle. "Since those merry days among the sandhills and on the plains," he continued, "Jack had settled down in life and married; and whether he could be induced to leave his wife and comfortable home, and to brave the hardships and dangers of a hunting or exploring trip to the far West, I was very much in doubt."[5]

The aristocrat was much delighted when he received his cowboy friend's reply letter that said simply he was ready for anything and would accompany Lord Dunraven anywhere. Jack indicated he would meet his friend at Charpiot's, a restaurant in Denver, in a few days. Finding Omohundro enjoying a whiskey when he arrived, Dunraven was glad to find that "Pork and beans and pickled cucumbers had failed to sour his genial smile; aesthetic dissipation had not dulled the lustre of his eye. Jack at Denver in broadcloth and white linen was the same Jack that I had last seen upon the North Platte, grim in an old buckskin suit redolent of slaughtered animals and bodily deliquescence."[6]

Jack's attire had changed significantly from his Nebraska days, in more than trading buckskin breeches for broadcloth and linen. Dunraven joked that, "While still some distance from the town I became aware of a great coruscation, which I took to proceed from a comet or some other meteorological eccentricity, but which on approaching nearer resolved itself into the diamond shirt-studs and breast-pin shining in the snowy 'bosom' of my friend Texas Jack, who had already arrived from the classic east winds of Boston to share the fortunes of the trip."[7]

Jack was adorned with various pieces of diamond jewelry purchased from Tiffany's during the previous acting season's residency in New York City. Jewelry was a weakness Omohundro indulged in at the conclusion of each dramatic season, and Dunraven, far wealthier than Omohundro, was always amused to see what huge diamond Jack would be sporting the next time they met.

Having reconnected, the pair determined that Jack would head to Salt Lake City, then called Deseret, to procure supplies and horses and a wagon for the expedition. Arriving there afterward, Lord Dunraven recalled that:

> *I acquired a considerable amount of second-hand renown, and, like the moon, shone with borrowed splendour. Jack was dressed in beaded buckskins and moccasins, fringed leggings and broad felt hat. Jack*

is a tall, straight, and handsome man, and in walking through the well-watered streets of Deseret in his company I felt the same proud conscious glow that pervades the white waistcoat of the male debutante when for the first time he walks down St. James's Street, arm in arm with the best dressed and most fashionable man about town. It was obvious to all that I was on terms of equality with a great personage, and on that account cigars were frequent and drinks free.[8]

After spending a few days in Salt Lake City and meeting with Brigham Young, Dunraven's retinue wended its way north from Salt Lake City to Bozeman, Montana, on their way to the Yellowstone. Dunraven was impressed by Jack's bronco-busting skill after he managed to break a horse they purchased at Sterling, Montana. "He was a native pony, of mixed Spanish and American blood," the lord wrote. "Like all half-bred mustangs, he was not destitute of the diabolical accomplishment of 'buck-jumping' and he exhibited a slight disposition to indulge in the past-time."[9] After a few minutes of effort on Omohundro's part, Dunraven watched from his buggy as "Jack on the newly acquired Broncho [*sic*], galloped gaily alongside in great form, full of spirit, singing, whooping, and yelling." Establishing a base of operations close to Bottlers' Ranch in Paradise Valley near Emigrant, Montana, the group ventured south and into the park.

The party that made its way south from Bottlers' into the park included ponies, mules, wagons, supplies, and a full retinue of the earl's friends, relatives, and servants. Along with Texas Jack and the earl was George Kingsley, Dunraven's personal physician and close friend. Fred Bottler, one of the two brothers who owned the ranch, agreed to join the expedition as Jack's assistant guide. Valentine Walter Bromley, a British artist, came along to document the trip, and his drawings, paintings, and etchings were used to illustrate Dunraven's book about the journey. Campbell, who the earl describes as "a limber-limbed Highlandman," traveled with the earl, as did Maxwell, an African-American man who served as Dunraven's cook and valet. Tweed, a collie who was Dunraven's favorite hunting dog, rounded out the group. Dunraven's cousin Captain

Charles Wynne joined the expedition at Mammoth Hot Springs, just south of the ranch.

Even offstage and away from the lights, Texas Jack Omohundro was an entertainer. When the group settled into camp in the evening, Jack regaled them with stories of his days as a cowboy in Texas or scouting for the army in Nebraska:

> *Jack, who is of course smoking—he always is smoking, except when he is eating, and the few minutes he is obliged to devote to mastication are grudgingly given—is holding forth to the rest of us, telling us some thrilling tale of cattle raids away down by the Rio Grande on the Mexican frontier; graphically describing some wild scurry with the Comanches on the plains of Texas; or making us laugh over some utterly absurd story narrated in that comical language and with that quaint dry humour which are peculiar to the American nation. Boteler [sic] is lying on his stomach, toasting on a willow-wand a final fragment of meat . . . he is greatly relishing Jack's story, except when some not over-complimentary allusion to the Yankees comes in; for Boteler served in the Federal Army during the great Civil War, while Jack, Virginian born . . . naturally went in for the Southern side.*[10]

In addition to his ever-present meerschaum pipe, Dunraven noted of Omohundro's morning ritual:

> *[A] little before sunrise, I was awaked as usual by hearing scratch, scratch, against the canvas of my tent door. "Come in," I said, with a sleepy and somewhat sulky voice at being disturbed, for I could feel by the stiffened and frozen condition of the blankets about my mouth that it was a very cold morning, and I was still tolerable warm. My "come in" was answered by the appearance of Jack's jolly cheerful face as he undid the strings that tied the tent door, and came in rubbing his hands and stamping his feet. "Good morning," says Jack; "it's about time to get up, it's a fine large morning, and going to be a great day for*

hunting." "All right, Jack, I will be up in a minute. In the meantime there is a pannikin, and there is the keg."

Jack, like most prairie men, invariably introduced himself to the Sun-god with a copious libation of whisky. To take a big drink of raw whisky in the morning, and to touch nothing more during the rest of the day, appears to me a most extraordinary perversion of principle. However, it is a part of the manners and customs of the country, and may be adapted to that particular region. I have often tried to acquire the habit, but have never succeeded. It is true that to take one drink of whisky in the morning induces modified intoxication for the whole of the day, and it is therefore an economical habit; but it makes a man so unpleasantly drunk that he is apt to become a nuisance to himself and a terror to his friends. After Jack had tossed off his tot of whisky with the customary salutation, "How," to which we replied with the polite rejoinder, "Drink hearty," we crawled out of our blankets. . . . [11]

As the party set off on the day's hunt, the group startled three white-tailed deer who quickly bounded away before any of the men thought to raise their weapons. Hunting being not only one of the goals of the expedition, but also the means by which the outfit sustained itself, Jack admonished them. "God Almighty damn, there goes our supper! Why the hell don't you fellows in front look out?"[12]

Chastised, Dunraven remained doubly vigilant for the remainder of the afternoon and managed to shoot an elk he encountered later in the day, bringing congratulations from the cowboy guide. Dunraven was unlikely to have received such a harsh rebuke in his own country, but here in the wilderness of America, the earl sought to be a peer of the cowboy, and he understood that if Omohundro hadn't considered him a friend, he likely would have been much more guarded about his choice of language. That Texas Jack treated him as an equal on the trail meant more to the earl than the deference of the men who bowed their heads and watched their words when he entered a room back home.

On the hunt, Texas Jack was unequaled. Lord Dunraven reported that at noon one day, the group spied objects on the side of a steep bluff that he estimated to be about five miles away. Initially afraid that the objects in question were Indians, the men soon realized they were elk:

> *As soon as we had made the joyful discovery we mounted our horses and galloped off, making a long circuit down wind, so as to come upon the game from the proper direction. Jack's instinct as a hunter stood us in good stead on this occasion. He brought us round beautifully to the exact spot where the deer lay, which was an exceedingly difficult thing to do, considering that when we first saw them they were four or five miles off, and were lying on a sand-hill exactly like hundreds and thousands of other sand-hills that surrounded us in every direction. There was not even the slightest landmark to point out the position of the elk, and having once got on our horses we never saw them till Jack brought us within a few hundred yards of the herd.*
>
> *I had no idea where we were, when Jack said, "Now be mighty careful in going up this hill, and keep your eyes skinned. We ought to be able to see elk from the top."*[13]

The party crested the hill to reveal a herd of elk, and the end of a successful day's hunt. The animals were butchered, and the meat brought back to camp to provide the evening's dinner. The discarded entrails and carcasses of kills left behind the hunters as they traveled enticed a local grizzly bear to follow, and one morning Lord Dunraven recalled that Jack came in from his morning scout quite early and looking rather flustered. Jack sat down, filled his pipe, and said, "Jesus! I have seen the biggest bear in the world. Damn me if he didn't scare me proper. Give me a drink and I'll tell you."

A member of the party rushed to fetch Jack's pannikin and unstopped the keg to fill it with Jack's beverage of choice. Whiskey now in Jack's hands, the group was regaled with a story:

> *I started out to try and strike some of those white-tail we saw coming up, for I'm getting pretty tired of elk meat, ain't you? Well, the patch of timber is quite small there, and beyond that is nothing but rocks.*

So when I found there was no fresh sign in the wood I took the back track for camp. When I got near where the first elk was killed I saw something moving and dropped behind a tree. There, within sixty yards of me, was a grizzly as big as all outside. By God, he was a terror, I tell you.

Well, I'd been walking fast and was a little shaky, so I lay still for some time to get quiet, and watched that bear, and I'll be doggoned if I ever saw such a comical devil in my life. He was as lively as a cow's tail in flytime, jumping round the carcass, covering it with mud, and plastering and patting it down with his feet, grumbling to himself the whole time, as if he thought it a burning shame that elk didn't cover themselves up when they died.

When he got it all fixed to his satisfaction, he would move off towards the cliff, and immediately two or three whisky-jacks that had been perched on the trees looking on, would drop down on the carcass and begin picking and fluttering about. Before he had gone far the old bear would look round, and, seeing them interfering with his work, would get real mad, and come lumbering back in a hell of a rage, drive off the birds, and pile up some more earth and mud.

This sort of game went on for some time. Finally, I got a fair broadside shot, and, taking a steady sight, I fired. You should have heard the yell he gave; it made me feel sort of kind of queer, I tell you. I never heard any beast roar like it before, and hope I never may again; it was the most awful noise you can imagine.

He spun round at the shot, sat up on his haunches, tore the earth up, and flung it about, boxed the trees with his hands, making the bark fly again, looking for what hurt him, and at last, having vented his rage a little and seeing nothing, turned and skinned out for the rocks, as if the devil kicked him.

No, Sir! You bet your life he didn't see me. I lay on the grass as flat, by God, as a flapjack until he was out of sight. Well, all right; laugh if you like, but wait 'til you see one, and then you'll find out how you feel. I don't want to have any more bear huntin' alone nohow. It's all well enough with the black bears down south; I don't mind them; but I ain't going to fool around alone among these grizzlies, I tell you. Why, with one blow of the paw they would rip a man and scatter him all over the place; you just look at the marks of his claws on the trees, and the furrows he has torn in the hard ground.[14]

The party was surprised when the same bear, made obvious by the injury it had sustained by Jack's shot, returned to the same carcass some days later, this time to meet his end by virtue of the cowboy's rifle. Dunraven told his cowboy guide that he very much wanted to claim a bear of his own before the hunt was over. "I told him that it would likely snow during the night," Jack said, "as it threatened it, and then he should have all the bear-hunting he wanted."

As I anticipated, there was a snow, and the ground was covered white in the morning, so we all set off on another hunt and soon struck a fresh trail.

We soon discovered the bear was not far ahead, for he was circling the spot where he intended to lay down, a habit of caution which grizzlies have.

Sending the party on the trail, the earl and myself cut across and came up on the other side of the hill, and in five minutes we heard a snarling in the brush, and instantly we jumped behind a big boulder, just as the largest sort of grizzly came out in full view, not more than fifty yards distant.

The earl carried a double-barrel Dougall rifle, and I told him to give Bruin both shots, which he did, after a long stare.

Instantly the bear set up a terrible howling, and started down the mountain, but turned as he saw us coming.

Having reloaded, the earl gave him another double shot, I holding my fire for emergencies, and determined to let my lord and the bear "fight it out on that line if it took all Summer."

Then the bear started toward us, but seeing the rest of our party coming up, ran down the mountain and hid in a willow swamp.

Instantly we surrounded the thicket, into which we could hardly see ten feet, and I ventured in, but finding that on foot I would have no chance if attacked, came out, and sent to camp after a pony, which soon arrived. . . . [M]ounting, I rode in, and the bear soon rose up in front of me with a growl and a rush.

The pony became frightened, reared up and fell backwards, rolling over me. I was not hurt, but sprang to my feet in a second, and found the bear at arm's length . . . I could easily see by his open mouth and glaring eyes.

I gave him a shot from my revolver in a twinkling, but he had aimed his blow, and his right paw grazed my cheek—I have considerable—and falling upon my chest, knocked me out of time.

It was some time before I remembered any more about the fight, and when I did, thought the bear still had hold of me, for I felt awfully cramped; but the bear was no where near, and I was happy, because I had begun to consider about passing in my checks.

I heard the boys yelling to know if I was hurt, but I had no strength to answer, and soon I heard the party coming toward me, for they had all determined to risk their lives to get me out.

I told them it was only a joke, my refusing to answer their call, to get them to come into the thicket; but my story wouldn't stick, for they saw the blood on my cheek, and that I couldn't get up.

I was taken to the edge of the swamp, and the doctor said I must have some brandy, and that was just what I had prescribed for myself. So they put me on the horse and led him to camp, and to account for my escape decided that the bear had given me one tap, and blinded by my fire had gone on after the pony, which he overtook at the edge of the swamp and tore from one of his hind legs a large piece of flesh, and although he carried me to camp, he had to be left in the mountains to hunt his own living. . . . [T]he next day my bear was found dead in the swamp, and as we had had enough of that kind of game for the present, we moved up the river.[15]

After several days of good hunting, the group found themselves beset by storms. The earl wrote that:

Jack and I had been wandering disconsolately about the sloppy valley all day long, sitting down violently and unexpectedly on the slippery

wet grass, our feet flying from under us on the smooth rounded sur-
faces of the fallen tree trunks, dislocating our bones and our tempers by
many and violent falls. When [we] got in, we found camp in a sorry
plight, everything soaked through—tents, bedding and all—and our
prospects for the night looked anything but cheerful. About dusk we
heard a shot, and visions of fresh venison steaks floated before our eyes.
About half an hour passed, but no venison or Kingsley appeared, and
then we heard another shot, and two or three minutes afterwards yet
another.[16]

Dr. George Kingsley, brother of British *Water Babies* author Charles
"Canon" Kingsley, was Lord Dunraven's personal physician. As the light
faded and the sound of rifle shots seemed to be getting further away, the
men decided that Kingsley was going in the wrong direction. "To be left
out on such a night might cost a man his life," the earl explained, "for it
would have been hard for even an old experienced mountain man to have
found material dry enough to make a fire."

Texas Jack and Fred Bottler, who with his brother owned the nearby
ranch and had come along with the expedition, set off into the darkness
looking for their lost compatriot, but dense storm clouds meant there was
no moon or starlight to guide them in the dark. It was almost morning
before Omohundro and Bottler returned to camp, carrying the injured
Dr. Kingsley between them. The doctor had fallen in the dark, slipping
down a wet hillside and injuring his leg. Attempts to make a fire with the
wet wood around him were in vain, and he had given up all hope of being
found when he'd heard Texas Jack yelling his name in the darkness. That
night the four men huddled beneath an elk skin pitched between four of
the animal's antlers, Jack regaling the cold company with a song about the
conditions, made up on the spot—a habit picked up on long cattle drives.

Assured by Dr. Kingsley that his injuries were mild, the group pushed
forward, arriving at last near Yellowstone Falls. Here Jack killed another
elk when two members of the party were unable to hit it. He then took
Dunraven and his men past Yellowstone Lake and Falls, through the
Grand Canyon of the Yellowstone, and into the land of geysers and
springs, where Dunraven took great care in documenting the geysers they

saw, with vivid descriptions and guesses as to their heights and temperatures. They would spend several weeks here, recording their stay.

Along with his other descriptions, the earl included one of the earliest descriptions of the famous Old Faithful geyser. A reporter for the *Spirit of the Times* later asked Jack to describe the park for that magazine's readers:

> *Beyond all power of description, grand and strange. You cannot imagine what it is like. The Yellowstone region is far more beautiful than any fairy scene in your plays here. The coloring is so vivid and surprising that if you did not see it you would not believe it possible. The Yellowstone is one of the wonders of the earth. I can't attempt to describe it. It is all red, pink, blue, and yellow, odd rocks and hot water springs. . . . It is so strange that I advise everyone to go and see it, for if anyone tells them about it, they will barely believe what they hear.*[17]

Preparing to leave the geyser basin, the party fished in streams for trout to cook in the hot springs and traveled northeast to hunt. They had successfully hunted for a few days before discovering that a number of Indians were in the vicinity. According to Texas Jack:

> *We camped in the hills . . . and I went out to follow up a fresh bear trail, and noticing that the track was long and smooth in the heel, I concluded that a redskin was trailing the same Bruin.*
>
> *But it soon got too dark to see and I returned to camp and put out double guards, taking the first watch myself.*
>
> *About ten o'clock, just as I was about to go in for a relief, I heard the rattle of hoofs, then a yell like forty wild cats on a spree, and away went all our ponies, stampeded by our Indian neighbors.*
>
> *Mounting the pony I had with me, I started at once in pursuit, and hailed the boys as I dashed by camp.*
>
> *Following the noise of running feet for about four miles, they soon halted at the base of the mountain, and I discovered that the Indians were trying to corner and catch the ponies, and with a yell and a dash I went at them, firing both of my revolvers in rapid succession.*

Turning the ponies quickly I started them in the run back to camp;
but whether I brought down any red game, I will not say, yet I found I
had an extra pony the next morning, with a lariat around his neck.[18]

Tracking back past Mammoth Spring, the party discovered that a
hotel advertised as immaculately kept and comfortable was instead a
single abandoned cabin, and as they trekked out of the park, the group
was unable to find game. Beset by bad weather, the entire company was
in bad spirits until they arrived back at the Bottler brothers' ranch, where
they were given fresh eggs, chicken, cream, butter, cheese, and imported
Japanese tea.

Dunraven recorded another incident at the ranch capturing Texas
Jack's fondness for whiskey:

The evening of our arrival [we] noticed a keg, but fearing that our
honesty might not prove equal to the temptation which a conversation
on the subject would have held out, we avoided the cask and the topic,
and asked no questions about it. We thought that if we resisted the
Devil he would "flee from us." We did resist that keg manfully, but it
did not budge an inch.

The next day Jack came in and hovered round it like a hungry fish
about the hook, getting bolder all the time. Finally, he tapped it to see
if it was full, and found that it was. It gurgled pleasantly when he
shook it, and that gurgle finished Jack. He asked Boteler [sic] what it
was anyhow, and Boteler replied it was some of the best whisky that
could be got in Bozeman, upon which Jack looked unutterable things
and walked away, speedily returning to renew the interesting conver-
sation. It turned out the keg was on its way to the man who used to
live by the Hot Springs.

"But!" we all cried in a breath, "there is nobody at the springs at
all!"

"Well," said Boteler, "I don't know anything about that. It was
left here for me to send on by the first chance. I don't suppose there
will be any chance now till next spring; and, if you fellows feel like
taking some and leaving ten dollars a gallon for it, I don't know that

there will be any great harm done; but you must take it on your own responsibility."

Jack was quite willing to take it on his own responsibility; and it was not long before there was an auger-hole in the head of that cask.[19]

The remainder of the party's time near the park was spent hunting sheep and camping in the Montana Absaroka mountains. While the rest of his group decided to head back to camp, their cowboy guide determined to crest one of the local peaks in search of bighorn sheep. In an account to *Forest & Stream* detailing the trip, Omohundro wrote:

Some distance further back in the mountains we struck a rough region and came to a high peak called Old Baldy. I had never seen Baldy before, and I never want to see him again. We camped near the foot of the hill, and I proposed to climb on top and see what it looked like. None of the party seemed disposed to tackle him, so I shouldered Kate (a favorite rifle) early next morning and started up alone.

It was a long, hard climb, and when I got on top I found out what it looked like—a dead jump-off of some fifteen hundred feet! That's just what it was on the other side. As it wouldn't be healthy to go further in that direction I concluded to lay there and gaze on the valley and scenes below (a long way below, I found out afterwards). It wasn't such a bad lay-out after all, provided a fellow was fond of looking over a heap of country at one time. Eventually I discovered a small band of sheep grazing by a little lake in the valley. They seemed almost straight down from where I lay, but how to get at them was something else. I meant to try it on anyway, so crawled along the edge of the precipice for a long ways, going down many rough, steep places, until I came to the lowest gap there was, and it looked mighty scaly, some eighteen or twenty feet nearly straight down; but there was snow to light on. I could get down, perhaps, but not up there again that I knew of. It was a go, anyway, so I reached Kate out clear of the rocks and let her drop. She struck, butt foremost, turned over and started down the snowbank; at first slow, but she soon went out of sight some two hundred yards away, going at the rate of about a mile a minute.

Next I came, but not to go coasting with Kate, for I struck square on my boot heels and stuck fast. It was kind of an edging job from there down. The snow was a little harder than I had counted on, and I had to stamp several times before I could get hold enough to risk taking up the other foot. It was no nice place to play sliding down the hill, all by myself, especially when I didn't know exactly about where I was going to haul up. At last I came on to Kate. She was lodged up against some loose rock at the end of the snowbank, and no bones broke. I now hurried on, sure of a sheep, but I felt sheepish enough when I found they were at least a mile further than I had calculated, and before I reached the place they had moved camp and were asleep perhaps somewhere up in the rocks.

The next thing was to get back to where I had started from. I thought it all over, and decided to try it round the other side of old Baldy, thinking it would be a better chance to scale the ridge; but how much I was mistaken—I can't tell you how much, just here, but it was the roughest place on earth, except one, and I don't think anybody has ever found that one. It looked easy enough when I started in, but before I got out—wait till I tell you.

The further I went along the mountainside the worse it got, and more of it, until I came to a point where I could see neither bottom nor top! I was just sticking up among the stones like something that had growed there! I had but one chance to go ahead, and that was to jump down off the rock, some ten feet. If I did that I should have no chance at all to go back. It is strange how a fellow will press forward when he gets into trouble, though he may know it will take him deeper and deeper into it.

I dropped Kate first, then swung myself down. I had but a few feet to drop, but that rolling business was what worried me the most. I struck all right. There was some earth and a small timber ahead, and I was hurrying along as fast as possible, when all of a sudden the rocks commenced rolling down all around me. Looking up, I caught sight of an old ewe's head and neck stuck out over the rock some two hundred feet above me. Up went Kate and down came the ewe clear over my head and lodged against some fir bushes quite a distance below.

I crawled down and took off a quarter. I was pretty tired, but had rather pack meat than go hungry. I had already made some calculations on doing like a dog on a deer hunt—eat and drink nothing, and lay out that night. After a good deal of hard climbing, nearly straight up, I reached the top of the ridge, or backbone, as we call it. One step would put me on the descent either way. I sat Kate down, straddled the rock, and dropped into meditation for a moment.

It was a strange scene; the sun had long since gone behind the mountain, and that peculiar yellowish green light (such, I believe, can be seen in no other part of the world) shone over the sky; that is, what I could see of it for the high peaks around. Not a sound to be heard, save the faint roar of the torrents far down in the deep dark hollows below! I looked to Kate, my only companion. Thinks I, "old girl, this ain't no good place to be in; if I drop to sleep and tumble off this rock I shan't wake up much before Gabriel toots his horn."

These thoughts put me in a stir! I hastily gathered up my little outfit and struck down the mountain; I was in for it now. The further down I went, the rougher it got, more the ledges and the greater distance I had to drop from one to the other. I got kind of desperate, and hardly stopped to look for a better place—just peep over, drop Kate, (always butt foremost) then the sheep, and I would follow. Darkness was gathering fast, the weather was turning cold, I was nearing the valley and hope began to brighten a little, when I came to a dead sticker. It was the last ledge! All below was loose stone that slanted away to the cañon below. I looked over—no use talking—over fifty feet in the clear; no pair of legs in America could jump down there and ever come out with a whole bone in them.

I scrambled along the ledge some distance one way; it got worse! Tried it the other, and found but one chance, and that a mighty slim one. It was where the water had cut a narrow crevice through the main ledge. If I could only hold on, it would take me within a reasonable distance of the loose stones below. It beat no chance at all, so over went Kate, meat next, and I commenced my descent bear fashion (tail foremost, of course, the same as I do everything), holding on in any way, or to anything that was fast, as long as there was anything, and then I went about half as far as I expected and hit twice as hard as I ought to. The loose stones began to slide, and away went me, Kate, sheep, stones, and all, some twenty yards down the hill. It was quite dark now, but I managed, by feeling around, to find Kate and the sheep, and rustled off up the hollow, though the darkness and over the rocks, with a few tumbles and skinned shins.

I reached camp, that is, where camp ought to be, but it wasn't there. Although it was very dark, I knew I was within a few steps of the right place, and there I stood, dumfounded [sic] for a moment, thinking to myself, if this is not me, who in thunder can it be? I knew I was not lost; the camp must be lost. Presently I saw a little spark, and crawling under some logs came on to a heap of smoldering embers, the only sign of human existence.

I gave the coals a kick, and a dim light glared around that made the old white logs loom up like so many ghosts. While gathering some brush forty different imaginations rattled through my brain. Indians? I thought first; somebody shot accidentally, or fell off the rocks and broke a leg; horses stampeded; everything; until I got a big light, when all was explained.

Right over the fire hung a big flask half full of the best!—with a note attached saying, "Come into the river, party started at 3 p.m." Old Whitey, my pony that was tied to a tree nearby and had been quiet all this time, now began to snort and tear around as much as to say, "get that saddle and outfit on here, and let's be off," and you bet I did, and was off in a hurry, and didn't forget the flask either.

Whitey took a near cut, and Kate took her chances along with me, through the thick timbers, up and down the steep rocks. Which ever way we went I don't know (as I was very busy settling up with the flask), but I do know that I was the first in to Bottler's Ranche [sic] on the Yellow Stone River, some eighteen miles from where we had been camped.[20]

The return from Bottlers' to Bozeman on the wagon coach was a foreign experience to Omohundro, a man well accustomed to his own steed. "Jack, best and cheeriest of companions," Lord Dunraven noted, "was for once out of humor. Fervent and frequent were his prayers, having reference to the future condition of driver, horses, coach, road, those that made it, the teams that had cut it up, and everything and everybody that had to do with the line."[21]

Jack Omohundro bouncing along miserably in the back of a wagon coach was not the lasting impression Lord Dunraven would share of his friend. Later in life, Lord Dunraven would remember his cowboy hunting companion as

> [a] good and kind friend to me, a cheery companion, as brave as a lion, as gentle as a woman, always ready for anything, always willing to work, cutting down mountains of difficulties into molehills, always in good humour, never quarrelling—a better hunting companion than Jack was in those days, or a more reliable friend, it would be hard to find. There was nothing mean about Jack: he was—to use one of his own Western phrases—a real white man. . . . Buffalo Bill and Texas Jack were as fine specimens of their race and class as could anywhere be found, and that is saying a good deal, for honest hearts and stalwart frames and handsome features are not rare among the pioneers of Western civilization.[22]

The earl and his party planned on spending the winter months in Canada hunting moose while Texas Jack returned to his wife and a dramatic season with Buffalo Bill. Dunraven and Omohundro talked about spending the spring in Texas and Indian Territory, with Jack leading the party through his old stomping grounds. "All of us delighted in the trip," wrote Jack, "and I perfectly willing to try it over again any summer as guide and hunter, into the great national park, whose wonders are yet unknown, and whose beautiful scenery is seldom gazed upon by either Indian or pale-face."

Asked by a newspaper reporter to describe the famous earl, Texas Jack Omohundro returned Dunraven's admiration, saying, "I like him very much indeed. He is a perfect gentleman, highly cultivated and most amiable. I enjoyed the trip with him." Then, paying the lord the highest compliment he could, Jack added, "He is so much of a man."[23]

Chapter Eighteen

Last Ride with Buffalo Bill

While her cowboy husband trekked through Yellowstone Park with the Earl of Dunraven, Morlacchi took her ballet troupe on tour during the first half of 1875, to the delight of audiences that had missed her during the past two seasons as she toured with *Scouts of the Prairie* and *Scouts of the Plains*. Once again, reviews were glowing. When Omohundro returned from the hunt, he joined his wife's tour, acting as manager for her ballet troupe.

During Omohundro's extended absence from the stage, Buffalo Bill continued touring, hiring an actor who called himself Kit Carson Jr. to fill in for Texas Jack. Kit Carson Jr. left Cody at the end of the dramatic season, attempting to establish his own Western drama, trading on his association with Buffalo Bill. For a few years, he attempted to run his own troupe, in direct competition with Cody and Omohundro, which upset Bill greatly. In one of his letters, Cody mentions that Kit Carson Jr. was arrested in Chicago for hitting his wife with intent to kill. Cody notes: "I should have expected as much."[1] A scribble in pencil on a portrait of Carson Jr. in the collection of James Earl Taylor, who illustrated the dime novel *Kit Carson Jr., the Crack Shot of the West*, indicates that Kit Carson Jr.'s real name was Jim Spleen, and that he had posed as the son of the famous scout Kit Carson to try and get into West Point. According to Taylor, General Sherman had confided in him that Spleen was discovered to be an impostor when he failed to pass the entrance examinations for either grammar or mathematics.[2]

Omohundro and Morlacchi happily rejoined Cody for the next tour, initially throughout the Northeast, but by November, venturing for the first time south, through North and South Carolina, Georgia, Tennessee, Alabama, and Louisiana, and as far west as Texas, where Omohundro showed off his old stomping grounds to Josephine.

Traveling together through the South was a kind of role reversal for Cody and Omohundro. Here Omohundro, the former Rebel, was afforded a measure of heroism that he hadn't immediately received from Yankee audiences. Theatergoers were well aware that Texas Jack had fought alongside their fathers, brothers, and sons with Jeb Stuart and Robert E. Lee. Omohundro and Cody, standing together on the stage as equals and friends, demonstrated for their audiences the possibility of unity. Sandra K. Sagala, in her book *Buffalo Bill on Stage*, says that, "After the war, when the South was warily reconciling with its northern neighbors, along came Cody, the Yankee, traveling with Texas Jack, the Rebel. Their friendship emphasized consanguinity and the rejection of separateness. Therefore, it's no wonder that southern reviewers echoed the acclaim Cody received elsewhere."[3]

In New Orleans, the pair of scouts attracted quite a bit of attention when they arrived at the city's Crescent City shooting club to compete against local marksmen. That evening, they offered the proceeds of their show at the St. Charles Theatre to the veterans of the Mexican-American War. The troupe's managing agent for their Southern tour was a veteran of that war, and the first several rows of the theater were reserved for the eighty servicemen who attended the festivities that evening.[4]

The tour looped north through Illinois, Ohio, Pennsylvania, and New York with Cody, Omohundro, and Morlacchi enjoying positive reviews and crowded venues at each stop. A review in the *Buffalo Evening Post* illustrates the continued success of the trio:

> As was confidently anticipated, a large and very enthusiastic audience greeted the appearance of the "Scouts of the Plains" last evening. The entertainment opened with the comedy "Thrice Married," which was well carried through, and the gem of which was Morlacchi's dancing. The Peerless has certainly few rivals in the ballet, and she was

repeatedly called back by her admiring audience. But it was when the curtain was rung up on the "Border Drama" that the audience went wild. Sensational the play is, certainly; a plot laid in the thrilling scenes of border life could not well be otherwise. The marvelous celerity with which the favorites handled rifles and revolvers extorted unbounded applause from the boys (irrespective of age), and after the curtain fell on one very thrilling scene, Buffalo Bill and Texas Jack were called out, and if it had been later in the season, they would have been smothered in bouquets, no doubt. The Indian fighting excited the audience to the most intense enthusiasm. When Texas Jack, tied to the death-stake, coolly defied his tormentors, laughing as his pard, Buffalo Bill, from his hiding-place, shot down in turn each brave who attempted to fire the pile of faggots around Jack's feet, when the prisoner tauntingly told Santanta the Comanche chief he'd better try his hand, and then as the redskin dropped from Bill's unerring rifle, how the gallery thundered, and the pit and dress circle took up the savage whoops. All the boys yelled and shrieked. There is no necessity for concealing the fact, everybody who went enjoyed the show immensely.[5]

Weeks later, on April 19, 1876, as the scouts were preparing to play in Springfield, Massachusetts, Bill Cody received an urgent telegram from his wife. Louisa urged Bill to depart immediately for their Rochester home, where their five-year-old son Kit Carson had fallen ill. The family doctor didn't think he would survive the night. The next train from Springfield wasn't scheduled to leave until nine. Cody, ever the consummate showman, performed the first set before rushing to the train station and heading home to hold his son in his arms one more time as he passed away. "My only darling boy is dead," read the telegram Cody sent to his partner, Texas Jack. "He was too good for this world," the disconsolate father explained. "We loved him too dearly—he could not stay. And now his place is vacant and can never be filled, for he has gone to be a beautiful Angel in that better world, where he will wait for us."

When Cody failed to make the next performance, a newspaper writer posited that he had gotten into an argument with a sheriff in Texas, that both men had drawn their weapons, and that Cody was gunned down after his own bullet went wide of the lawman. The report further stated that as Bill sank to the floor, he had grabbed his rifle and killed the sheriff. Others embellished this already false story by saying that Buffalo Bill and Texas Jack had come to blows, and either Buffalo Bill had been killed or was in jail for the murder of his old friend. Furious after reading these reports, Texas Jack dashed off letters to the editors of several prominent newspapers, defending and confirming the still-living status of his pard:

> *Dear Sir,*
>
> *In Tuesday's edition I find the following extract from the New York Sun:*
>
> *"W. F. Cody—'Buffalo Bill'—a few weeks ago went to Texas, and after he had been there awhile the sheriff of Young County attempted to arrest him; but he resisted. The sheriff and he drew their weapons at the same moment and fired together. The sheriff's shot took effect, but Buffalo Bill missed his mark. He grasped a rifle, however, and fired, the shot piercing the heart of the sheriff, killing him instantly."*
>
> *The above is prefaced by the following:*
>
> *"This explains why Buffalo Bill was not at the theatre on Saturday night."*
>
> *Beside the moral, if not legal, libel in the use of W. F. Cody's name in connection with such an affair in Texas is the perfectly uncharitable and heartless conclusion you hastily jumped at, after the explanation personally given your reporter by me, is to say the least, a criminally careless violation of the injunction to "comfort the afflicted." Your reporter and the editors were truthfully informed of the reason [for] Mr. Cody's absence, and he painfully feels the injustice you have done him in this, his first great sorrow, of coupling an absurd gossip with his irremediable affliction; I therefore send the following extract from the Rochester Democrat, in corroboration of the death of his darling boy.*

With each copy of the letter he mailed, Jack included a clipping from the *Rochester Democrat and Chronicle* newspaper, reporting on the death of Kit Carson Cody.

I refer to the gentlemen of the Springfield press to show that he was with us the first night in Springfield, and give them and you liberty to search the authentic telegrams in your respective cities received from Rochester by Mr. Cody and by us from him. I also desire you to state that he has joined us today, and, God willing, will appear with us every night through New England, and also that the affair in Texas had no more existence than the original "three black crows." As your publication is liable to seriously affect his reputation and his business prospects, I hope you will do him the justice to publish this. Ascribing no malicious intent on your part, I think it right and shall be glad to see you make this reparation to a man whose character so far stands unsullied.

Believe me, yours respectfully,
J. B. Omohundro
Texas Jack[6]

The death of his young son took the wind out of Bill Cody's dramatic sails, and he confided to his partner that the idea of an extended stage tour no longer appealed to him, telling Omohundro that when the current season ended he might never return to the stage again, and perhaps would retire to Nebraska to manage his fledgling cattle business. In her biography of her brother, Helen Cody Wetmore wrote: "Very glad was the sad-hearted father that the theatrical season was so nearly over. The mummeries of the stage life were more distasteful to him than ever when he returned to his company with his crushing grief fresh upon him. He played nightly to crowded houses, but it was plain that his heart was not in his work."[7]

Texas Jack, Buffalo Bill, and the Peerless Morlacchi headlined one final show at Wilmington, Delaware's Grand Opera House on Saturday, June 3, 1876. Newspapers reported that Buffalo Bill was heading to North Platte to meet General Crook, and then heading into the Black Hills "to assist in suppressing the Indian troubles there."[8] Buffalo Bill and Texas Jack would never appear on the same stage again.

Jack and Josephine likely discussed the idea of a dramatic tour of their own, but a desire to start a family combined with commitments by

Jack to lead a party on a hunt out West ensured that any dramatic plans they made wouldn't reach fruition for almost a year, providing time to plan and construct a play showcasing their unique talents.

Jack and Josephine left their Billerica farm and headed for Philadelphia, where they purchased a small home on the west side of the city, into which Omohundro had invested their fortunes.[9]

Chapter Nineteen

Centennial 1876

As America approached one hundred years since the signing of the Declaration of Independence, the city that hosted the ratification of that historic document prepared to mark the occasion with the Centennial International Exhibition. This was the first World's Fair in the United States, and from May to November of 1876, over ten million people visited the exhibition halls built in Philadelphia's Fairmount Park. Though many detractors worried it would be impossible to provide adequate funding or for American exhibits to compete with those of European countries, the Exhibition would prove to be a rousing success for the city of Philadelphia.

Three years earlier, in 1873, Philadelphia's Fairmount Park Commission had set aside some 450 acres of the west side of the park for the Exhibition, which was originally scheduled to begin on April 19 to commemorate the Battles of Lexington and Concord. The International Exhibition of Arts, Manufactures, and Products of the Soil and Mine was opened officially on May 10 by President Grant, after some construction delays. Grant and Brazilian emperor Pedro II opened the ceremony by turning on the power to a specially built Corliss Steam Engine that powered the entire Exhibition through shafts totaling over a mile in length.

The Exhibition showcased many things that are so ubiquitous in modern life that to consider their simultaneous debut is astounding. For the first time, Americans could use Alexander Graham Bell's telephone to speak to each other from one end of the massive Main Building to the other. When Emperor Pedro II first tested the machine, he exclaimed,

"My God, it talks!" For most of the spectators, it was the first time they had seen the Remington Typographic Machine, which would become well known as the typewriter. The second-oldest soft drink still made in the United States, Hires Root Beer, made its debut and earned many new customers when its creator, Philadelphia pharmacist Charles Elmer Hires, gave away free glasses of the beverage, claiming that the combination of sixteen wild roots and berries would purify the blood and ensure rosy cheeks. The horticulture exhibit at the Japanese pavilion introduced Americans to an ornamental bush that was easy to grow and said to prevent soil erosion. Kudzu is now estimated to cover as much as seven and a half million acres of land in the United States. A local company introduced a bottled version of a table sauce that took an incredible amount of preparation. Advertised as "blessed relief for Mother and the other women in the household," Heinz Ketchup was an immediate success.

Americans saw for the first time a sculptured torch-bearing arm designed by Frédéric Auguste Bartholdi. When the arm arrived in August, it was listed in some of the written material as Bartholdi's Electric Light, or Colossal Arm. Bartholdi called it Liberty Enlightening the World. Visitors could make a small donation to climb the arm and look out above the fairgrounds. These donations contributed to the erection of a stone pedestal for the finalized version of the sculpture in New York, where it became known as the Statue of Liberty after its dedication in 1886.

To cope with the mass of humanity expected to swarm Philadelphia, the city's mayor, candy magnate William Strumberg Stokley, instructed his officials to encourage the building of new hotels and the addition of rooms to existing hotels in the city. A new city organization called the Centennial Lodging-House Agency was created to create a list of all the hotels in the city. As the Exhibition neared, the agency queried local citizens and added to its list of hotels an additional list of Philadelphia locals who would be willing to rent a room to an individual or family traveling to the city for the event. It became quickly apparent that even with these counted among the city's rooms for rent, there would not be enough hotel space in the city for the expected number of guests on any given week. The situation was further complicated by the fact that the majority of the area's hotels were centralized around the city center, far from the Exhibition site in Fairmount Park, west of the Schuylkill River.

New hotels started to be built on what was then Elm Avenue (now Parkside Avenue), the street that formed the park's southern border. With mere months left before the opening of the Exhibition, builders rushed to complete the new edifices. An article bearing the headline "Buried in the Ruins," appearing in the *Philadelphia Times* on March 14, 1876, demonstrates the inherent problem:

> *The three-storied building in course of erection for Bachelor Brothers, at Forty-second street and Elm avenue, fell shortly after 11 o'clock yesterday morning, in consequence of imperfect foundations. There were a number of mechanics engaged upon the structure at the time, and when the entire mass fell, almost without warning, four carpenters and a carter were buried in the ruins.*
>
> *Their companions quickly set to work to remove the debris, and in a short time extricated the unfortunates. Three of the men were seriously injured and two but slightly. . . . [T]he wounded men were conveyed to the Presbyterian Hospital.*[1]

The easiest solution to the problem of erecting stable brick buildings in the time remaining was to put up wood-frame buildings, but the city of Philadelphia had outlawed wood buildings due to concerns about fires after the disastrous conflagrations that had ravaged Boston and Chicago. Despite Mayor Stokley's protests, the city council determined that the need to provide adequate housing outweighed concerns over fires and granted several applications to build wood-frame structures near the Centennial site. The *Philadelphia Inquirer* reported on one of these meetings:

> *The Police Committee of City Councils met yesterday afternoon. Several applications for the privilege of erecting frame buildings in the vicinity of the Centennial grounds were read, and all, excepting one, referred to subcommittees. The exception was in the case of the application from the projectors of a new hotel on Elm avenue. That was ordered to be reported favorably.*[2]

This exception was granted for a hotel registered to Omohundro, Erb & Lafferty. Their two-story building, called the Hunters' Home, was a combination of hotel and saloon, with room for just over one hundred patrons at a time. In addition to supplying money for the investment, Jack sent to the hotel many of his own weapons and trappings of frontier life. Patrons could fire Texas Jack's guns at the indoor shooting gallery before retiring to the saloon, which was well stocked with wines, lagers, ales, and whiskies. John M. Burke, dressed in the wide-brimmed hat and fringed leathers of his scout friends, assisted Texas Jack in the attraction's operations.

An exhibit by the New York delegation on the Exhibition grounds, called the Hunter's Cabin, purported to show real frontier life, with a bear chained to a nearby tree and men in buckskins showing off their revolvers and bowie knives. Omohundro and his partners may have thought to capitalize on his fame, believing that authenticity would win over hotel and saloon patrons just as it had theatergoers in every major city for the past four years. To ensure this authenticity, Omohundro invited several Indians to stay at the hotel for the duration of the Exhibition.

Omohundro himself was likely planning on staying in Philadelphia throughout the Centennial Exhibition, as city records show him maintaining a residence at 614 North 44th Street, just a mile from his hotel on Elm Avenue. Morlacchi was engaged to perform both *The Black Crook* and *The French Spy* at the city's New National Theatre for the duration of the centennial celebration. Omohundro was in Philadelphia as the Centennial proceedings got under way. On June 5, Texas Jack was present, "sporting a huge sombrero," to watch a man attempt to ride his horse sixty-five miles in under three hours. At the end of June, Jack represented himself at the trial of a man who had stolen one of the cowboy's guns from his new hotel. A notice in the *Philadelphia Times* about a legal proceeding in small claims court in the city details the incident:

> *Thomas Murphy, a stranger in this city, was arraigned on the charge of stealing "a silver mounted barking iron" from "The Hunter's Retreat," a saloon in the vicinity of the Centennial Buildings. "Texas Jack" and "Lasso Bill," proprietors of that ranche [sic], were in attendance as the*

prosecutors. The trial went over, however, as the accused asked for time to send for money to retain a lawyer.[3]

The *Times* also reported that "Buffalo Bill was in Philadelphia on or about the 4th of July. He has been engaged in no business, but has been interested in the support of the Indians at the Hunters' Home."[4] The Indians in question were Donald McKay, his Warm Springs Scouts, and perhaps half a dozen Cherokee (DhBƟꞶT).

Texas Jack and Buffalo Bill did not spend the remainder of their summer in Philadelphia. As the date of the nation's centennial approached, so did news about the defeat of General Custer at the hands of the Sioux (Očhéthi Šakówiŋ) and Cheyenne (Tsêhéstáno) at Little Bighorn. Both of the scouts headed west to join the conflict, Cody to General Crook in Wyoming, and Omohundro, to General Terry in South Dakota. Working both as a scout for Terry and occasionally submitting reports on the action to the *New York Herald*, Jack would not return to Philadelphia until late October.

As the hotel buildings that had been granted exceptions were being built on Elm Avenue adjacent to the exhibition's Main Building, enterprising businessmen who had failed to get such exceptions ignored the law and built wooden structures between the hotels, filling the spaces with everything from exhibition halls holding huge canvas paintings and exotic animals to brothels, restaurants, barbershops, and beer halls. The owners of the existing buildings complained to the City but were told that the offenders would have to be taken to court and told to remove the structures.

On September 9, well after Omohundro had bid good-bye to his wife in Philadelphia and trekked toward Montana to join General Terry on the trail of the Sioux, a correspondent for the San Francisco *Daily Evening Bulletin* described the scene on Elm Avenue during the late summer:

The side-shows have picked up wonderfully during the last few weeks. A great impulse has been given to business in this direction. It is 9 o'clock in the evening and Elm avenue is in full blast. On the other side of the street is the main exhibition building, dimly lit here and

Texas Jack. Taken in Philadelphia just before the 1876 Centennial Exhibition. Jack opened a Western-themed hotel, saloon, and shooting gallery on Elm Street, across from the main grounds. (COWAN'S AUCTIONS)

there, silent and deserted. So is the sidewalk fronting it. Over the way is seen a long range of wooden buildings. Their fronts are of many and incongruous styles of architecture. No two are alike; the entrances are in many cases without doors or windows; the life within is plainly seen; there are lights, red and blue and green; flaring oil lamps and calciums darting their brilliant rays up and down the street. Cross over. The sidewalk is densely thronged.

For half a mile there is a succession of saloons, beer gardens, free minstrel shows, shooting galleries, hotels, restaurants and scores of other localities and appliances for amusing and comforting humanity. There is little of the more sober and practical business of life done here; no marketing, no buying of clothes or provisions. This is a Centennial crowd. They are gathered from all quarters, and bent only on enjoying themselves. Nor is this Philadelphia. It is a city by itself—a city of the Centennial. . . . Here is the saloon of Texas Jack: "The Hunters' Retreat," with many life-size wood cuts of Texas Jack pasted on the walls. Texas Jack, rifle in hand! Texas Jack, swinging the riots. Within sits an Indian woman in a brilliant red costume adorned with beads and furs; without is a burly Indian, still more brilliant in red leggings, hunting shirt and head dress of feathers. On the curb another Indian, more glaring still in red, silently offering bead-work for sale.[5]

Just after 4 p.m. on September 9, the day after the above report was printed, thousands of visitors near the entrance to the Centennial Exhibition noticed smoke rising south of them. Initial fears that the Main Building had caught fire were quickly dispelled, but as the throng of people rushed toward the fence, it became obvious that some of the wood buildings on the south side of Elm Avenue were on fire. The fire had begun at the Broadway Oyster House when a cook had grabbed a can of gasoline for the stove and carried it too close to the flame. The ensuing explosion quickly spread to encompass the surrounding buildings.

The first alarm went out from the nearby Globe Hotel at twenty minutes past four, but despite having shown their speed of response the day before by racing steam-powered fire engines down Elm Avenue, it was another twenty minutes before firefighters arrived to begin battling the blaze. When they ran their hoses to the nearest fire-plug, it was found to be clogged with sand and filth and had to be cleaned before it could be used at all. Fifteen minutes later a second alarm sounded from the United States Hotel further down Elm Avenue.

As the fire raced toward the Transcontinental Hotel to the west and the Ross House to the east, many of the one hundred thousand visitors crowding the park that Saturday gathered to watch the conflagration. The people packing the street made it hard for the firemen to move, and police were dispatched to push back the crowds. As the pine buildings burned, the flames became so hot that Exhibition fences across the street on the north side of the avenue were scorched. This heat made it impossible for the firemen to continue combating the flames. Two fire engines that had made it to the scene were kept inside the park fences, in case the winds shifted and made their way to the Main Building.

Buildings along Elm Avenue were consumed so quickly that most of the proprietors were only able to grab their cash boxes before escaping, leaving valuables and personal belongings to the flames. One zoological exhibition contained two sea lions in an enormous tank, which was far too heavy to move. Spectators watching the fire from inside the park reported hearing the animals crying above the noise. Blanchard's Amazon Theatre, Wylie's drinking pavilion, California Cheap John's clothing and junk shop, and Madame Duclos' female minstrels were all burned out, dancers of the latter being forced to flee in costume onto the Exhibition grounds. The fire's eastward spread was halted by the solid brick walls of the Ross Building, though the interior of that building was consumed in the blaze as well.

The third alarm at a quarter to five was sounded from within the Exhibition grounds, as the fire continued to consume buildings along Elm Avenue. A bowling alley, a shoe shop, more beer saloons, restaurants, and a stable were consumed before firefighters were finally able to contain the flames. The following morning's newspapers, in addition to recounting the story of the fire, pondered its origin. Arson, either on the part of the oyster house staff or from a city official determined to shut down the less-family-friendly establishments contained in the area, was the primary guess as to the beginnings of the blaze. One writer opined that this was exactly the opportunity that Mayor Stokley had been waiting for. Insurance estimates ranged from $50,000 to $200,000 in total losses, and many of the insurance companies simply refused to pay on grounds that the illegal buildings in the vicinity had violated the terms of their contracts.

Some of the owners immediately started replacing the burned wooden structures, most of them using brick instead of the pine they had used before, hoping to be allowed to continue doing business. One proprietor put up a large sign with the word "Phoenix" in bold letters above a smaller announcement reading "Loss by the fire $10,000." Inside he continued selling beer and cigars. The mayor proposed tearing down every building east of the Atlas Hotel, a temporary building with room for five thousand guests west of Jack's establishment on Elm Avenue, stretching from 52nd to 48th streets.

Other city officials argued that the mayor did not have the authority to declare buildings a public nuisance and then have them torn down without the court's involvement. In court a lawyer representing one of the building's owners argued that as there were laws prescribing certain penalties for infractions, it was illegal for the mayor to threaten penalties beyond the scope of those prescribed and without judicial hearing. The lawyer argued that the court should ensure the mayor would not be allowed to carry out his threatened demolishing of the remaining buildings.

Another lawyer argued that the city had been guilty of negligence in permitting the various parties involved to invest their capital in these buildings and the businesses carried on in them, and to remain there for months without complaint, and that the injured parties were therefore entitled to as much favor from the court as the city authorities were. The city solicitor offered his opinion that the burned-out building owners came before the court as "willful violators of the law" and were not entitled to equitable relief. He reasoned that because many of them were in violation of the law, and that their buildings were now to be viewed as clearly risking extreme peril to life, to the city, and to the valuable property contained within the Exhibition, it was the court's and the city's duty to protect these at the expense of the investments made by the business owners.

The court adjourned by giving Mayor Stokley discretion to clear out those businesses he deemed to be a "public nuisance." The mayor immediately set out to destroy what was now referred to in Philadelphia papers as "Shantytown." The buildings were separated into three classes. The first class was listed as "those buildings which have been erected without authority or pretense of authority of law." This class contained the majority of businesses, including hotels and entertainments, as well as small restaurants and bootblack stands. Between fifty and a hundred businesses fell into this category, with the vast majority being small booths or stalls between the larger buildings.

The second class was comprised of "those buildings which have been erected under what is claimed by the owners or occupiers thereof a permission received from the Building Inspectors of the city of Philadelphia." The city council had not ratified exceptions for these buildings, and most of them had no such permission from city building inspectors. In general, these were the wealthier business owners who believed that if they stalled for time they could replace their wooden buildings with brick edifices and avoid demolition altogether. Twenty or so businesses fell into this category.

The third class of buildings, listed as "those which have been erected under authority of ordinances of Councils," comprised the only three legal wood-frame buildings on Elm Avenue. These were the Jourdan Brothers establishment at 4120 and 4122 Elm, the Elm Avenue Hotel, and Texas Jack's Hunters' Home at 4188 Elm.

A local judge, in speaking to the mayor, presented his opinion that "as to the first two classes, I have no hesitation in directing you to follow the request, as the chief executive officer of the city, in accordance with your duty, to remove, as speedily as possible, the nuisances complained of. As to the third class, they may exist under a doubtful right, and it would be as well to allow them to remain for further consideration." This further consideration meant only that before it was razed Omohundro's business partners were given a few hours to empty the building of its contents.

The *Philadelphia Times* reported that "the buildings torn down by the police on Friday were the 'Fish House,' 4030–4034 Elm Avenue; the 'Bee-Hive,' 1222 Forty-first street; five stands adjoining 4188 Elm Avenue; two low frame structures on Elm Avenue, near Forty-ninth street, and three buildings just east of Fiftieth street."[6] These buildings were not all saloons and restaurants. Some housed minor attractions prior to the fire. Just as patrons had come to see the Indians and scout trappings at the Hunters' Home, they also crossed from the Exhibition to Elm Avenue to view George Washington's private carriage in a building on Forty-first Street or Commodore Perry's flagship at 4118 Elm Avenue. The city solicitor decided that the document presented to him by the proprietor of the Tivoli Garden, Mr. Aronheimer, ostensibly an appeal of his case to the Supreme Court, was not adequate protection, and his building was also razed.

On Friday, September 22, while the destruction of the buildings on Elm Avenue began, the *Philadelphia Times* noted that "Texas Jack is still with Terry terrifying the Indians."[7] By the beginning of October, all that remained to do was to empty the building. A notice in the *Times* read "Lease of ground, Building, Good-will and Fixtures of the Hunters' Home, 4188 Elm Avenue, will be sold at public sale, on the premises, Thursday, October 5, at 10 o'clock."[8]

It is likely that Texas Jack was unaware of the fire and loss of his hotel and fortune until he returned to the city in mid-October. Outside of mentioning sometime later that he had lost "$6,000 hard earned money," Jack didn't discuss his failed investment at the Centennial with reporters. That this venture escaped the notice of both Omohundro biographer Herschel Logan, as well as every historian to write about Cody and the early border drama years, speaks to Omohundro's seeming reticence to dwell on it. Many of those who lost their fortunes never moved on. Mr. Aronheimer, the theater proprietor whose Supreme Court appeal failed to halt the mayor and his police from tearing down the Tivoli Garden, shot himself soon after the Exhibition closed.

Texas Jack's venture at the Centennial Exposition failed because of his absence and because of fire. Jack could not have known that his idea—a Western-themed entertainment staged just outside the grounds of a major world's fair—would eventually succeed beyond his wildest imagination. Seventeen years after the Hunters' Home closed in Philadelphia, Buffalo Bill's Wild West opened just outside another Exposition in Chicago. According to the *Chicago Tribune*, "The pinnacle of Buffalo Bill's Chicago career coincided with the World's Columbian Exposition of 1893. On a city block adjacent to the fair, Cody staged the latest incarnation of his show, billed by that point as 'Buffalo Bill's Wild West and Congress of Rough Riders of the World.'"[9]

Like Jack's saloon, shooting gallery, and hotel, the *Wild West* was under the watchful eye of John M. Burke. "With its magnificent pageantry," writes historian Joe Dobrow, "the *Wild West* would fill the arena twice a day, every day, for the next six months, attracting 3 million visitors and clearing $1 million in profit. Many visitors who attended the *Wild West* believed that they had actually been to the Exposition."[10]

Texas Jack's hotel had failed at the nadir of his career, but Buffalo Bill and his cowboys—stand-ins for Cody's "Pard of the Plains for Life"—reached their zenith replicating his idea.

CHAPTER TWENTY

General Custer and Wild Bill

WHILE THE NATION CELEBRATED ITS CENTENNIAL ON THE FOURTH OF July, 1876, news reached the East about the death of General Custer and the defeat of his troops at the Battle of the Little Bighorn—known to the Lakota Sioux (Thíthuŋwaŋ), Cheyenne (Notameohmésêhese), and Arapaho (Hinono'eino) tribes that fought there as the Battle of the Greasy Grass—on June 25. Earlier that month, during the ceremonial Sun Dance on Rosebud Creek in Montana, Thatháŋka Íyotake, a Hunkpapa Lakota holy man known as Sitting Bull, had a vision of soldiers "as thick as grasshoppers from the sky" falling into the Lakota camp.

Bill Cody told a reporter for the *Rochester Democrat and Chronicle* over the summer that "The Indians do not care for the march of the United States troops through their country, but when they see a miner with a pick and spade they know he comes to stay."[1] Gold had been discovered in the Black Hills, which had been designated by the Treaty of Fort Laramie as part of a large territory for the exclusive use of the Indians, with a clause forbidding the intrusion of any non-Indians into the territory. After the discovery of gold in 1874, the Cheyenne and Lakota had been ordered to return to the confines of the reservation by the end of January 1876 so that the government could broker a sale of the gold-laden Black Hills. Bands opposed to a further reduction of their guaranteed lands refused to return, and Washington sent troops as early as March to force compliance. This initial military excursion ended in defeat at the Battle of Powder River.

Early in June the government sent generals Crook and Terry, Lieutenant Colonel Custer, and Colonel Gibbon, along with companies from the 2nd, 3rd, and 7th Cavalry and the 4th, 6th, 7th, 9th, and 17th Infantry divisions into the Montana and Dakota Territories to force the various tribes to return to their reservations. The three-pronged approach saw Gibbon's forces approach from Fort Ellis, Montana, to the west, Crook's column from Fort Fetterman, Wyoming, to the south, and Terry and Custer's men from Fort Abraham Lincoln, to the east.

On June 17, General Crook's companies, as well as allied Shoshone (Newe) and Crow (Apsáalooke) scouts, traveling along the Bozeman Trail met a force of mainly Lakota Sioux and Cheyenne warriors at the Battle of the Rosebud. The Cheyenne call this the Fight Where the Girl Saved Her Brother, as during the battle a Cheyenne named Buffalo Calf Road Woman (Mutsimiuna) rode to rescue her brother Chief Comes in Sight (Ôhme'ehnęstse) after he was left on the battlefield by the retreating Indians. Northern Cheyenne tradition holds that Buffalo Calf Road Woman, who was later at the Battle of the Little Bighorn, landed the blow that unhorsed General Custer before his death. Oglala Lakota Shirt Wearer, or war leader Thašúŋke Witkó, known as Crazy Horse, had warned that he would be forced to fight the army troops if "Three Stars," their name for General Crook, crossed the Tongue River, which he had on June 8. Though Crook claimed victory in the battle due to the retreat of the native forces, he was forced by his loss of troops to retreat south and await reinforcements, leaving him far away from the Little Bighorn River eight days later.

Scouts under Custer reported on June 25 that they could see smoke rising from a village some fifteen miles from their current vantage point. The assumption of the army was that these were the eight hundred braves known to be with Sitting Bull. Custer's plans for an imminent surprise attack were thwarted when it was discovered that Sioux scouts had discovered his troops' trail and possibly seen the smoke from their own cooking fires. Unknown to Custer, the Sioux that had been reported on his trail were departing from the village on the Little Bighorn and had not alerted the village to Custer's presence. Under the assumption that the natives now knew his location, Custer ordered an immediate attack, despite having received orders to wait and unite with Terry and Gibbon within a day.

Custer divided his companies into three battalions under himself, Captain Frederick Benteen, and Major Marcus Reno. As Custer devised his plan of attack, one of his scouts warned him that "General, I have been with these Indians for thirty years, and this is the largest village I have ever heard of." Weeks earlier, many of the "reservation Indians" had left the confines of the reservation to join Sitting Bull on the summer buffalo hunt, swelling the village at Little Bighorn to contain as many as twenty-five hundred warriors. Custer, determined that the Indians shouldn't be allowed to scatter and re-form later, insisted on pressing the attack in broad daylight.

The results were disastrous. Custer's battalion became separated from Benteen and Reno, who were unable to reinforce Custer's troops. Custer and his soldiers came under immediate fire from the assembled warriors and quickly retreated to a defensive position on the high ground that has become known as "Last Stand Hill." Within an hour of the start of the battle, the Cheyenne and Sioux had annihilated Custer's force and left him dead, with wounds to the left chest and temple. Lakota tradition holds that Custer committed suicide rather than risk capture and torture, though modern investigation has largely discredited this version of events due to the inconsistency of Custer's wound placement in view of his right-handedness.

A reporter in Philadelphia interviewed Texas Jack and Donald McKay just after news reached the city about Custer's defeat. McKay was of the opinion that "General Custer trusted too much to his own dash and too little to his Indian scouts." The reporter asked Jack for his thoughts on Custer, whom Jack had met while assisting Cody during the Grand Duke's buffalo hunt, and his enemies the Sioux:

Texas Jack said the Sioux are, with perhaps the exception of the Comanches, the bravest Indians on the plains. He saw one fighting once on the Loup river, when there were eleven United States soldiers around him, and although wounded in half a dozen places, he still had strength to fire a parting shot at Cody (Buffalo Bill)—a shot which

would have finished Cody's career, but that a bullet which entered the
body of the Indian at the moment he fired somewhat disarranged the
aim.[2]

Showing his typical modesty, Omohundro failed to mention that the bullet that entered the Sioux warrior and saved the life of Buffalo Bill was fired from his own gun. When a reporter asked Jack what he thought had happened to Custer, Omohundro said:

I think Custer was badly surprised . . . and I can imagine just how it
was. Custer having parted with Reno, found the village apparently
unsuspicious of his presence. But I believe that all along his march, the
Indians were perfectly well aware of every event that took place—
that they knew his strength to a man—and laid out their plans
accordingly. Letting him get to a certain point, the Indians, before
he could think of it, rose from all sides and poured in such a fire as
to slaughter half his command. Then, instead of trying to cut his way
through with the remainder—if such a course had been practicable—
he tried to retreat. Then rose the Indians on every side—in front and
rear—and there was nothing left to tell the tale but the bodies of those
slain.[3]

The defeat of Custer spelled the beginning of the ultimate end to the Plains Indians' traditional way of life. Fearing a reprisal from the military, the village at Little Bighorn was disbanded and scattered within forty-eight hours. Following the buffalo-hunting season, the "reservation" Indians returned to their families, leaving only six hundred braves noncompliant with the government's orders. In October, General Nelson Miles took command of the military effort, and continued fighting led to Sitting Bull's escape into Canada, Crazy Horse's surrender at Fort Robinson, and the end of the Great Sioux War after Miles defeated a band of Miniconjou Sioux on May 7, 1877. The Manypenny Commission required that the Sioux cede the Black Hills to the federal government or face a withdrawal of the rations they relied on without access to their traditional hunting grounds.

The later US Supreme Court decision in *United States v. Sioux Nation of Indians* acknowledged that the Black Hills, called Paha Sapa by the Sioux, had been unfairly taken without compensation. The Court ordered a monetary reimbursement, which the Sioux declined, as acceptance would legally terminate the tribe's demands that the land be returned to them. The fund was placed in an interest-accruing account and, as of August 24, 2011, was worth more than $1 billion.

The death of Custer at the hands of the Sioux came as a shock to the nation and to the various scouts and soldiers who had served under and known "The Boy General." "Custer was almost idolized by all who knew him," Omohundro told a reporter several months after the battle. "His cruel murder will cause much sadness among his many friends." Jack immediately offered his services, as well as those of his friend and later theatrical partner Donald McKay, as a guide for General Sheridan seeking to avenge the defeat. It was clear to Omohundro that after Little Bighorn, the Sioux threat could not be overstated. "The band of Sioux under Sitting Bull probably numbers three thousand warriors, and Crazy Horse has half as many more. They are very ferocious and wage a continual war on the whites, and also upon any peaceable Indians who come within their reach. They can never be kept down, and the government should send a sufficient force to clean them out entirely." Texas Jack, it seems, had never forgiven the Sioux for their massacre of the Pawnee during his first year onstage.[4]

In a piece in the *New York Sun* reporting on that city's reaction to the news of Custer's death, one reporter wrote that "a large, empty cart serv[ed] as a roosting place for a dozen noisy boys, who, perched upon the driver's seat, or lying in the bottom of the box, shouted, sang and told stories, some of which were about the gallant Custer, who, one youngster maintained, was 'a bullier Injin fighter than Texas Jack!'"[5]

Texas Jack and Buffalo Bill immediately headed west to join the action and lend their hands as scouts for the army as they chased the remaining Indians—Cody, to an encounter with a native warrior called Yellow Hair, and Jack, scouting for General Terry and carrying dispatches for James O'Kelly of the *New York Herald*. By August, both men were in South Dakota, and a concerned Cody wrote to his friend:

There is going to be the damnedest Indian war ever known, and no man can say when it is going to end. The Indians have thus far whipped every command they have met. They have one village that numbers 10,000 fighting men. They boast that in mountainous country they can whip all whites that may come against them, and many a white man will turn up his toes before they are conquered. I expect to hear of volunteers being raised![6]

While Texas Jack was on his way to meet up with General Terry, his old friend Wild Bill Hickok was murdered in Deadwood, Dakota Territory, an illegal settlement on Lakota Sioux land that had sprung up after the discovery of gold in the Black Hills. Though General Sheridan had reminded would-be settlers that the military intended to prevent whites from moving into the area, the promise of gold lured thousands of fortune hunters to the hills. Custer City was the first boomtown, but by April of 1876, more than five thousand of the miners had set up camp in Deadwood Gulch.

Hickok's friend Charlie Utter, who was then working as a wagon train driver, partnered with Wild Bill in Cheyenne after the gunslinger retired from acting. They arrived in Deadwood in July, with Utter running a train service back to Wyoming, charging 25 cents to deliver a letter, and sometimes carrying as many as two thousand letters in a forty-eight-hour round-trip. Hickok had married the widow of a circus magnate named Agnes Thatcher Lake in March, and imminent biographer Joseph G. Rosa believed that:

Hickok must have realized that he was now fast approaching a stage in his life when he would want a more stable existence, to put down roots, and to settle. And if his eyes were acting up on him, it would only be a matter of time before some young fool would try to back him down to make a reputation. Hickok was the first to admit that bluff and a reputation could only go so far. Thus the gold rush to the Black Hills must have seemed the best way out. If he could once make a strike, he could return to his wife perhaps to retire or engage in less dangerous pursuits.[7]

According to Hickok's nephew Howard, Bill realized that the $1,600 he had left to his name "would not go far in making a home consistent with the one his wife already had. He resolved to go into the Hills and win a stake more commensurate with a higher standard of living. He had old-fashioned ideas of honor, and living on his wife's money was contrary to his ideas of honor and decency."[8]

Hickok had thrown his lot in with Utter, and when their wagon train passed Fort Laramie, they may have picked up another traveler, Martha Jane Cannary, better known to posterity as Calamity Jane. Jane had ended up in Fort Laramie when she rented a buggy in Cheyenne for a one-mile ride to Fort Russell, but she was so drunk that she missed Fort Russell altogether and arrived at Fort Laramie, some ninety miles away. Utter later claimed that while he was riding with Hickok in Deadwood Gulch, the gunman had said, "Charley, I feel this is going to be my last camp, and I don't think I'll leave it alive." Hickok had long been paranoid that someone with either a vendetta or wanting to make a name for themselves would take it upon themselves to shoot down the famous Wild Bill. As far back as his days in Hays, Kansas, when he'd first met Texas Jack, Hickok had been cautious and wary, walking only down the center of the street, worried that anyone seeking to make a name for themselves as the man that took down Wild Bill might lurk in the shadows, alleys, and doorways he passed. Hickok refused to go to the same saloon two nights in a row, worried that a potential threat would learn his patterns.

In Deadwood, Hickok ran into his old scouting partner California Joe, and the pair likely talked at length about their time with Custer, the general's recent death, and perhaps even reminisced about walking the streets of Hays with Texas Jack. Hickok may have indeed had some premonition about his death there in Deadwood. Shortly before he was murdered, he reportedly wrote a brief letter to his wife.

Agnes darling,

If such should be we never meet again, while firing my last shot, I will gently breathe the name of my wife—Agnes—and with wishes even for my enemies I will make the plunge and try to swim to the other shore.[9]

A report that Omohundro wrote for the *New York Herald* says that he was headed for the Indian Territory on August 4, 1876, so he was not in Deadwood when his friend was murdered. His account of his brief tenure scouting with General Terry in the summer after the Battle of Little Bighorn doesn't mention traveling to the mining camp at all, but an account of Hickok's assassination that Omohundro gave to a *Herald* reporter suggests that he may have gone to Deadwood soon after he heard of his friend's death and received accounts of the murder from California Joe or Charlie Utter:

> *Texas Jack, a well known and respected scout, who, when not employed by the government or by private parties in the wilds of the Indian country west of the Missouri, lives quietly near Philadelphia, was long and intimately connected with Wild Bill, for whom he entertained a generous admiration. He has furnished to the Herald correspondent the following narrative of the cowardly assassination of the renowned and patriotic scout, as follows:*
>
> *"Early in August Wild Bill was at Deadwood City, Dakota, where there is about the roughest and worst population in the West, made up largely of outlaws, gamblers and roughs. Here he met one Jack McCall, a cross-eyed fellow, who was a gambling sharp and a sort of 'no-good.' He challenged Bill to a game of poker, in which Bill beat him. At the last deal in the game, McCall overbet his hand; that is, he bet $10, and when Bill called him and took the cards McCall had only $7.50. Bill mildly remonstrated with him, saying, 'You don't want to overbet your hand. That's no way to play cards.' McCall said he hadn't another 'red,' upon which Bill kindly gave him enough to pay for his lodging and his breakfast.*
>
> *"Next day Bill was sitting in the saloon playing a quiet game with a party of gentlemen. The play was proceeding pleasantly enough, with several looking on, McCall being in another part of the room. Suddenly, before anyone noticed him, McCall stood behind Bill, who remained seated at the table. To draw his revolver, place it within a few inches of the back of Bill's head and to fire, exclaiming, 'Take that, damn you!' was the work of a few seconds. The ball entered*

a little to the right of the centre at the back of the head, and came out below the right eye. Bill stiffened himself and fell back in his chair dead, without a groan, and probably never knew who had killed him. The cowardly deed was so quickly done that before those present could seize the murderer he had begun backing toward the door, holding his revolver in front of him and threatening to kill any man who moved.

"The bullet that killed Bill passed out below his right eye and buried itself in the arm of his opponent in the game, a steamboat captain on the Upper Missouri. The ball entered at the wrist and passed upward to the elbow, where it remains wedged in between the bones of the forearm in such a position that it cannot be extracted, and the man will probably be disabled for life.

"McCall was subsequently arrested and put through the form of a trial by a miners' court chosen at hazard in an impromptu, informal manner. He was acquitted. After McCall's acquittal California Joe, General Custer's old guide and a good, honest fellow who was a friend of Bill's, met McCall on the street and told him very significantly that he thought he had stayed in Deadwood long enough. McCall thereupon left town, and California Joe was subsequently killed in the same feud.

"McCall probably went direct to Custer City, where, being heard to say that he was the man who had shot Wild Bill, he was arrested by a United States Deputy Marshal and taken to Yankton Jail. He was tried at a regular court and condemned to be hung [sic] on the first of March. The only excuse he gave for his crime was the assertion that some years ago Bill had killed his brother.

"Bill had a large funeral, and was very much mourned by the law-abiding people of Deadwood, by whom his death was regarded as a great calamity."[10]

William Littlebury Kuykendall, who was known as "Judge" to his friends after a stint as member of the Wyoming territorial legislature and probate court judge, placed Omohundro in Deadwood just after Hickok's death. Kuykendall was the principal promoter and organizer of the 1870 expedition into the Black Hills and served as the elected commander of the group. Kuykendall's group was eventually stopped by two companies of United States cavalry on orders by General Grant to keep settlers out of Sioux territory.

Not to be deterred, Kuykendall and his companions returned later, avoiding detection and settling in the Dakota Territory. He was in Deadwood in 1876 and was later elected to the territorial council for the Dakota Territory. In his memories of the time, recorded as *Frontier Days: A True Narrative of Striking Events on the Western Frontier*, Kuykendall recalls being present at the Deadwood trial of Jack McCall:

> *When the jury was in place I asked the foreman if they had agreed upon their verdict. He answered yes. "Mr. Foreman," I said, "you will pass the verdict to the clerk, who will read it." The verdict was, "We, the jury, find the defendant not guilty." McCall hurried out through the back door and was soon on a swift horse, fleeing the country in the darkness with California Joe and Texas Jack, friends of Wild Bill, in hot pursuit. He escaped, was arrested a few days afterwards in Laramie City, Wyoming, taken to Yankton by the United States marshal, indicted by the United States Grand Jury, tried and hanged for the crime. While I was a member of the Legislature of Dakota, I was shown the four posts where the hanging occurred.* [11]

"That was a cowardly and brutal murder, wasn't it?" asked a journalist some time later. "Indeed it was," answered Texas Jack, "Yet all of us border men are continually in such danger. It is only a question of time when we must yield to that common fate . . . to become the marks of some cowardly bullet, or die like men while obeying duty's command." [12]

According to Omohundro's account, much of August was spent trying to get to Terry's force in Sioux territory. He set out from Philadelphia at the beginning of the month, making his way to Bismarck where he purchased a pony and a pack mule. In his account of the campaign, he reported that:

> *At that time there was no certainty as to where the army was. It had left the Rosebud and no news had been received of its movements. I*

Left to right: Wild Bill Hickok, Texas Jack Omohundro (standing), and Buffalo Bill Cody. The three famous western men appeared together in *The Scouts of the Plains*. (COWAN'S AUCTIONS)

determined to go up the Yellowstone as far as I could by boat and then take to the country with my pony and pack mule. I took the steamer Josephine on the evening of the 15th of August, and we started on our journey in company with another boat, the Yellowstone. General Whistler was on our boat with two companies of infantry, and another on the Yellowstone. His errand was the same as my own—to learn the whereabouts of the army, and, if possible, join it. We moved up the river as far as Fort Buford, where we arrived on the 18th. There we learned that the Indians had fired into the boat which went ahead of us a few miles below Buford, on the Missouri River. There was great excitement among the people there. They had run off some woodchoppers' stock and created great alarm.

Nothing could be learned of the whereabouts of the army here. The first news we got was on the 20th, when we met some half dozen soldiers in a small boat, from whom we learned that Terry's entire command was at or near the mouth of the Powder River, within twenty miles of us. This was good news, and we felt well over it, but things changed when we learned further that both sides of the river were lined with Indians. They had not, however, fired into the soldiers. We continued our journey without disturbance, and tied up that night without any preparations for defense except a temporary guard to protect the pilot. It was a fortunate thought, for a bullet afterwards struck the pilot-house, and would have killed him but for the protection it afforded.

The next morning, I got on shore to follow some deer that had run to an island, and found some fresh Indian trails. Coming out of the timber I went to the open sand bar, and got there just in time to see a volley fired into the Yellowstone from the opposite side of the river. She was about a quarter of a mile from our boat, and coming toward us. I was directly in range of the firing from the other shore, and could see the bullets skipping along the water.

She was not more than eighty or a hundred yards from the shore, and I could see the smoke curling up from the high bluff banks of the river. Other Indians were discovered a little further below and near the Josephine. I ran to the brush and made my way hurriedly back to her. There was so much noise and bustle on board that they had not heard the firing. On my way I saw Indians on our side of the river, and had to hasten for fear of being cut off.

Just as I got aboard, the Yellowstone came up alongside of us and reported what had happened. There was one man lying dead on her deck, and several bullets had passed through her. The Indians soon made their appearance again on the bluff immediately opposite, not more than 300 yards off, and we sent a volley into them from both boats that drove them off.

No more of them were seen on our side, and hasty breastworks were thrown up around the boats. We had no means of estimating their numbers. Two or more at a time might be seen riding, and a head or two would look out over a bank, but that was all. Some of the soldiers reported that they saw one or two fall and others lift and carry them off. Later reports showed that a large village had been encamped behind the bluff. We remained behind for three or four hours, till all of them had disappeared, and then steamed up the river a short distance and camped for the night.

The next morning, six or eight miles further up the river, we picked up a wounded man and a small boat lying on the shore. The man was bleeding and exhausted. He was barely able to tell his story, and proved to be a deserter from Terry's command. He and a companion deserted together, and the evening before they became separated in a chase by some Indians. During the night he returned to find his friend, when he saw his body scalped and cut into pieces.

On the 23rd we met the steamer Carol coming down from Terry's old camp near the mouth of the Powder River. She reported that Crook had left the day before, and Terry, that day, moving in a southerly direction. Dispatches were at once sent from our boat to Terry. He reported back, ordering all further movements of boats and wagons stopped.

His command came up the next day, the 24th, and crossed over to us. Crook in the meantime was to follow the main trail, leading about east, and then bearing off south toward the Little Missouri. After remaining two days in camp Terry's command marched off nearly northwest from the Yellowstone River, and, after making a big detour, arrived again at Glendive, on the river, about halfway between Buford and the mouth of the Powder River, expecting to meet Crook there or encounter the Indians he might drive across the Yellowstone.

Colonel Rice, who was entrenched at Glendive, reported that no Indians had been seen for several days and nothing had been heard of Crook, whom we confidently expected to meet. We remained several days in camp, but could learn nothing of him.

Colonel Reno took command and commenced a march down the Yellowstone, with the general understanding that we were going to Buford. Terry and his staff, after remaining with us during the first day's march, went on by boat. When within 35 miles of Buford a courier reached us with dispatches that the hostile Indians were crossing the Missouri at Wolf Point, about 18 miles below Fort Peck, after a hard march. Two miles below Wolf Point, we found fresh trails and bull boats, which the Indians had used for crossing the river. The boats had been taken back to the side from which they crossed and left there, as if others were expected to follow. About half a mile further below, before we came to the boats and trails, two Indians appeared on shore and made signs of peace. They said they saw the large moving columns and came to see what it was, fearing we were hostiles and in that case not wishing to let us cross.

They were, no doubt, runners for the hostiles to spot out our movements, because runners left Buford the moment our movements became known there. They were unsuccessfully pursued by a Lieutenant and two scouts, and the two we met were very likely from Buford.

From the runners and friendly Indians at Wolf's Point we found that Long Dog's band of twenty-three lodges had crossed the river several days before, and were making for Cypress Mountain, near the Canada line. They acknowledged at Wolf's Point that at one time we were so close to them that they were compelled to fly with bare ponies and guns, leaving everything else behind them. When I found out this it confirmed a belief I had at one time, that we were near them.

While making the detour to Glendive, we came on a herd of buffaloes, and began a promiscuous firing on them. An old Montana scout, named White, and myself went off some distance to have a shot by ourselves. Pretty soon I took down a cow and a calf at about 150 yards range, and was about to go on and secure some of the meat, when I became suspicious, for what reason I can hardly say; but, taking a glass, I saw two specks on a distant bluff, which I believed to be Indians. I told White what I thought, and he stood guard while I ran to secure some of the meat, which I was determined to have. I cut away the tongue and tenderloin, and hurrying back, found the two specks had disappeared. This convinced me I was right, and we hastened to join the command.

They had moved some distance, but, mounting a hill, we caught sight of the column and made for it with all speed. An officer who, like ourselves, had been some distance from the column, saw two Indians riding about. If we had fired upon them when we saw them, we would only be blamed for disturbing friendly Indians or frightening hostiles away; so we couldn't do anything.

The Indians, when they arrived at Wolf's Point, were well armed, but evidently short of ammunition. They were refused supplies, and said they would go where they could not get them. A Sioux agent, who visited their camp on Porcupine Creek, not far from Wolf's Point, reported them as very bold and impudent. They searched his belt for ammunition and offered to trade a pony for 100 rounds. They further promised to return in the Spring, when they would have fresh supplies, and fight the soldiers "plenty." They carried with them a number of cavalry pistols, such as were used by Custer's men, and which they were anxious to trade off, as they had no ammunition for them.

The following incident will show how bold and suspicious they are: a white man, who was taking one of the pistols in exchange for a coat, accidentally pointed it at the Indian with whom he was making the exchange. On the instant two rifles were pointed upon him and only removed when the mistake was explained.

Our troops were now out of rations, but Terry arrived by boat with supplies and ordered Reno to return by the opposite band of the river to Buford. The campaign was evidently over for the season.[13]

On September 15, General Terry and Texas Jack Omohundro, aboard the steamer *The Chambers*, arrived at Fort Peck, Montana, on the Missouri River. There they met Major Reno, who had marched with his troops from the Yellowstone to the fort, where they had run out of hardtack. With the soldiers unable to pursue them, the Sioux crossed into British Columbia where, low on ammo, they had been forced to trade their ponies for enough ammo to hunt for food. Jack was eager to pursue, convinced that there were bands of Sioux that had not yet crossed the border. The cautious Terry chose to keep his scouts on the boat with him, and they departed back down the Missouri.

A frustrated Omohundro complained that "none of us could comprehend the meaning of any of the movements we made, and everything was kept very secret. It is the first campaign in which I could never make out the object of any movement. Perhaps if I knew the object that might explain them, but as it was the Indians might have roamed around for twenty years and lived comfortably. They made no use of the scouts to any purpose, while among the Indians spies were watching us from every hilltop, and were in no danger of being caught unless they wished to be."[14]

As he left Montana, Omohundro unexpectedly met Buffalo Bill when the steamers that both men were taking back down the Yellowstone landed at the same time and the men spied each other on the dock. Cody had initially been with Lieutenant Carr and the 5th Cavalry on the Cheyenne River, when they received information that as many as three hundred Cheyenne warriors under the leadership of Morning Star (Vooheheve), who was also known as Dull Knife, had left the Spotted Tail and Red Cloud agencies with their families to join Sitting Bull and Crazy Horse.

Having felt insulted by the newspaper critics who insisted that real scouts didn't wear the bright and flashy colors that Cody and Omohundro had worn on their latest stage tour, Cody took to the trail in his full stage garb, including a bright red shirt and black velvet pants with red ribbon seams and silver bells. If any of the soldiers thought the outfit was outlandish and impractical, no one was willing to tell the most famous scout in the country that he looked like he didn't know what he was doing.

With Cody acting as lead scout, the 5th Cavalry intercepted the Cheyenne warriors en route to join the Sioux just after dawn on July 17, 1876. Scattered groups of Cheyenne crested a ridge and were descending the ravine toward Warbonnet Creek, unaware that troops were so close.

Cody rode ahead of the troops, and as he rounded the hill came within a dozen yards of a warrior in a long feather headdress. Both men raised their weapons and fired. The warrior's revolver shot missed Cody, but Buffalo Bill's Winchester rifle shot true, injuring the warrior's leg and killing his pony. Turning to take aim, Cody's horse stumbled, and the scout was thrown to the ground. As Cody rose he could feel a bullet pass within inches of his right ear. He dropped to one knee, brought his rifle to his shoulder, and fired once more, this time landing a fatal shot to the brave's face.

Cody rushed forward, pulled out his bowie knife, and removed the scalp from the dead Cheyenne warrior, screaming "The first scalp for Custer!" as he held the bloody souvenir aloft. This is Cody's account, among many divergent versions of the "Duel With Yellow Hair," some ending with the Cheyenne brave and Cody locked in hand-to-hand combat, Cody with a bowie knife and Yellow Hair (Heova'ehe) with his tomahawk. Some accounts claim that Yellow Hair was instead killed by one of the other soldiers and that Cody had merely scalped the dead Indian.

Whatever the truth, Cody sensed an opportunity.[15] Though he had determined after his son's sudden death to leave show business to spend more time with his family, tending to his business interests in Nebraska, his time as a scout had both reinvigorated him and provided him with a new tale to tell. After showing his friend Texas Jack the gruesome scalp and long headdress he had claimed from his foe, Cody explained his plan to Omohundro. They could use the artifacts as advertising for a new show, a dramatic retelling of Custer's defeat, Buffalo Bill's triumph, and Texas Jack's adventures on the Sioux trail. Buffalo Bill must have been surprised when his partner told him that he couldn't join him this time.

It is impossible to know exactly what reasons Texas Jack gave to explain his reluctance to join his friend, but there were circumstances that contributed to his decision. He had agreed to lead a hunt for a few English friends of the Earl of Dunraven in the early winter and wanted to follow through after giving his word. Alexis, the Grand Duke of Russia, had intimated in letters to the cowboy that he had read Dunraven's writings on the trip to the Yellowstone and would like to travel to the national park himself. After the death of Cody's son and his subsequent insistence that he was done with acting, the Omohundros may have already begun planning and scheduling a tour. The cowboy and the scout shook hands and parted as friends, neither knowing that the "Pards of the Plains for life," Texas Jack and Buffalo Bill, would never appear on the same stage again.

ACT III

Perhaps he was fully satisfied with what he had accomplished, for to the plainsman nothing is more dear than notoriety, of which Jack secured his measure. To read his name in print was intoxication to him. To hear himself spoken of in terms of praise for his courage delighted him beyond bounds, for he had all the conceit of the ranger class, and loved to be regarded as one whose mention would thrill the listener. More refined than Wild Bill, more modest in asserting himself than Buffalo Bill, he stood on a plane above both, and though he recognized the fact that better fighters and better scouts than he were still content with the hardships of the prairies, he felt a superiority of education and a deep capacity of enjoyment that they could never attain.... On the ranches of the far West, and occasionally among the rolling stone scouts, one finds genuine manhood, braced by intellect and backed by thorough-breeding.

—BROOKLYN DAILY EAGLE
JULY 1, 1880

CHAPTER TWENTY-ONE

On the Hunt

JACK SPENT THAT WINTER HUNTING WITH ENGLISHMEN SIR JOHN RAE
Reid, 3rd Baronet, his cousin, Charles P. Eaton, and Samuel Ralston, son
of San Francisco banker William C. Ralston. Reid, whose father was
governor of the Bank of England, hired Jack based on the description in
his friend Lord Dunraven's book. They met in Rawlins, Wyoming Territory, named after the general who had stopped there in 1867 looking for
a drink of cold water. His men had scouted the local hills and discovered
a spring. Declaring the water from the spring the most refreshing drink
he had ever tasted, General Rawlins had expressed the hope that "If anything is ever named after me, I hope it will be a spring of water." Rawlins
Spring and the community that sprang up around it was the last stop
for water on the Continental Railroad before it crossed the Red Desert
to the west. Omohundro often used Rawlins as a last stop before taking
hunting parties into the Sweetwater, Wind River, and Bighorn ranges.

For this particular excursion, Texas Jack invited Tom Sun, also known
as Indian Tom, to accompany him and his English guests. Sun was born
Thomas De Beau Soleil in Vermont and owned a large ranch on the
Sweetwater Creek near Devil's Gate, one of the areas that Omohundro
planned to hunt. Sun's ranch would eventually grow to encompass more
than eighty thousand acres, with several thousand head of cattle. Like
Jack and Buffalo Bill, Indian Tom served as a scout, based out of Fort
Fred Steele in Wyoming. Tom was at the fort in 1868 when generals
Grant and Sherman came west with General Sheridan to meet with
Union Pacific officials Thomas C. Durant and Sidney Dillon.

Omohundro had invited his fellow scout and Indian fighter as a precaution, as he intended to take Reid, Eaton, and Ralston into the heart of the Sioux territory. During the time he had spent with General Terry, Omohundro had come to two conclusions: The vast majority of the Sioux had either submitted to the government and returned to the Wounded Knee reservation or escaped to Canada, and without the Sioux there to hunt them, elk were abundant. Officers at Fort Steele tried to dissuade the cowboy guide, warning his guests about the danger that the Sioux presented to anyone traveling in their territory. The threat of scalping did not deter the hunters, and Jack remained convinced that the few Sioux remaining on the plains that fall had by now retreated to the reservation for the winter.

Northeast of Rawlins the hunting party came upon elk, white-tailed deer, and mountain sheep. Jack estimated that one of the elk herds numbered three thousand head, and the hunting party tracked it for eight miles, allowing Reid and Eaton ample opportunity to take down trophy bucks. Jack told a reporter that "most of them were does and fawns, with a few bucks scattered around. In a band of three thousand head there would not be more than thirty or forty bucks, for these elk have more wives than Brigham Young."[1]

Asked about the difficulty of hunting elk, Omohundro laughed, noting:

> *Elk are about the stupidest animal in the world, and you can get all you want by either sneak-hunting or stalking. When they first see you, they are so silly they will walk right toward you, but at a shot they start off, always in the face of the wind, so that they can smell ahead and see behind. Their natural gait is a trot; when they are harried and frightened they sometimes break into a clumsy run, but they can't travel near as fast that way. I have timed elk trotting eight miles in twenty-four minutes, over rough ground.*
>
> *When you get a band started, you charge into them, ride your ponies into the midst of the animals, press those you don't want aside by pushing their flanks with your hand, and make for those with fine antlers. They never show fight to men, but are the timidest beasts in*

the world. The only danger you are in is that your horse might stumble,
and then you would be trampled to death by their sharp hooves.[2]

Indeed, one night a herd of elk chanced into the hunters' camp, and the mules the men used to carry their supplies attempted a stampede. Leaping onto his bronco, Jack was in his element, riding around and gathering the animals. Though it had been some years since his cowboy days on the Chisolm Trail, he hadn't lost a step.

Traveling north, the group continued to hunt before turning west toward the Sweetwater River, where they pitched their permanent camp near Independence Rock, long a popular stop on the Oregon, Mormon, and California trails. Many of the travelers who had passed had taken time to carve their names in the stone face, and for a time a few local stonemasons had set up shop, charging money to chisel the names of the pioneers heading for Portland, Salt Lake, or San Francisco. The area was abundant with elk and black-tailed deer.

Some of the specimens that Sir Reid sent on to Omaha for transportation to first New York and then London had antlers that he measured at five feet long from skull to tip, with a spread of four feet. On Christmas Day Reid and Omohundro were hunting high in the Wind Rivers when Jack alerted the Englishman to the largest buck they had seen during the expedition. When they returned to camp that evening, the head was preserved, and the rest of the animal roasted and served as Christmas dinner.

As the hunt concluded, a Chicago paper reported that during the course of the excursion, 276 elk, 73 black-tailed deer, and a large number of antelope, bear, and various small game had been killed by the party. The large number of animals killed prompted the following response from the *Santa Fe New Mexican* newspaper:

We hope the time will come, and that soon, when no newspaper in the
United States can with truth publish such an item as this. Here are
three hundred and forty-nine of the largest animals which roam the
western wilds, besides "a large amount of bear, antelope, and small
game"—possibly a thousand animals in all—wantonly slaughtered

*for the gratification of some English sportsman, who in his own coun-
try would not dare to shoot a rabbit without license.*

*The elk has been nearly obliterated in this country, and the black-
tailed deer is scarcer, yet any foreigner who has more money than
humanity is allowed to come here and buy a "Texas Jack" to lead him
to the preserves in order that he may make havoc among them so that
he may go home and boast of his success. If Congress does not soon pass
a law stopping this kind of slaughter, there will not be a wild animal
native to the country within its bounds half a century hence.*[3]

When Jack returned to New York, a reporter for the *Spirit of the
Times* magazine asked him about the hunt, and after describing Sir Reid
and Mr. Eaton as "about the most sensible men and best hunters I ever
piloted over the plains." Jack added, "They were hunting for trophies
more than anything else, and didn't kill any game and leave it to rot
on the ground."[4] On this, as well as most of the hunts that Texas Jack
managed, none of the animals that were hunted were wasted. Generally,
the hunters were seeking prize specimens to display when they returned
home. Other animals were killed to provide food for the hunting party.
When one of the guests took a trophy, often the head was preserved
and the rest of the meat was eaten. On this trip, what meat wasn't used
by Omohundro, Indian Tom, Sir Reid, and their guests was carefully
packed and sent back to Fort Steele. The grateful fort used the game to
feed the troops during the cold winter. After the camp was fully supplied
with elk, deer, and sheep, the remaining meat was sent on to Omaha,
where it was sold to the poor at the bargain price of eight to ten cents
a pound. The wild game purchased this way was often the only meat
affordable to disadvantaged citizens, as beef from the Texas cattle that
Jack had once driven north to waiting markets was more than twice that
price.

When asked about the slaughter of animals by other hunters, Omohundro told a reporter that he had seen some parties slaughtering animals needlessly. "But I don't think there has been much of that sort of
thing done lately. I know our party killed nothing but what they wanted,
and these Englishmen were good shots, and brought down a buck when

they drew a bead on him. There is a fine of $30 for leaving any game on the ground."[5]

The weather during these winter hunts could get brutally cold, and one newspaper reported that on the Christmas that Jack and Reid dropped their biggest trophy elk the temperature in the Wyoming interior was close to zero. Within a week it had dropped to an estimated 25 degrees below. With flurries of snow falling around the hunting party, Omohundro led the expedition out of the plains and toward Rawlins, where they arrived on New Year's Eve. Parting ways, Sir Reid and his cousin Mr. Eaton along with Sam Ralston boarded a train west to San Francisco, where they split up, Ralston remaining while Reid and Eaton chartered a boat to India. Indian Tom Sun returned to his ranch, and Omohundro returned east to meet his wife in Lowell.

Jack was pleased that his estimation that the hunt would not encounter any Sioux proved to be correct:

> We didn't see any Indians, though, all the time we were out, and I wasn't a bit sorry for that. . . . [T]hey all seem to have gone North, and I reckon are up to the Canada line. We didn't see any Indian signs all the time we were out. You see the buffalo have all been driven north, and the Indians have to follow them, for they can't be on the warpath without buffalo. They don't like elk and deer and small game well enough to live on it, but give them plenty of buffalo meat and they are happy. You know they consider them as their own property. A redskin will speak of buffalo as "my cattle," and as long as they can swell around, on horseback, in paint and feathers, and kill one of their cattle whenever they want food, they're all right; but cut them off from this, and they'll soon come into the agencies, get beef and beans, and be "good Indians." The wild Indian and the buffalo are pards, and when one dies the other must. If the Government had put all its soldiers to killing buffalo, instead of trying to kill redskins, and getting butchered themselves, the Indian question would have been settled long ago.[6]

In 1889, some twelve years after he hunted with Texas Jack, Tom Sun and five other men kidnapped and lynched a local Wyoming homesteader named Ella Watson and a business owner named James Averell, claiming that the pair were cattle rustlers. Although when he was arrested Sun admitted to what had happened and named his accomplices, the case was adjourned when none of the four witnesses could be induced to testify against the men. Today, Sun's ranch is owned by the Church of Jesus Christ of Latter-day Saints and contains the largest remaining uninterrupted stretch of the Oregon Trail. It has been designated a National Historic Landmark and is frequented by visitors.

Omohundro spent the first few months of 1877 in Philadelphia with his wife, expecting to accompany the Grand Duke Alexis on a return trip to the Western hunting grounds, predicated by the duke's desire to replicate the Earl of Dunraven's Yellowstone expedition. Unfortunately for Texas Jack, the Grand Duke was soon promoted to commander of the Russian Naval Forces on the Danube in advance of the Russo-Turkish War that began early in April and was unable to return to the American West to hunt. A Washington newspaper wrote that Texas Jack "stands in no awe of the Russian, but treats him as hail fellow, well met."[7] According to another report, Jack was overheard telling a companion, "I wonder what on earth is the matter with 'Lexis! I write him, but hain't got no answer."[8] The frustrated cowboy set off to hunt and returned with several antelopes, throwing a feast for members of the Philadelphia press.

Bill Cody and William Frank "Doc" Carver, the sharpshooter who would later tour with both of the famous scouts at different times, visited the camp of Omohundro on his return from a hunt in March of 1877.[9] Likely Cody had returned West between theatrical seasons, where he met Carver, who had spent the last year or so in California competing as a sharpshooter and making a name for himself. The two had mutual acquaintances from Cody's days in Fort McPherson, and Buffalo Bill was never a man to forego a challenge or a bet when it came to shooting or horse racing.

Omohundro, who knew Carver primarily as the sometimes romantic partner of Ena Palmer, nonetheless spent a little time with Doc, likely teaching him the finer points of marksmanship and showmanship, the former of which Carver mastered quickly, and the latter, which he fabricated by co-opting the real-life heroics of Cody and Texas Jack, just as

Ned Buntline had used the real-life facts of Wild Bill's story to enlarge the legend of Buffalo Bill in his dime novels.

Once again, Cody asked Jack to join him onstage, and once again Omohundro declined. Cody seems to have been upset by his friend's refusal, perhaps believing that like Kit Carson Jr., Jack was leaving him to strike out on his own, in direct competition with the Buffalo Bill Combination. In one way, Cody's fears were well-founded: The Texas Jack Combination with Donald McKay would embark on a series of shows that year, playing the same kind of shows—and, in some cases, the exact same play, but for a few alterations in the characters' names—that Cody and Omohundro had been touring for the past four years.

What Omohundro was perhaps unwilling to tell his friend was that because of his desperate financial situation after the loss of his investment in Philadelphia, the Combination wouldn't be under Texas Jack's control at all. He was simply a hired actor in a show that billed him as the star and traded on his fame to fill seats. Ever confident in his own abilities, Omohundro was likely convinced that after a season of well-attended shows, he'd be able to stop touring and enter into the realm of theatrical management, as he'd told a local Lowell newspaper that he had secured a company to stage European operas in Boston that had not yet appeared stateside. The plan was for his wife to act as leader of the incidental ballet attached to the opera, allowing the couple to live in Lowell while they worked in Boston, an arrangement conducive to eventually raising the children both likely hoped would soon come.

CHAPTER TWENTY-TWO

The Texas Jack Combination

LARRY McMURTRY NOTES IN HIS BOOK *THE COLONEL AND LITTLE MISSIE* that "Cody always had too much raw star power for Texas Jack to compete with, but when it came to organizing a modern theatrical troupe, Texas Jack for a time pulled ahead. He had, for one thing, his charming wife."[1] Joy S. Kasson goes further, writing that "Texas Jack was even better placed than Buffalo Bill to succeed in the theater. Judson had written a serial featuring him, Morlacchi was performing in his plays, and the brilliant John Burke continued to work for him as a manager. Over the next four years, Omohundro continued to star in border dramas such as *Texas Jack in the Black Hills*, *The Trapper's Daughter*, and *The Scouts of the Plains*. . . . [H]e was not so hungry as Cody, not so eager for fame and money, and perhaps that is why he did not pursue his stage career so aggressively."[2]

For the new tour in 1877, his first full dramatic season without his old friend and partner, Buffalo Bill, Texas Jack recruited a stable of actors and performers to complement his strengths and shore up his shortcomings. The first role to fill was that of his second man. Knowing that there was no scout or Indian fighter in America that would not pale in comparison to Buffalo Bill Cody, Omohundro convinced John Allen, the company's manager, to hire Donald McKay, who Jack had become close friends with over the course of the past year.

Donald McKay was born in 1836 to a prominent fur trader named Thomas McKay and a Cayuse (Liksiyu) Indian mother in eastern Oregon. Donald's father Thomas and his grandfather Alexander had come to Oregon in 1811 with the Pacific Fur Company of John Jacob Astor. Donald grew up hunting in the Willamette Valley, and in the early 1850s worked with the army as a translator and scout. In the 1860s, Donald's brother William served as captain of the Warm Springs (Tinaynułáma) Indian Scouts, and Donald soon commanded his own company of Warm Springs natives for the army, serving against the Northern Paiute (Numa), Bannock, Shoshone (Newe), and other northern tribes. He also served as a translator for the government when they treated with the Warm Springs, Klamath, Yurok (Olekwo'l), and Karuk tribes in Oregon and northern California.

During the Modoc War, McKay worked as a scout and translator, carrying messages between the army and Kintpuash, who was called Captain Jack. Just before hostilities reached a boiling point, McKay traveled alone into the lava beds in an attempt to convince Captain Jack of the futility of fighting the white soldiers. Captain Jack disagreed, and in the ensuing battle McKay was shot off his horse, only to spring to his feet and save the life of a white soldier who had fallen nearby. Though he was unsuccessful in preventing hostilities, and the resulting battle saw the loss of life of many Modoc, Warm Springs, and army soldiers, McKay's bravery was recounted in newspapers covering the uprising, with pictures of himself and his Warm Springs Scouts viewed nationally. Donald and his brother William capitalized on this celebrity and began competing in sharpshooting events and demonstrations, their army wages being insufficient to sustain their families back in Oregon.

The success of Cody and Omohundro in *The Scouts of the Prairie* ensured that many border dramas sprang up within months of their December 1872 debut. As news of the army's fight with Captain Jack dominated newspapers in the east in 1873, dramatized versions of the events of the Modoc War appeared, such as *Captain Jack of the Modocs* and *White Hair; or, The Last of the Modocs*. The body of Captain Jack was stolen from its grave and embalmed and was now touring the East as a circus and carnival attraction. When an actor named Oliver Douglas Byron toured with a drama entitled *Donald McKay, the Hero of the Modoc War* in 1874, the McKay brothers decided it was time they played their own drama as themselves, just as Buffalo Bill and Texas Jack had done two years earlier.

When their first traveling Indian show failed due to poor management by the reservation agent the brothers had hired, William went back to his family in Oregon while Donald was briefly imprisoned in Boston for debt. When he was freed, he traveled to Europe with a drama called *Donald McKay, the Hero of the Lava Beds*. McKay returned to America in 1876 to visit the Philadelphia Centennial, where he and his daughter were among a group of Indians staying at Omohundro's Hunters' Home hotel.[3]

When McKay and Omohundro met in Philadelphia just before the Exhibition, they discovered that they had a great deal in common. While both had been celebrated in Northern newspapers for their exploits, they both felt like outsiders—Omohundro, as the former Confederate soldier whose Virginia sensibilities clashed with Yankee urbanity, and McKay, the half-breed Indian scout who was viewed as a hero for his work against other Indians, ensuring he was fully accepted by neither the native people of his mother or the white people of his father. Both men had seen dramas produced by professional actors impersonating them, without benefiting from the productions in any way. Both viewed their native heritage proudly but had worked tirelessly against the Indians they saw as standing in the way of their country, of which both men were equally proud.

Staying at the Hunters' Home hotel and recounting their dramatic endeavors, Omohundro and McKay likely discussed the mutual benefits of forming a dramatic partnership. With Buffalo Bill Cody determined to retire from acting after his son's death, Texas Jack must have been acutely aware of the benefit in having a real Indian war hero standing on the stage with him. During their last dramatic season together, Cody and Omohundro had pared back the wholesale depictions of Indian slaughter in favor of more-realistic border stories, with less gunpowder and more of the kind of acting both men aspired to. With McKay and his Warm Springs Indians, the Cherokee (DhBꙨꭰT) that were with them in Philadelphia, and the Pawnee (Chaticks si Chaticks) that Jack had hunted with in Nebraska, perhaps it would be possible to stage a show that was closer to real life on the frontier than the blood-and-thunder dramas that Ned Buntline and Fred Maeder had written for the scouts.

Between acting projects, McKay was engaged in selling a cure-all called Ka-Ton-Ka for Colonel T. A. Edwards, who had worked as a circus manager before becoming a Union spy deep behind Confederate lines during the Civil War. Edwards managed McKay's shows in Europe and arranged his appearance at the Philadelphia Centennial Exhibition. Although Edwards and McKay claimed the snake oil they peddled was made by Donald and William McKay at the Umatilla Reservation in Oregon, in reality it was manufactured in Pittsburgh. The fantasy that the Oregon Indians had an ancient deep woods remedy was hugely appealing to Eastern crowds, and Edwards's Oregon Indian Medicine Company did brisk business, advertising via traveling shows and also offering their products wholesale through general stores and catalogs. Having experienced the life of a frontier scout, a touring actor, and a cure-all salesman, McKay vastly preferred the stage.[4]

At the Centennial, Omohundro was introduced to an endurance and trick rider named Maud Oswald who had acted in border dramas like *Indian Life; or, Chase for a Wife* during the last dramatic season as a member of P. T. Barnum's Great Roman Hippodrome. When Omohundro viewed the performance in Philadelphia, he was impressed by Miss Oswald's horsemanship, watching as she raced her pony against four other riders in a hurdle race, as well as participating in the chariot races that Barnum staged.[5]

Texas Jack, Morlacchi, Donald McKay, and Miss Maud Oswald, together with ever-present fixture John Burke, now billed as "Arizona John," practiced the show in Chicago after Jack returned from his latest hunting trip in the Bighorns of Wyoming and debuted at the Bowery Theatre in New York on April 2, 1877. The *New York Dispatch* reported on the opening performance:

> *Texas Jack (J. B. Omohundro) made his first appearances before a succession of audiences that tested the capacity of the building and attested the popularity of this young and experienced hunter, trapper, guide and scout, who but lately returned from the heart of the Bighorn Mountains. "Shot out of a gun" is nothing compared with the manner of Jack and his pony Modoc's flashing appearance on the scene. If*

ever a horse and rider were in accord and knew how far to go—and no further—knew how to go it, and so quick—the perfect safety, yet terror of the orchestra stalls, the delight of ye enthusiastic "gods," the anticipation of the medical auditor, and the admiration of all, they are "Lone Star John" and his mustang.

It's worth a month's lessons to see Jack mount and dismount. If anything approaching them can be found it is in Maud Oswald and her dancing, prancing Firefly, who waltzes on and off with such fiery energy that their "beautiful finish" brings a sigh of relief from the assembled admirers of the daring equestrienne. These two novelties to the stage, with the winsome, gifted child of Italy, the energetic Morlacchi, in her personation of an impressible maiden of La Belle France transported to the wilds of the American frontier and subjected to the teasing, yet pleasing attention of an amorous son of "ould Erin," and the terrors of capture, torture and death at the hands of a band of veritable "sons of the forest," led by the genuine red-skin hero, Donald McKay, backed by a play with a simple story, few impossibilities, and withal practicable, formed an entertainment enjoyable and natural.[6]

Other reports of Texas Jack's opening salvo on the dramatic world as the single star in a combination bearing his name were equally favorable. The *New York Sun* offered this report of the evening's performance:

Oceans of applause greet "Texas Jack" at the Bowery Theatre. The teeming terraces of men and boys belched sonorous admiration for two hours. And Texas Jack unquestioningly deserved it, if only for his tireless industry in killing savages. He made his entree upon the stage mounted upon an Indian pony whose real live Simon pure Indian pony performance put to shame all previous attempts to make a horse a dramatic animal. Ordinarily this noble beast falls off most miserably in his theatric exploits. He balks at the orchestra, backs up against the scenes, and if he is slaying the role of the blooded Arab barb has to be pricked from the wings to make him go.

The noble pony of Texas Jack crosses the back of the stage on a wood bridge at full speed, carrying his master, and, bounding into

*view, circles the ample stage, and is pulled up suddenly at the foot-
lights with his mouth agape and one fiery eye looking down sideways
at the frightened double bass, while the sinewy rider bows under the
storm of applause.*

*As to the play, Texas Jack probably wrote it himself in an idle
literary moment with coyote's blood in some canyon. All the Indians
in it are bad Indians, and they all die. Texas Jack kills nearly all of
them with his eagle eye and regulation revolver. It may be said, in
truth, that the steady stream of death is something unusually exhila-
rating. The unbroken slaughter appears to be enjoyed by the miserable
red skins. The alacrity with which they die in groups and tribes at the
shake of a navy revolver bespeaks a preference for extinction that is
deeply interesting.*

*Texas Jack is supported by Mlle. Morlacchi, whose French accent
gives a pleasant flavor to the Black Hills society. The rest of the company is well known to the Bowery habitués.*[7]

Though the two friends never seem to have had hard feelings about
the dissolution of their dramatic partnership, writers and critics often
framed the tours of Omohundro and Cody as competitive and rivalrous.
A St. Louis critic wrote:

*Texas Jack's play beats Buffalo Bill's play all hollow. We don't think
Texas Jack is any more of an actor than Buffalo Bill—in fact, if we
had a five year old boy that couldn't act better than both of 'em put
together, we'd shoot him at sunrise. But Texas Jack's play has more
dying in it than Buffalo Bill's. It probably has more dying in it to the
square inch than any other piece in America—not even excepting one
of Shakespeare's tragedies or Ned Buntline's stories. Why, people die in
it seemingly for the simple fun of dying. At the end of the first scene in
the first act, the corpses lie around so thick on the stage that it looks like
a morgue in cholera season. One dies of the sunstroke, another of the
jim-jams, another because he can't find his mother-in-law, three are
struck in the stomach by Texas Jack, four scalped by an Irish comedian
disguised as the great Tonkay, two die of camp colic, while ten drop*

down without any provocation whatever—just because it seems kind of fashionable like to die. The red fire—peculiar, we believe, to Indian warfare—is plentifully distributed throughout the piece, and between acts, two bow-legged boys, dressed in the imposing habit of Choctaw squaws, pass among the spectators selling photographs of Texas Jack and his troop of living men.[8]

The play, titled *Texas Jack in the Black Hills*, incorporated elements of Omohundro's scouts for General Terry in Montana, as well as an exposition of the incidents McKay had been a part of during the Modoc War. Reviews were generally good, but Omohundro experienced the same problem that Buffalo Bill was experiencing on his dramatic tour at the same time. After the first show, which was inevitably well received and performed to a packed house, the parquet floors of the venues steadily decreased over the course of the show's run, though the galleries were still brimming with the voracious devourers of Texas Jack dime novels. This necessitated fewer performances per city, and more cities over the course of a month, depleting the energy of the performers. With only a single performance booked in a given theater, and fewer daytime matinee shows than had been performed with Buffalo Bill, the show was constantly on the brink of failure. If a show was poorly attended due to weather or poor advertising, the actors weren't paid. If the actors weren't paid, the board bills at their hotels went uncollected, and when the board bills went uncollected, hotel management sought recourse through the courts and the police.

Texas Jack had never been a particularly thrifty man, spending his money on jewelry, fine horses, nice clothes and showering his wife with gifts. This generosity spread to his friends and family as well. Whenever he traveled through Virginia, his brothers and their families would receive small tokens of Texas Jack's success. A treasured pocketknife for a nephew or a diamond ring for his stepmother were reminders that while he was Texas Jack to the rest of the world, he was still Johnny, the boy who had set off for Texas as a young man, to the Omohundro clan in Virginia. Several of Bill Cody's favorite guns, and a fine set of Colt revolvers that Wild Bill carried before his death, were gifts from Texas Jack.

Despite these risks, the tour continued to enjoy modest success through the summer and into the fall of 1877. The majority of the cities that the combination visited were in New York and Pennsylvania, with scattered shows in St. Louis and in other states. After performances in twenty-eight cities, a break of three months was planned to allow Jack to return to Yellowstone Park with another Bitish lord and a captain in Her Majesty's Armed Forces. When the show premiered at Chicago's Adelphi Theater, the critic for the *Daily Inter Ocean* wrote:

Texas Jack . . . there is evidently magic in the name of this Western hunter. He is a veritable specimen of the modern pioneer, and it is a singular blending of realities and unrealities to see this intrepid scout and his Indian associates making sport, like a group of blind Samsons, for the Philistines. Samson got his death by it, but Jack makes money. The Adelphi Theater was crammed last night from pit to dome, and hardly standing room, to see Texas Jack and his braves acting on the stage what none of them would ever dream of enacting in open air. The play if played by ordinary actors would be treated with ridicule, probably. Played by sun-browned veterans of the plains and the mountains, it is surprising how fresh and real the scenes appear. There was no end of enthusiasm over the valorous deeds of these heroes last night. Jack and his comrades commanded the greatest audience that has been seen within the walls of any theater in this city for many days.[9]

At the end of October, the tour returned to New York's Bowery Theatre for another run of shows. By now Jack was growing increasingly restless performing the blood-and-thunder type of border drama he had been involved with for the past five years. As she prepared for her role as Desdemona in a version of Hugo's *The Hunchback of Notre Dame*, Morlacchi mentioned to a reporter that her husband often helped her by performing in pantomime the part of Quasimodo, hunching himself over and changing his voice to affect the qualities of that titular character.

"My husband can act also very well," she enthused to the reporter in her Italian accent. "You see, he belongs to the Indian race, which pantomimes wonderfully, and also to the French, who are born actors. You will scarcely believe me when I tell you that he can act Quasimodo to perfection, although he won't play it in public. He cripples himself up to look like a hunchback, and it is a capital performance." The skeptical interviewer replied that "We can ill imagine such a superb man acting the role of a hunchback."[10]

Regardless of that man's skepticism and Omohundro's initial reluctance to forego the confines and security offered by portraying a stylized version of himself onstage, by the time he made his return visit to the Bowery footlights, J. B. Omohundro for the first time portrayed someone other than Texas Jack before an audience larger than his wife. The critic for the *New York Times* offered the following review the next day:

> *The Bowery Theatre was the scene of a remarkable dramatic event last evening: Mr. Texas Jack making his first appearance as Mohammed, in "The French Spy." The cast was a strong one, as regards the stars, being Henri St. Almé, Mlle. Morlacchi, and Mohammed, Mr. T. Jack. The play gave this eminent tragedian full scope for the play of his wonderful powers. His striking attitude, statuesque positions, graceful motions, and deep, intoned voice, combined to make the play one of surpassing interest, full of surprises from beginning to end. . . . [T]he opening scene is on the battlements of Algiers, with a wide expanse of sea in the distance; and one of the most striking points in the act is the moment when, the spy having been discovered, Mohammed, in his deep bass voice, shouts:*
> *"He's a spy, he's a spy!*
> *By heaven he shall die!"*[11]

After *The French Spy* concluded, the regular cast and Texas Jack performed their standard border drama as well, to equally favorable reviews. The *New York Times* reviewer continued:

> *It being a benefit night for Texas Jack and the fair Morlacchi, they appeared in a thrilling drama, written expressly for them, entitled* Life in the Rocky Mountains, *in which are included several such*

An advertisement for the Texas Jack Combination from appearances on September 21 and 22, 1877, at the Globe Theater in St. Louis. (BUFFALO BILL CENTER OF THE WEST, CODY, WYOMING)

lively and entertaining characters as Big Turtle, White Dog, and Lit-
tle Thunder. This play is full of dramatic incident and tragic situation,
no less than four men being victims of their own folly and weltering
in their own gore before the curtain goes down after the first act. One
of the most thrilling situations is in the second act, when, one batch of
enemy just having been slain, the party are about to start out for fresh
fields to conquer, and Texas Jack, striking an attitude, asks:
  "Now, are we all ready?"
  "We are," replies a trembling squaw.
  "Then forward! Be careful; and don't waste your ammunition!"
This scene at once brings down the house and the curtain.[12]

One aspect of the play that received much attention and positive
reviews was Jack's handling of a horse onstage. The earlier plays with
Buffalo Bill didn't include live animals, but perhaps because he had added
equestrian Maud Oswald to the stage, Texas Jack was now making his
entrance on horseback. The *New York Herald* informed readers that "the
handling of a horse upon the stage by Texas Jack is a sight worth double
the price of admission." The *New York Sun* went further, stating, "The
horse has always been a failure on stage until introduced by Texas Jack."[13]

Near the end of the dramatic touring season, Texas Jack reached
out to "The Poet Scout," Captain Jack Crawford. The former scout had
partnered with Buffalo Bill in late 1876 and early 1877 after Omohundro
and Cody had parted ways as dramatic partners. An Irish immigrant who
had come to America as a teen and then joined the Union Army before
eventually finding work as a journalist and serving as a scout in the Black
Hills, Crawford had been introduced to Texas Jack by Bill Cody during
the Black Hills campaign and had maintained correspondence ever since.
Crawford's partnership with Cody had come to an abrupt end at a performance in Virginia City, Nevada, in 1877, when Crawford accidentally
shot himself in the groin during a combat scene staged on horseback with
Cody. Crawford blamed the incident on Cody's drunkenness and sought
the sympathy of Texas Jack.

In a letter to Crawford, Jack explained that he felt for the man and
understood his frustration, but that time spent apart from his old Pard of

the Plains had not diminished his affection for Buffalo Bill Cody, who once again was intimating a retirement from the dramatic stage:

Dear Crawford,

Yours read today. Very glad to hear from you. What you say about your treatment is nothing more than I expected. I have been there myself and I have been a damn fool to lose time and reputation. So much for having a good heart and meaning honest.

I can't help but like Bill because he is honorable, and I gave my own reputation to support him, but I don't believe I would ever do it again for anyone else. Such is life. I will do anything for a man I like, and suppose you will do the same. . . .

If you have got nothing to do and there is no more Indian trouble, come and join me. I will certainly be more liberal with you than $20 per week if I make money. Bill I suppose is going to settle down in the farming or cattle business. I think he ought to do well. I hope so, but I will bet all that I have got that he don't stay out of the show business three months. . . .

Excuse me for haste, Jack, and try to run down to Chicago. Write to Bill and the Boys. Madam and Burke are well.

As ever yours,
Texas Jack[14]

Jack Crawford never joined Omohundro on stage and never forgave Buffalo Bill. At the end of the theatrical season Texas Jack prepared for another visit to Yellowstone Park with another set of aristocratic Englishmen. Dunraven's writings about the park and his cowboy guide had raised significant interest in Texas Jack's services, but neither the earl's recommendation nor the fame of his theatrical exploits could prepare Jack for his most challenging western expedition of his life.

CHAPTER TWENTY-THREE

Return to Yellowstone

BETWEEN ACTING SEASONS, JACK MAINTAINED THE LONG CONNECTION
with the Western wilderness he had grown to love as cowboy, scout,
hunter, and guide. In the 1870s there was no more sought-after guide
for parties traveling to the wild areas of Wyoming than Texas Jack Omohundro. Expeditions led by Jack generally approached Yellowstone Park
from the north. After traveling to Bozeman, Montana, by rail and pro-
visioning the party there, Jack would lead his guests south to the Bottler
Brothers' Ranch and proceed into the confines of the park, hunting for
food and sport while taking in the majestic sights unique to that part of
the country.

While spending the spring with Josephine in Lowell, Omohundro
must have concluded that the most financially viable way to spend his
summer was guiding another group of wealthy British hunters. The past
season's trip with Sir Reid had been arranged because of a mutual friendship with the Earl of Dunraven, but desperate to pay back his debts and
position himself to support a family without constant theatrical touring,
Jack ran the following advertisement both in *Field & Stream* and *The
Spirit of the Times* publications in America, and in London's *The Field*
magazine:

J. B. Omohundro
"Texas Jack"
*The services of this experienced Guide and Hunter are offered to parties
desiring to hunt in any of the wilder portions of the United States or*

Canada. He can be addressed in care of this office at any time, or until May 1, 1877 at No. 614 North Forty-fourth Street, Philadelphia, PA.[1]

By the summer of 1877, Omohundro had received responses from several wealthy English hunters, and he rode west toward Rawlins, Wyoming, to meet a pair. On the hunt with these English noblemen, Jack wrote to his friends at the *New York Herald* detailing one of their more memorable encounters:

I came near getting into a scrape with two grizzly bears the day before yesterday. One of the Englishmen (he is out with a large party) and myself saw them at a distance, and headed them off with our ponies. When we came up they were both lying asleep under the shade of a scrubby pine. The ponies were so frightened that I had to hold them while he shot. One fell dead, but the other made for us. My horse wheeled, I fired and struck him while he was coming up to my friend. The shot stopped him, but he recovered soon, and we had a lively time rushing around through the brush for a little while. He eventually hid and we lost him, but the other one's skin is lying in camp, and I don't think the Englishman will want to see any more bear very soon.[2]

In September of 1877 the Texas Jack Combination was scheduled to open its theatrical season with a weeklong run at Chicago's Adelphi Theatre. When the curtains rose on opening night, the role of Texas Jack was played by the show's manager. Omohundro showed up two days late for his own tour loaded with what a reporter for the *Chicago Tribune* called, "twenty pounds of rifle, four pounds of revolver, seventy-six and a half ounces of Bowie knife, and a perfect freight of news."[3] The news was that as his party explored the wonders of the Yellowstone in August, Nez Perce (Niimíipuu) warriors attacked two different parties in the park, capturing or killing several visitors, injuring others, and shooting a man named George Cowan in the head at point-blank range. Omohundro was leading the party of Captain C. E. Bayley—"the son of an eminent English nobleman" who "possesses no less than three million dollars in his own right"—and Lord B. Birmingham, Esquire of London.[4]

"Let us see the wildest of your blasted country!" one of the Brits had requested, and Jack obliged, leading the English lord, captain, and company for six weeks through the Wind River range in Wyoming, to Clark's Fork of the Yellowstone River, and then past Soda Butte Creek in the Lamar River Valley portion of the park.

"There," wrote Jack, "we cached our heavy baggage and struck for the Yellowstone Park. There we met the Radersburg party, eleven of them, and they were the first that told us the Nez Perce were on the war-path. The party consisted of Mr. Cowan and his wife, Frank Carpenter and his sister (a young girl of fourteen), and several folks from Centreville, Deep Creek, Montana. They were there to visit the geysers and other curiosities of the National Park."[5]

Frank Carpenter, who recorded the trip in a recollection entitled *The Wonders of Geyser Land*, described his first encounter with the scout:

A man emerges from the bushes ahead. He is a tall, powerfully built man, and as he rode carelessly along, with his long rifle crossed in front of him, he was a picture. He was dressed in a complete suit of buckskin, and wore a flaming red neckerchief, a broad sombrero, fastened up on one side with a large eagle feather, and a pair of beautifully beaded moccasins. The costume of the man, his self-confident pose, and the quick penetrating glance of his keen black eye, would give the impression that he was no ordinary mountaineer. We meet; Houston recognizes him, it is the world renowned Rocky Mountain hunter and scout, Texas Jack. While Houston was in conversation with him, our party sat silently staring at him. This is our first sight of the man, whom, above all others, we were anxious to see, and we were in a measure excusable for our seeming impertinence. He inquired for "spare grub"; we had none to give him or sell, but told him that Storey and Riche's party were but a little ways ahead of him, and he could be provided for by them. He bade us good day and pushed ahead.[6]

In August of 1877, as multiple parties of tourists headed to the Yellowstone sites that Dunraven had so vividly described during his trip just three years prior, a band of 750 Nez Perce led their horses through the park pursued by the US Army, on their trail since the Battle of Big Hole in Montana earlier that month. White visitors to the park were taken captive. "Nez Percy Joe," as Texas Jack called Chief Joseph (Hinmatóowyalahtqit), ordered that they be released unharmed, but several were left for dead, with more injured.

"I went on with my party to the geysers," Jack reported, "and there met [Nelson] Story, a wealthy Montana man, owner of the boat *Yellowstone* and 1,400 head of horses, and his party and another small party, with ours, camped right on the geyser basin. This was on the 23rd [of August]. Next day we had to hunt for swan meat, and I wanted to go back toward the Yellowstone."[7]

The next morning, Jack and his group broke camp early and again passed the Radersburg party. When they reached the foot of the mountains, they heard gunfire behind them. "The Indians had jumped the Radersburg party," Jack told a Chicago reporter. "Oldham, a miner, was the first man shot. [George] Cowan was the next—he was shot through the leg. His wife rushed to him and took his head in her lap when an Indian came up and shot him through the head. Mrs. Cowan was dragged to the Indian camp, along with Ida Carpenter and young Frank Carpenter, who was out gathering specimens. They tied him to a tree and he would have been killed but for a sign he made, by which Chief Joseph recognized him as the son of an old Indian trader. He unloosed Frank from the tree and sent him back to his sister."

Marching his own party toward safety, Jack's entourage met the Helena party, which reported that it had been jumped by the same band, with two killed and three wounded. The rest of the party had lost their stock and escaped toward McCartney's cabin at Mammoth Hot Springs. Frank Carpenter and his sisters discovered a group of soldiers and were soon reunited with Texas Jack and his British guests at the Hot Springs.

"Before daylight several of those who had escaped from the Helena party came in," Jack told a reporter, "three wounded and several worn out stragglers. We pulled out of the springs that morning with the ladies—on a wagon—and some photographers that had come along with me. Saw Indians in the rear. Tried to pass me. Sixteen shots. Broke my saddle. Overtook wagon and took the ladies to Boteler's [*sic*] ranch for safety.

There we met scouts from the Government. Jack Burnett said the Crows were coming up."

All told, Jack believed that two members of the Radersburg party and two of the Helena party were dead, with several more wounded, and he had heard reports of twenty others from separate parties captured or killed. In reality, George Cowan had survived both the initial shot to the leg that had knocked him from his horse, the subsequent bullet to the head, and a third round to his hip before crawling back to safety in the company of his dog two weeks later. By then, Omohundro and his group had affected a harrowing exit from the park, spending two days looking over their shoulders for signs of pursuing Nez Perce.

Having returned his party to the safety of Bottlers' ranch, Omohundro was anxious to depart for Chicago where his theatrical combination was scheduled to rehearse the new season's drama. Leaving the party in the capable hands of Boney Earnest and Tom Sun, Jack made his way to Bozeman, Montana, where a telegraph was awaiting him informing him that his wife was seriously ill. The worried Jack immediately set off to meet her in Chicago for rehearsals before setting off to New York for that season's debut.[8]

An article from the *Times of London* newspaper listed as simply "From a correspondent," but likely penned by Lord Birmingham, included a description of Rawlins and the Wyoming hunting area, along with an account of Texas Jack's persona:

> *Owing to its convenient situation as a starting point for sportsmen, many persons who like to hunt large game make a halt here on the way to and from the resorts of wild animals, and several guides congregate for the purpose of accompanying them. These guides are generally men of long experience who have undergone great hardships and many adventures. One of the most notable is Texas Jack, who dresses for the part in a costume copied from the Mexicans, and has the look of a hero on the stage or in a novel. He boasts of his powers and achievements with so much openness that the hearer suspects him of romancing. I found that he was not a dead-shot when he handled a rifle, and I inferred that he was not always to be trusted as a story-teller. The*

character which he bears among the citizens here is not faultless; but,
then, they regard him as a stranger and almost an interloper. It is only
recently that he has appeared here, and the conservative feeling of the
independent Western citizen leads him to look with suspicion upon a
newcomer. Certainly Texas Jack is a good story-teller, and he may be
a good guide and hunter as well as a handsome man. . . . Tom Sun, a
Canadian from Montreal, enjoys an excellent reputation as a guide
and hunter, and he is a great favorite among those persons who are
fond of sport on the plains and among the mountains. He is as reticent
and modest as Texas Jack is talkative and boastful.[9]

Texas Jack was in the middle of two weeks of full-house performances at New York's Bowery Theatre when the following article
appeared in the Sunday edition of the *New York Sun* on October 21,
1877, reprinted from the *Sioux City Journal*. The headline was "Dime
Store Jack," with the subtitle "A Stage Indian Fighter Accused of Cowardice on the Plains":

B. T. Birmingham has returned to this city from Rawlins, Wyoming,
where he has been collecting specimens to send to England. He and
Captain Bayley will be remembered as the two Englishmen who left
this city in the early summer for the great unknown country of our
Northwestern frontier, under the guidance of the notorious Texas
Jack. If they should ever go again, they would not go under the guid-
ance of Texas Jack.

When they employed him it was with the understanding that he
had been all through the Yellowstone Park and the adjacent regions,
but it was discovered that, instead of his having explored even the
Park, he had simply gone on the ordinary wagon road as far as the
Mud Volcano, and then returned the same way. He professed full
information in regard to the Geysers, but the only knowledge he
exhibited was what he had probably collected from books and maga-
zines. The result is that he was no guide whatever for the party, either
in the Park or in the surrounding country—in fact, he had them lost
for three weeks.

Jack is a fair shot when he has his gun leveled at clawless game; but when it comes to attacking anything which is able to fight, he prefers to let it alone. By some correspondences forwarded to Eastern papers he sought to make it appear that in a contest with two grizzlies he gave the Englishman a sample of what real courage is. The real circumstances were that he didn't want to stir the bears up, but Birmingham told him that it was for just such fun he had taken the trip; and so while Jack held his horse the Englishman slipped up and killed one of the animals, wounded the other, and pursued it into the sagebrush. This and other episodes knocked the stilts from under Jack's pretensions of being a hunter.

Fortunately for the party, there was not much difficulty with the Indians during the trip. When within about thirty miles of Bozeman, it was feared that there was some danger, and Jack then wanted to leave the party. He was told that right then was the time he was most needed, because every man counted when it came to such a conflict as appeared to be imminent. He replied that he could look out for himself, and the rest might do the same for themselves; and he quit the party abruptly in the very contingency for which he had been engaged as guide and guard.

From this his employers came to the conclusion that the stories about Texas Jack being such a terrific Indian fighter are rather on the dime novel order. They met two other guides, who exhibited real bravery and acquaintance with their surroundings. These were Boney Earnest and Tom Sun, both of whom make their headquarters at Fort Fred Steele. These old hunters made no boast of their prowess, but were on hand in every difficulty, while Jack's chief glories were won with his tongue. He is now in the East displaying them on the stage, where there is no chance to disprove his claims in actual service.[10]

Texas Jack was incensed. His reputation as a real hero sustained both his stage career and his summer guiding business, and articles like these threatened both his livelihood and his pride. The following day's edition of the *Sun* recounts just how upset the scout was in an article headlined "Texas Jack in War Paint":

Texas Jack had evidently seen the extract from the Sioux City Journal *in the* Sun *yesterday, for he walked into the editorial room in the
afternoon, and after slinging his broad-brimmed hat upon the table,
and tossing back his long hair, he pulled up a chair, unfolded a* Sun,
*and pointing with a much-scarred finger to the extract, said, "That's
the most outrageous lie I ever read."*

*The article was carefully reread. Its first sentence merely says:
"B. T. Birmingham has returned to this city from Rawlins, Wyoming,
where he has been collecting specimens to send to England." Further
on the reporter for the* Journal *says that Mr. Birmingham and Capt.
Bayley had intimated that they would never go out again into the
frontier under the guidance of the notorious Texas Jack, several little
episodes having knocked the stilts from under Jack's pretensions to being
a hunter. This was, no doubt, what caused Jack to put on his war paint.*

*The article had hardly been read before Jack planted his foot on
the corner of the table and exclaimed, "It's a lie from beginning to end,
and I can't see how any man could have the cheek to write it." Jack was
now deeply in earnest. His long legs were drawn back, one on each
side of the chair, and he leaned forward and shook his head until his
ringlets fell around his shirt collar, which was a stand-up.*

*It was mildly suggested that the language was rather strong,
but in following Jack's glance at the word "coward" in the article, an
excuse at once presented itself. That little word of six letters had caused
all the trouble. Jack did not sweep the room with his eagle eye, because
he has no eagle eye, and his moustache did not bustle out Frenchy,
because he has a very slim moustache. He depended on his fist, which
is large, in convincing his interviewer that he had been most outra-
geously insulted. He didn't thirst for blood, except stage blood, in New
York, but he did desire to have the truth told. He had cooled his anger
to a temperate heat, and proposed that what he had to say should be
taken down verbatim.*

*"I ain't much of a newspaper man," he said, "but I can tell a story
and you can take it down and fix it just as you want to. That's what
I say—that's a lie. I would be willing to wager a year's salary that I
know that country of which this thing speaks better than any living*

man, and yet this thing makes it out that I don't know anything at all about it.

"I'll tell you my connection with that party of Englishmen, and of that trip. I told 'em when we started that no man knew definitely the route to the Geysers; but I could and would take them safely through to the Yellowstone Park; and I did it. I can't understand how any person could get up such a tissue of barefaced lies, for all their statements I can prove to be untrue.

"In the first place—in the first place it is stated that I had never gone to the Mud Volcanoes, as a guide, through the wilderness, but simply by the ordinary wagon road. Now I can prove beyond all question that there isn't a wagon road within twenty miles of the Mud Geysers. Again, I can prove that I took the men without trouble right to the Mud Volcanoes, and then we were jumped by the Perces [sic] Indians. I took them safely out of the basin just in time, for we had barely left the region when the Cowan and Carpenter party were massacred. The very day, in fact, on which we left the basin the other party were shot down. We made a long march that day of twenty-six miles, and went into camp after I had gone out and killed a deer for our supper.

"By the way, that was the most remarkably cooked deer I ever heard of."

"Why?"

"Well, I'll tell you. Just as I shot at it, it leaped into a boiling spring, and before I got it out its hair had been completely boiled—"

"Boiled?"

"Yes, boiled off; and it was ready to be eaten. In getting it out I had all the trousers boiled off my legs, and my skin was badly blistered. I have got the remnant of the trousers now. That looks like neglecting my party, doesn't it?

"Now we'll keep to the story. The article says that I was afraid to tackle a grizzly bar [sic]. That is the biggest lie of all. I'll take my Bible oath that of all the bars killed on the trip, I killed more than half single-handed."

"How many were killed?"

"About twenty-two, and I'll bet I killed nearly twenty. Now, on the day when they said I refused to go out with Birmingham to tackle a grizzie, I was sick in camp, and I had also had a row with him in the morning on account of words he had given me. That same day I was attacked by a bar, the biggest I ever saw—must have weighed over 2,200 pounds. I wounded him, and he clawed me, and I just escaped with my life.

"About my wishing to leave the party, it is just here. On the very day when I was expected to be on a Chicago stage practicing with imitation Indians in my play, I was in the heart of the wilderness surrounded with Nez Perces. With our repeating rifles we kept them at bay from a rampart of the rocks, and I took them safely, with all my pack horses, twelve in number, out of the reach of the redskins. Every other party in the region either lost their lives or had their stock stampeded.

"And yet this article says that as an Indian fighter I am no good? I telegraphed my wife that I had escaped the massacre, as it was reported that I had been killed together with my party. I also sent word to my manager in Chicago that I would be in that city on a certain day, and then I told my party that I must go back to the settlement at once. On the strength of this, it is asserted that I wanted to desert my party."

"Where did you leave them?"

"I saw my party safe in Bozeman before I left them. On the way to that place I escorted Mrs. Cowan and Miss Ida Carpenter, who had escaped the massacre. I protected the rear, and several times we were fired on by Nez Perces Indians. I had my stirrup shot away and a ball shot through my hand."

"Where?"

"Right here, see. It isn't healed yet."[11]

Not content to set the record straight only in New York, Jack penned a letter to the editor of the *Sioux City Weekly Journal* on October 23:

Journal Editor,

Though I may not lay all actual blame to you for the publication of the cowardly and scandalous article about me which appeared in your paper some time since, I ask you to do me the justice to contradict it. If you do not see fit to do this, at least do me the justice to give me the name of your informant. I suspect that the information was given by B. T. Birmingham, whom I consider to be a renegade Englishman, and because I did not give him credit for acts of bravery that he never performed, he has taken a mean advantage of my absence, which he never would have dared to have done had I been in his neighborhood.

Birmingham wanted me to put his name in the papers some time since and I refused, but now I will oblige him, and when he sees it in the different papers throughout the United States he will regret the fact that he ever tried to injure me. Let me further add that I regard Capt. Bayley as a perfect gentleman, and I greatly wonder that he should ever have been mixed up with such a blot upon the western frontier as Birmingham.

If you will take the trouble to interview Boney Earnest and Tom Sun, they will vouch for the fact that I have always proved myself what I represented myself—a man, a gentleman, and a scout. And let me further add that I denounce all of Birmingham's statements as a tissue of lies. In regard to all Indian difficulties, I refer to Mr. Frank Carpenter and his two sisters, Mrs. Emma Cowan and Miss Ida Carpenter. If they do not say that I aided them during the Nez Perces [sic] trouble, then I am willing that I should not be considered what I now am.

Permit me to state further that my character can and will be vouched for by any of the old frontiersmen, or any of the army officers with whom I have served as guide.

My address at present is the Grand Central Theater, Philadelphia, Pa.

Respectfully,
J. B. Omohundro
TEXAS JACK[12]

To a third newspaper, Jack reported that "A sneaking coward named Birmingham wrote up a pack of lies for the *Sioux City Times* in which he accused me of cowardice before the Indians, said I was no scout, and did not know the country as I professed. Then some enemy of mine caused the same story to be published in the *New York Sun*. It was done to ruin my reputation as a guide, and to injure me before the people to the advantage of would-be rivals.... [E]very season I act as guide for parties from the old country, as they have faith in my knowledge of border life. [Birmingham] thought that if he could injure my reputation, he could palm himself off as a scout and guide and take my place at the head of these parties."[13]

For his part, Frank Carpenter, who along with his sisters Ida and Emma managed to escape from the Nez Perce after they shot Mr. Cowan in the head and left him for dead, recorded a version of the events that coincides neatly with Omohundro's own. Having narrowly escaped from the Nez Perce, Carpenter wrote that his trio

> *emerged from the canyon and, crossing the river, were soon at the springs and with friends.*
>
> *Here we found Texas Jack's party. . . . Calfe and Catlin, two photographers, came and told us that if we would wait until ten o'clock they would take us to Bozeman with their four-mule team. This was good news, as neither Emma nor Ida could walk or ride horseback.*
>
> *When we had reached the summit of the hill below the springs we saw Texas Jack looking through his spy-glass up the canyon towards Gardiner's River. Looking in the direction I saw two persons running towards us in and out of the bushes skirting the river.*
>
> *"Who is it?" I asked, "Indians or white men?"*
>
> *"I think it is two white men," he replied, "but I think there are five or six Indians following them."*
>
> *We afterwards learned that the two men were Detrich and Duncan.*
>
> *Jack, turning to us, said, "You go on and overtake our party which is not far in advance, and I'll go back and give those Indians a shot or two."*
>
> *We now started down the mountain towards the Yellowstone three miles distant. Just as we began the descent we heard firing in the rear. This frightened Emma and Ida, and they became very nervous*

Back row, left to right: Boney Earnest, Texas Jack, Captain Bailey, Mr. Birmingham. Front row, left to right: Ida Carpenter, Emma Cowan, and Frank Carpenter.
(NATIONAL ANTHROPOLOGICAL ARCHIVES, SMITHSONIAN INSTITUTION)

again. Calfe rode up behind us saying, "Drive fast, Catlin, I guess the Indians have attacked the Springs."

Down the mountains we went pell-mell, and we soon reached Henderson's Ranche [sic], eight miles from the springs. Here we were rejoined by Texas Jack, who told us that he had shot two of the Indian ponies and driven the Indians back. This news relieved our anxiety considerably and we began to breathe easier. We soon drove down into the canyon of the Yellowstone, a wild and rugged place, just suited for an ambuscade for Indians. We feared trouble here, but Texas Jack went in advance scouting for us, and about midnight we emerged on to Boteler's [sic] Ranche. The Boteler Brothers showed us every possible attention, and an old Scotch lady was very kind.

The next morning many friends from Emigrant Gulch and the surrounding country came in, and the ladies cheered up Mrs. Cowan considerably. Ida had fully recovered the use of her feet [she had injured her feet during the escape] and here Texas Jack presented her with a pair of beautiful moccasins. They were very acceptable.[14]

Omohundro's response was about more than just pride, it was about reputation. Since he had started acting in the winter of 1872, each summer season had been spent on a hunt with a wealthy European aristocrat, with the exception of 1876, when he had joined General Terry to serve as scout for the army. Though hunting wasn't quite as financially rewarding as acting, it did contribute handsomely to Omohundro's income and, unlike his current dramatic endeavors, was solely controlled by Texas Jack.

It is important to note that the vast majority of news articles were not attributed to their authors, and this allowed reporters the option of penning damning and libelous reports without fear of reprisal. It was not often that the subject of such pieces walked into the editorial room, flung his Stetson down, pounded his fist on the desk, and demanded that his version of events be given column space in order to clear his name. It seems that Texas Jack took questions of his integrity personally and saw anything that damaged his public reputation as a threat to his livelihood, both in the wilderness and on the stage.

Reunited with Josephine after Jack's Yellowstone trek, which had brought to his wife at least one news report that he had been killed by Indians, the pair set out to rehearse in Chicago before debuting their new show at New York's Bowery Theatre.

CHAPTER TWENTY-FOUR

Texas Jack's Troubles

IN MAY OF 1877, THE TEXAS JACK COMBINATION, WHICH HAD PLAYED to full houses in New York, Boston, St. Louis, and Chicago, and fifteen other cities in April and May, hit a streak of bad luck in Cincinnati. With warm weather encouraging theater patrons to remain outdoors, the week's booking at Wood's Theater in Cincinnati played to increasingly light houses. Failing to raise enough money to cover the costs of printing their advertising materials and paying their board bills, the troupe was disbanded by its manager. The *Cincinnati Daily Star* reported that the Texas Jack Combination had left the city in arrears to J. J. McGrath, proprietor of the St. James Hotel. When the combination failed to pay the board bill, McGrath refused to return three trunks that Morlacchi had asked him to keep safe while she was staying at the hotel. Josephine complained that she shouldn't be held responsible for the payment of the troupe's full bill, but offered to pay her own board. Texas Jack returned the next evening and complained to the constable about the seizure of his wife's possessions, but McGrath could not be convinced to return the trunks without full payment of the outstanding bill.

The unsettled board bill continued to haunt Jack as he gathered his combination that September for a week of shows at Chicago's Adelphi Theatre, followed by a series of shows across New York State. After months without receiving his payment for lodging the troupe in June, the angry hotel proprietor enlisted a Cincinnati law firm to recover the $103 he claimed he was owed. The firm issued an attachment for the possessions of the current iteration of the Texas Jack Combination in an effort to sell the troupe's effects to pay the delinquent board bill. The *Syracuse Sunday Morning Times* issue of October 7, 1877, carried the details:

> *It is not a common thing that a man with so extended, if not exalted, reputation as that attaching to J. B. Omohundro, alias Texas Jack, is arraigned before His Honor; so there was a good deal of interest felt when his name was called, and he responded. There is not, perhaps, in all America today another man whose profile is such a "counterfeit presentment" of that of England's great poet Shakespeare, as is that of this same Texas Jack. Note the resemblance, next time you see him— in jail.*
>
> *Jack is a Virginian by birth, and is only thirty-one years old, an intelligent fellow, with feet as small as a chinaman's, from the effect of a life spent almost entirely in the saddle. He is one of the best shots in America, is the best scout on the Western plains, not excepting Buffalo Bill, and can throw a lasso with all the accuracy of the historic South American on his nature pampas; all this when he is himself. But he don't know so much about business—show business or any other kind—as a mud turtle. With all his efforts, and all his income from other sources during Summers, he finds himself after several years experiences in blood-thirsty theatricals, without a dollar; and he has been going down hill ever since his first year on the road with Ned Buntline and Buffalo Bill, when the trio made so much money they scarcely knew what to do with it. Show business of any kind, except something strictly first-class, is not what it was then.*
>
> *Well, this continuous down hill travel has brought to Texas Jack, as one of its results, a habit of drinking to excess at times. Not only this, it has left behind him in one or two instances, unpaid hotel bills, etc. One of these, amounting to $103, is held by a man in Ohio and is in the hands of a Cincinnati firm for collection, who last week sent it on to Messrs. Beach & Brown, with instructions to attach the property of Texas Jack's present show. This trip is under management of John R. Allen, a Chicago show-managing beat, who also left a little claim of $40 in the west, and which also came in the same hands for collection.*

Attachments were issued by Beach & Brown last Saturday, and put in the hands of Constable Booth, with instructions to serve them just at the same time of the opening of the box office; but the constable was a little late, and when he reached Park Opera House, the show was in progress. The constable and an attaché *of the law office applied at the stage wicket for admission, which was at first denied; but which was finally gained by the constable's intimation that he was going on the stage if he had to break down the door. Allen was not to be found; he kept his precious head out of sight, and when poor Jack asserted that everything connected with the show belonged to him, the constable whipped out and presented the attachment against him. Jack, having previously imbibed a little spiritual inspiration, promptly snatched the legal document, tore it into fragments, and drew a loaded stage revolver and ordered Booth off the stage at its muzzle.*

Had not an actor grasped the scout and wrested from him the revolver, it is quite probable that other blood than that of the painted aborigines belonging to the company would have spattered the stage. Of course this sort of conduct towards an officer of the law isn't strictly formal, and a warrant was sworn out on Monday morning by Mr. Brown, and Texas Jack was arrested thereof in Auburn and brought back to this city. He was arraigned and pled not guilty, and was released on bail.

In his soberer moments he expressed himself as willing to do anything in his power to straighten up the matter; but he was absolutely without money. It is to be hoped that whisky and other bad habits may not get the advantage of a man who is otherwise one of nature's noblemen.[1]

Perhaps as a result of some combination of his financial and legal difficulties, his worry about his wife's health, a nagging pulmonary problem, and the pain from his many wounds received at the hands of Union soldiers, Comanche (Nʉmʉnʉʉ), Sioux (Očhéthi Šakówiŋ), and Nez Perce (Niimíipuu) foes, lassoed buffalo and angry bear, Jack was drinking far more of his favorite beverage than usual. Omohundro may have also been in the early stages of the disease that killed his mother. Consumption, as tuberculosis was known at the time, was prevalent, and sufferers often turned to the bottle for relief. Whiskey had been Jack's drink of choice since he'd set out from his father's farm for the cattle trails of Texas, and a combination of hard drink and hard living were now catching up with the old cowboy.

The tour that began in Chicago in September of 1877 continued throughout the winter, with weeklong stays in Philadelphia, Washington, DC, and Boston, and a two-week residency at New York's Bowery Theatre. Most of the supers employed as Indians since *The Scouts of the Prairie* had debuted six years earlier had been replaced by actual natives from various tribes for a show called *The Trapper's Daughter*. Unlike *Texas Jack in the Black Hills* before it, this drama was less a rehash of *The Scouts of the Prairie*.

The tour initially saw modest receipts, traveling through Massachusetts, New York, Pennsylvania, and Connecticut, and with another two-week-long residency in New York City, this time at the Olympic Theatre in late February. But by March the financial strain of playing long strings of shows separated by weeks of one-night-only appearances showed on Texas Jack and his combination. An article in the March 17, 1878, edition of the *Brooklyn Daily Eagle*, then the most read paper in America,[2] bore the headline "Trapped—'Texas Jack' and 'Arizona John' Hemmed In," and noted another unpaid board bill creating trouble for the outfit:

> *Yesterday afternoon, while Wood's Theatre, on Court street, was echoing with the howls of the Hibernian warriors who travel under the leadership of "Texas Jack," Scout and Actor, an official more implacable than the most boisterous of red men, entered the stage door . . . the official was a deputy sheriff.*
>
> *The scene which presented itself was, to use the words of the local reporter in describing a surprise party's attack on a clergyman, "full of weird and startling interest." At the foot of a ladder-like stairway stood a number of gaudily painted savages, conversing in guttural tones; now and then, the reporter, a man who has travelled in Red Hook, and is consequently, slightly familiar with the language of the natives, caught the muttered remarks:*

"Hey Patseywhoisthatsonofagun?"

"Ithinkthatroosterisfromthesheriffsoffice."

"Is Texas Jack in?" queried the Deputy Sheriff sternly, at the same time eyeing the savages cautiously.

"Youkinfollerhistrailupstairs," replied one of the warriors and then the procession moved ahead.

Texas Jack's trail led directly up the stairs, and it seemed quite fresh and unpleasantly slippery. Upstairs the trail crossed several other trails, which appeared to concentrate in the neighborhood of an immense stone cuspidor.

"What do you want, young feller?" queried a stoutly built individual, whose principal article of attire was a wig, the luxuriant locks of which were streaming over his shoulders.

"I want 'Texas Jack' and 'Arizona John,'" said the Deputy Sheriff sturdily.

"I am 'Arizona John'! What do you want of me?" said he of the hair.

"Well, sir, I have got an attachment for you and 'Texas Jack.' I want you to settle a board bill."

A shudder ran over the stalwart frame of *"Arizona John"* as he murmured, *"A—a—board bill?"*

"Yes, sir; a board bill of $100, which Mr. Pierce, of the Imperial Hotel, Washington wants to collect," answered the official.

"Arizona John" was speechless.

Just then a tall, finely built individual, attired in scout's costume, his manly face flushed with excitement, stepped forward: *"What's that you say about a board bill?"* said he.

"I want to collect Mr. Pierce's bill against you for board had in Washington. If I don't get $100 I will have to seize on the property belonging to the Texas Jack Combination," was the answer.

"I'm Texas Jack! You kin seize on all the property you find b'longin' to me. I wish you could show me whar I could find any property b'longin' t' myself."

"We haven't got a dollar's worth of property," joined in Arizona John.

"Wail, yes, we hev. I've got a $16 suit of clothes," said Texas Jack, jocularly. "Now, look yar, strawnger," he added, "Look yar. I've paid Mr. Pierce $50 on account, an' I'll pay him the rest when I get money; but you can't pay money when you hain't got it. I'll be back in a minute."

A moment after there was a rapid discharge of firearms and a series of unearthly yells. The party of three immediately turned toward the exit . . .

"That's nothin'," said Arizona John, reassuringly. "It's only Jack a pepperin' some redskins."

By this time the members of the Texas Jack Combination, through some mysterious system of telegraphy, had been made aware of the object of the official's visit.

The warriors of the party cast ominous glances at the sturdy little official, and kept up an angry muttering in their strange tongue. Said one burly savage, rendered somewhat conspicuous by the loss of a portion of his ear:

"Thesonofagunoughterbefiredout."

This drew out a chorus of

"Youkinbetheorter."

At this alarming juncture Texas Jack came back, followed by a gang of braves whom he had a moment since left weltering in their gore on the stage boards. Said he:

"Strawnger, I see ye ain't gone yet. Now I've told you God's truth, I ain't got a cent. I've been in hard luck. All the stage property belongs to Mr. Augustus Piton. It's kinder hard to push a man so."

While the Deputy Sheriff was conferring with his assistant the reporter asked:

"How do you like this business of acting, Mr. Texas Jack?"

"Don't like it at all. But I'm in it, and I can't git out. I've lost six thousand dollars hard earned money, and I've got to try and make it up somehow. I've had to sell my clothes to pay my bills, and it's kinder tough."

Texas Jack . . . is a magnificent specimen of a man physically, and his manner is that of a straightforward, honest backwoodsman. There is no swagger about that man, and his voice is singularly soft and *pleasant. He entered the dramatic field, if it can be called such, with Buffalo Bill. Shortly after his debut he fell in love with Mademoiselle Morlacchi, the premier danseuse, and married her. She travels with him now, and performs in the same company. They are said to be devotedly attached to each other.*

Arizona John's real name is John Burke. He is a stout, good natured fellow, his jolly features being somewhat marred by a broad scar caused by the slash of a bowie knife.

The Deputy Sheriff's conference was interrupted by the arrival of Mr. Augustus Piton, the manager of the Texas Jack Combination. He declared that he owned all the property of the company, including scenery, costumes and arms, and warned the sheriff against seizing any of the same. Said he:

"You can seize this property tonight, and I will replevin [sic] it and give bonds on Monday morning. Then I will sue your bondsmen for damages."

"Texas Jack" seemed very much annoyed, and in a quiet gentle-manly way protested against any seizure. His warriors, however, seemed to thirst for the gore of the pale-faces—perhaps it was for beer instead of gore—but at all events they flourished their stuffed clubs and tin tomahawks menacingly. Fortunately, a bottle of lager appear-ing on the scene diverted their attention for a few moments.

A messenger was sent to Mr. Minturn, counsel for Pierce, for instructions, and he sent back word that if the property was seized, he would give bonds to indemnify the Sheriff. Mr. Piton grew wrath-ful, whereupon there was a clattering of tomahawks and the muffled sound of stuffed clubs. Mr. Piton glared. The Deputy Sheriff glared. Patrick, clenching the half of a brick, glared, and Texas Jack smiled— over a bottle of lager.[3]

The next day a follow-up article in the same paper opined that the reason for "Texas Jack's Troubles" was that in becoming actors, he and Cody had "got into a line of business for which [they] were not qualified. . . . Success on stage is by no means an evidence of fitness for it." Even here, the author felt the need to blunt his criticism of the man, if not the actor. "The public will be inclined to sympathize with Mr. Jack," he wrote, "far less because he is a broken actor than because he is a courageous, manly fellow, who has 'done the State some service.' As heroes, such men should be confined to the plains and appear in literature only in boys' story papers."[4]

Regardless of Jack's ability as a thespian, it was clear that his financial house was far from in order. In April, Lieutenant Frederick Schwatka, who met Jack while both were serving at Fort McPherson, mentioned to the *Indiana State Sentinel* that he was preparing an expedition north at the behest of the American Geographical Society to search for traces of Rear-Admiral Sir John Franklin. Franklin's ships HMS *Erebus* and HMS *Terror* had disappeared on an Arctic expedition meant to finalize exploration of the Northwest Passage. According to Schwatka, there was room on the ship *Eothan* for perhaps six men, one of whom would be Texas Jack. Jack was to serve primarily as the group's hunter, ensuring that the men were provided with fresh meat and protected from predators like the grizzly bear that roamed the Canadian Arctic. Jack, increasingly unhappy with his management, his financial situation, and his success as an actor, may have intimated to Schwatka that he was ready to head out into the wilderness again.

It is interesting to note that had Omohundro been a part of this expedition as planned, he would have been returning from the Canadian Arctic in early 1880 and not in Leadville, Colorado, where he and his wife would occupy two of the city's theaters with their performances. Perhaps the length of time this journey would have taken him away from his wife discouraged Jack from making the trek. Though they failed to find the main party of Sir Franklin, Schwatka's expedition did make the longest sledge journey recorded up to that point, traveling 2,709 miles in just over eleven months.

Whether he spoke about it or not, it was obvious to others that the stress of losing not just his own but also his wife's money in his failed Centennial venture troubled Omohundro greatly. A newspaper reporter from Oswego, New York, wrote a brief article about Jack's arrival in town:

Texas Jack in 1878, on a stop in Gettysburg, Pennsylvania. (BUFFALO BILL CENTER OF THE WEST, CODY, WYOMING)

Yesterday afternoon, the quite famous "Texas Jack," J. B. Omohundro, who married Morlacchi, the danseuse, arrived in town wearing a white sombrero and a black velveteen suit with brass buttons. On the legs of the wide trousers near the bottom in the outside seam, were striped of a color very fashionable in Mexico, but quite out of character in portions of Ireland and Canada. . . . His long unkempt hair lacks the raven luster that it had when he appeared before our citizens as one of the "Scouts of the Plains" and killed two or three hundred thousand Indians and ruffianly "pale faces" in the Academy of Music.

"Jack" says that he is fresh from the plains and from the hills beyond. He says that he was taken with chills after striking the low malarial land, and is still suffering from a complaint that is hard to shake, although nearly all the victims shake easily. He is working his way, by easy stages, to his home in Massachusetts. He reports sport, "Indian hair lifting," as rather tame in the "Rocky" this season, as the red devils are too quiet for scouts.

After scanning "Jack's" story we are inclined to discredit it. . . . He does not look like the "Texas Jack" who was here two or three times with "Buffalo Bill." Instead of having the bearing of a "scout of the plains" he looks like a plain scout, who, for a long time had been on the scent of "spiritual" game of a fluid nature, or had served as "a sad example" for an itinerant intemperate temperance advocate to show to rural gatherings.[5]

It was clear to both Jack and his wife that a break was needed from the constant stress of relentless touring. Their current tour had stretched over ten months and at least 200 shows. The couple was engaged for weeklong stays in Toronto, Montreal, Cincinnati, and then Boston from May until June of 1878. It was in Boston, during his weeklong residency performing *The Trapper's Daughter* at the Howard Athenaeum, that Omohundro was offered the chance to escape the stage for a brief time by a chance encounter with a familiar, if unexpected, face from his past.

CHAPTER TWENTY-FIVE

Dr. Carver

TRAPSHOOTING HAD BEEN GROWING AS A SPORT SINCE IT WAS INTRO-
duced in the early 1830s at the Sportsmen's Club in Cincinnati, Ohio.
There, men would shoot at passenger pigeons or sparrows, seeking to
demonstrate their skill and proficiency with various firearms. By the end
of the decade, the New York Sportsman's Club held its first trapshooting competition. The 1860s marked two huge advances in trapshooting
circles. The first was the introduction of the glass target ball, brought to
America from England. Glass balls were filled with feathers, but initially
were viewed as inferior to live animals by shooters who complained that
the balls did not provide an adequate challenge, as they were far more
predictable than pigeons. In 1868, Fred Kimble invented the choke-bore
shotgun that could take down a duck at eighty yards, and this became the
preferred weapon for competitive shooters like Captain Adam Bogardus.

Bogardus was already a prolific shooter when he invented the first
glass ball trap that would fling the balls into the air in a long arc, mimick-
ing the flight paths of real birds while maintaining a uniform weight and
size that ensured every shooter was given an equal challenge at shooting
the targets. Bogardus modified the glass balls to add ridges, ensuring that
a bullet would shatter the globe rather than glancing off it. Not merely
an inventor, Bogardus was also a showman and competed in challenges,
killing 500 pigeons in under 645 minutes or downing 500 clays in under
45. Endurance challenges were a part of the captain's exhibitions, and
at one performance at Madison Square Garden in New York, he broke
4,844 of 5,000 glass balls in eight hours and twenty minutes without

cleaning the barrel of his gun. Bogardus offered to accept all challengers at the Philadelphia Centennial, and Texas Jack had planned to accept the challenge until he was called to Montana to scout for General Terry.

While Bogardus was the master of the shotgun, the champion pistol shot was Ira Paine, who joined the Texas Jack Combination for shows in 1877 and 1878. Paine was a Massachusetts native who initially worked as a plumber and pipe fitter (his obituary went so far as to call him "one of the finest in the state") before becoming a professional singer with a traveling vocal quartet. He joined his local yacht club's pigeon-shooting group, quickly becoming known as the finest shot in the club. Paine was proficient with the shotgun, rifle, and pistol and mastered shooting with both his left and right hands, allowing him to make shots that many witnesses had previously assumed were simply impossible. Some of his more-popular stage feats involved shooting a small glass ball from the top of his wife's head while she walked across the stage, shooting the numbers from playing cards she held in the air, and splitting a card in half when it was held with the edge facing him.

Doc Carver began shooting competitively in California in 1877 and quickly established himself as a crack rifle shot. By all accounts, Carver was one of the undisputed masters of target shooting at the time, but acknowledgment of his skill never seems to have satisfied Carver, who had witnessed the frontier celebrity of men like Texas Jack, Buffalo Bill, and Wild Bill from his dentist office in Nebraska. As Carver made a name for himself with his feats of marksmanship, he also began to invent a backstory that would render him every bit the real-life hero of those men he had so envied while pulling teeth.

Born William Frank Carver in Winslow, Illinois, in 1851, Carver added a decade to his life when talking to reporters, and alternately claimed that Doc was either his birth name or that he had been nicknamed "Doc" by Sioux Indians (Očhéthi Šakówiŋ) who had deemed him "bad medicine." Raymond Thorp, Carver's biographer, echoed Carver's claims that he had left home as a young man to travel to Minnesota on a quest to take back a piece of land that he claimed the Sioux once granted his grandfather. According to these claims, the Sioux came to recognize Carver as the greatest shooter that had ever lived, with Spotted Tail bestowing upon the erstwhile dentist the nickname "The Evil Spirit of the Plains" in recognition of his deadly rifle skills after witnessing Carver fell a white buffalo.

Carver's opinion of himself is obvious from the first page of his own autobiography, which bears this preface:

> *With the universal interest that the unparalleled marksmanship of Dr. Carver has suddenly awakened, naturally comes the question, "Who is this wonderful man, who rides like a Centaur, shoots as unerringly as Death, and combines the modest courtesy of a true gentleman with a more than savage genius for the chase, and cool, courageous skill in the use of its weapons of destruction?"[1]*

When storytelling wasn't enough to inflate the legend of the Evil Spirit, Carver simply took the real-life exploits of Texas Jack or Buffalo Bill and added himself, ever present and positioned to surpass the feats of the legendary cowboy and the famous scout. Carver's autobiography claims that, "In buffalo-killing, Dr. Carver eclipsed the famous Buffalo Bill, who good-naturedly acknowledged him as a superior shot." The truth was that Cody, supremely confident in his own abilities as a hunter and with the hard-won sobriquet to back up his claims, would never have readily accepted Carver or any other man as the superior hunter, even if at the time Carver had been buffalo hunting on the frontier and not inspecting cavities in North Platte.

Carver's self-promotion meant that not only did he need to position himself as the better rifle shot than his heroes, which he was, but that he had to best them in their areas of expertise. Just as he claimed that Cody had acknowledged him as the superior buffalo hunter, he wrote that when he and a partner were hunting elk, they came across traces of Indians. As the pair examined the signs, Carver wrote:

> *A horseman suddenly came in sight on the hill above, looked down at them for a moment, and then came on at full speed. As he drew near, they were delighted to recognize, in the dashing horseman, the fine proportions and handsome face of Texas Jack.*

He was in a great hurry, having come for the Doctor to help him in following the trail of a band of Indians who had stolen some horses at the fort.

"I went after them," said Jack, "and followed the trail easily enough for a ways, but then they separated, and I got confused, and I'm blest if I can see any trace of them."

"Come back to camp, Jack, and I'll soon be ready," said the Doctor, promptly.[2]

Similarly, Carver would later claim to have been in Deadwood with Wild Bill Hickok before his death, but to have departed after beating the old lawman at cards and just before he was assassinated, lamenting that he could have prevented his friend's death if he had been there. Most of Carver's self-created legend was published after Omohundro's death, and when Carver and Omohundro met in Boston, it was as former citizens of frontier Nebraska.

The cowboy was happy to see a familiar face from the plains when Carver traveled to Boston's Beacon Park for a shooting exhibition in early July of 1878. Ira Paine, who had traveled with the Texas Jack Combination for the past season, was engaged as Carver's shooting coach, and when he invited Jack to join the pair for a round of target shooting, Omohundro jumped at the chance. With the dramatic season done for the summer and no hunting out West scheduled until later in the fall, Texas Jack had grown restless while spending the second half of June at the Billerica farm.

Carver was immediately impressed with Jack's ability with a pistol and rifle and quickly realized that having the veteran scout in his party drew larger crowds, ensured more newspaper coverage, and lent him the authenticity he so badly desired. Standing next to Texas Jack served to make the visitors to his shooting exhibitions and reporters alike believe that Doc Carver was every bit the Western hero he purported himself to be, and as Omohundro and his old pard Bill Cody were.

Doc Carver was initially described by reporters as "seemingly a refinement of the 'Buffalo Bill' and 'Texas Jack' type of accidental manhood; not so theatrical as those professionally ferocious worthies, but obviously of their fraternity."[3] One newspaper went so far as to say that "his makeup is so much like that of Texas Jack that we can almost imagine him sending a postal card to that gentleman from the west asking, 'How's things in New York?' and Jack replying, 'Good, but you must wear a broad brim, and put it on thick.' The long hunting hair, the velvet shirt, and the wild expression, as of a man constantly battling with wild beasts, are all there."[4]

Carver's version of his invitation for Texas Jack to join him at his forthcoming shooting exhibitions is characteristically inaccurate, but offers additional evidence of Omohundro's worsening alcoholism. In recounting the moment to his biographer, Raymond Thorp, Carver, who seems to have been the rare individual not completely taken by Giuseppina Morlacchi, reported that:

> *Doc . . . travelled to Boston. Here, in the city of beans and culture, the "Evil Spirit" received the shock of his life. He was visited by his old partner, Texas Jack. The famous plainsman and hunter, who should never have left the land of the bison for the glittering tinsel of cheap Eastern shows, was penniless, broke and down and out. As Doc had predicted, his marriage with Mademoiselle Morlacchi had "gone on the rocks." Doc added Jack to his roster of helpers.*[5]

Regardless of the circumstances of the meeting, Carver immediately invited Omohundro to join him for his next exhibition in New York. The exhibition at Brooklyn's Deerfoot Park took place on Saturday, the Fourth of July, with Carver demonstrating his remarkable accuracy against glass ball targets while Texas Jack reloaded rifles and entertained the crowds. The *New York Sun* featured a lengthy article on the showing exhibition under the headline "The Magical Marksman," and in the reporter's conclusion he noted that:

> *When the writer left Deerfoot Park, twilight was approaching; but the fever was still on the Doctor. Texas Jack and he were shooting at silver quarters with a revolver that looked as though it might be owned by a German shoemaker. In this match Texas Jack was holding*

his own. Quarters were struck every minute, and sent bounding into
the air, to the delight of a dozen little urchins who were hopeful of
picking up the stray ones.[6]

The *New York Herald*'s version of the following day's exhibition was much the same, though they noted that Doc Carver's "expressions while shooting were at times comical. He would call for Texas Jack in true Indian style, and frequently make remarks in the true broken Indian phrase, such as 'Heap good Sioux,' and 'Bad Injun.'"[7] Carver's use of these clichés reveals the fact that his own experience with Indians was largely limited to what he read in dime novels.

When a reporter appeared at the hotel near the Brooklyn Driving Park where Jack and Doc Carver were staying, he found that they had left to visit Coney Island. The hotel's proprietor Hiram Howe told the reporter how wonderful he thought the pair were. According to Howe, after their exhibition was over, the two would return for supper and then go right back to the park with their rifles and revolvers, offering to shoot anything the kids threw into the air. Howe said that "it appeared to him that they could not remain quiet except for a bath or a good square meal, and when in their rooms they would fire rifles out of the windows at minute objects." As proof, Hiram walked the reporter to the street, demanding that he look at his hotel sign. As they approached the sign, the reporter told the hotel proprietor that he didn't see anything amiss, but stopped as they got closer, noting that the dot of the letter "i" in Hiram Howe's name on the sign had been shot through multiple times.[8]

Though Doc Carver was the star of the show, and an imposing man at six-foot-four—a *New York Times* reporter noted that Carver was "taller and more powerful than Texas Jack . . . rigged out in an immense sombrero, much larger than Texas Jack's"—the people who came out to watch could not help flocking to the famous cowboy turned scout who, the *Times* reporter noted, "was on the grounds, and with his flowing ringlets, keen brown eyes, and face blackened by exposure to the prairie sun, attracted much attention."[9] The *New York Sun* noted that "Texas Jack rejoiced in black trousers, a white shirt, open down the back, that caught the breeze delightfully, and black slouch hat that shaded his flashing eyes and bronzed cheeks."[10] The next day, Jack was described by the *Brooklyn Daily Eagle* as

> *costumed in a pair of dark woolen pegtop trousers, a dark blue flannel shirt, thrown open at the throat to catch the breeze, and a broad brimmed light felt hat that looked as though it had seen its best days. A silk bandana encircled his sun browned throat in lazy folds, and one of the same material peeped forth from a hip pocket. Jack seemed to draw immense satisfaction from a short dudeen [a short-stemmed Irish clay pipe] that he whiffed with evident gusto.*[11]

It wasn't just his looks that caught the attention of visitors and reporters. Omohundro's easy manner when talking to people, especially children, along with his unassuming Southern charm were on display as well. When the reporter for the *Daily Eagle* arrived to witness the last day of shooting, he noted that

> *the Doctor was not visible. He kept his room in the hotel until the last moment, preferring to remain quiet and composed until the time for action had arrived. Texas Jack, however . . . mingled with the company as soon as they began to arrive . . . Jack spinning frontier yarns to the eager crowd as they gathered about him to listen. He recounted several hair breadth escapes from the "reds" and other wild "varmints" during his career as a scout, and told everything with a modest assurance that carried conviction with it.*[12]

Though he was likely concerned with the level of attention Texas Jack was drawing at what were being advertised as Doc Carver shooting exhibitions, Carver couldn't deny that the draw of the well-known scout was adding to his own coffers.

An offer was extended for Omohundro to join Doc at a series of shows in the Deep South. Anxious to earn some money to offset his debts, Omohundro told Carver that he would be glad to join him after he returned from a previously scheduled trek to Wyoming with another European aristocrat, this one a German-born businessman who would play his own part in America's cowboy legend.

Chapter Twenty-Six

The Cowboy, the Count,
the Wizard, and the Doctor

In late July 1878, the scientific world converged on Rawlins, Wyoming, to view a total solar eclipse. Traveling on a special Pullman car reserved for the astronomers was the young inventor Thomas Alva Edison, a year removed from his invention of the phonograph. Newspaper coverage had ensured that Edison was well-known throughout the country after he had turned selling his "quadruplex telegraph" to Western Union for $10,000 in 1874 into the world's first industrial research lab at Menlo Park, New Jersey. Edison had been invited to Wyoming by astronomer Henry Draper to test a new invention, a device Edison called a "tasimeter," designed to measure small changes in solar temperature. Edison hoped to use the device to detect minute changes in temperature associated with the sun's corona during the eclipse.

Edison later recorded his first night in Wyoming:

There were astronomers from nearly every nation. We had a special car. The country at that time was rather new; game was in great abundance, and could be seen all day long from the car window, especially antelope. We arrived at Rawlins about 4 p.m. It had a small machine shop, and was the point where locomotives were changed for the next section.

The hotel was a very small one, and by doubling up we were barely accommodated. My room-mate was Fox, the correspondent of the New York Herald. *After we retired and were asleep a thunder-ing knock on the door awakened us. Upon opening the door a tall, handsome man with flowing hair dressed in western style entered the room. His eyes were bloodshot, and he was somewhat inebriated. He introduced himself as "Texas Jack"—Joe Chromondo [sic]—and said he wanted to see Edison, as he had read about me in the newspapers.*

Both Fox and I were rather scared, and didn't know what was to be the result of the interview. The landlord requested him not to make so much noise, and was thrown out into the hall. Jack explained that he had just come in with a party which had been hunting, and that he felt fine. He explained, also, that he was the boss pistol-shot of the West; that it was he who taught the celebrated Doctor Carver how to shoot. Then suddenly pointing to a weather-vane on the freight depot, he pulled out a Colt revolver and fired through the window, hitting the vane.

The shot awakened all the people, and they rushed in to see who was killed. It was only after I told him I was tired and would see him in the morning that he left. Both Fox and I were so nervous we didn't sleep any that night. We were told in the morning that Jack was a pretty good fellow, and was not one of the "bad men," of whom they had a good supply.[1]

Seeking out Omohundro at the Railroad Hotel the following morn-ing, the pair were disappointed to find that the famous cowboy had already left town early that morning on his hunt with the German count who had hired his services as a guide for the summer.

Despite weeks of careful preparation, Edison's tasimeter immediately failed, variations in coronal temperature being much higher than he had accounted for in his design. Locals in Rawlins, Wyoming, as well as a memorial plaque along the highway there, hold that when the tasimeter failed, Edison decided instead to go fishing, and that it was in casting the line from his bamboo fishing pole that he first had the idea to use bamboo filament to incandesce in his electric lightbulb.

As Omohundro headed west, he laid the groundwork for his forth-coming exhibitions with Doc Carver. He wrote letters to some of his contacts, men involved in shooting clubs that Jack and Bill Cody had met and shot with as their dramatic tours of the past six years had traveled throughout the country. A letter that Jack penned to the president of the New Orleans Gun Club is an example of his promotional work:

Dear Sir,

As many days [have] passed since I heard from you or any of the club only through the press, I write this to say that I am still in the land of the living, and would be pleased to hear from you once more.

At present, I am with Dr. Carver, the champion rifle shot from California. I suppose you have seen full accounts of his marvelous shooting. I was with him July 4 when he broke ninety-nine glass balls out of 100 with a Winchester rifle, balls thrown in the air, rifle loaded with regulation cartridge, powder, and ball.

He is certainly a wonder of the world, and I would ask if you will be so kind as to let me know what kind of a crowd you think he would draw in your city, to give an exhibition of his fine and fancy shooting; also what ground he could secure to shoot in.

I shall not be on the stage for some time, but hope to get around before a great while to see you all, and that I may find you in the same health and spirits as when we parted.

Remaining as ever, yours truly,

J. B. Omohundro

Texas Jack

P.S.—Dr. Carver is an old friend of mine from the plains.[2]

That Omohundro felt the need to add the postscript is telling. The fact was that likely Jack did not know Carver exceptionally well from his days on the Nebraska plains, other than as a rival suitor for the affections of Ena Palmer. Carver had been present on at least one occasion when Omohundro taught Miss Palmer to shoot. In her diary, Ena recalled one tense moment when Omohundro was walking through Cottonwood Springs with Annie Snell and noticed Ena and Carver together. Ena wrote that she was embarrassed that the sight of Omohundro had so distracted her from the attentions of Mr. Carver. Carver seems to have joined one of Buffalo Bill's hunts between Cody's theatrical tours in 1877 and most likely met Omohundro again when Cody visited Texas Jack's camp at the conclusion of his hunt.

Shooting with Dr. Carver would have to wait until after Jack's Wyoming trek with Count Otto Franc von Lichtenstein, a German-born aristocrat who emigrated to the United States just after the Civil War, and Dr. Amandus Ferber of New York. The pair had been introduced to Jack by George Bird Grinnell and the editors of *Forest & Stream* magazine, and Ferber documented the trip in letters published throughout August and September. The count engaged Omohundro on this visit to Wyoming not only to hunt and explore, but also to ask the cowboy's expert opinion on the possibility of raising cattle in the Bighorn Basin. The first of the group's two treks through Wyoming led south toward the Colorado border and into present-day Medicine Bow National Forest, where they hunted and fished along Battle Creek, making their way to Battle Lake on the western side of the Continental Divide. While Jack's recent acquaintance Thomas Edison pointed his tasimeter at the sun's corona during the eclipse, the count recorded in his diary that "we caught some trout and went back to camp; while cooking the fish the Eclipse sets in and we have a very good view of it, Jack calls it a damned humbug and put up job, because our tent and blankets caught fire while we were looking at the sun, we lost a blanket, burned holes in the tent and some blankets and besides burned our hands in trying to extinguish it."[3]

For this first leg of their trek, Texas Jack hired a local guide named Henry H. "Tip" Vinson. Franc's diaries and Ferber's published letters show that Vinson was an asset to the hunt, scouting for game and camping sites with Jack and hunting and fishing with him to keep the group well fed. When Jack led the men back to Rawlins after three weeks, he asked Tip to join them for the northern portion of the expedition. Tip agreed, but was delayed by officials from the Union Pacific Railroad, who asked him to assist them in seeking out a band of ruffians that had attempted to derail a train. Tip, acting as special railroad detective, and Deputy Sheriff Robert Widdowfield trailed the men into Rattlesnake Canyon near Elk Mountain, where the fugitive gang of "Big Nose" George Parrott opened fire, killing both men, the first lawmen to be killed in the line of duty in the state of Wyoming. Parrott and his associate "Dutch Charlie" Burris were both lynched by Wyoming mobs for the murders.

After returning to restock their provisions in Rawlins, the group's path wound north through the Wind River Canyon toward the Bighorn Basin, traveling toward the hot springs region of present-day Thermopolis. Just four days out from Rawlins, Franc set off alone to hunt bighorn sheep when he ran into trouble, fearing that he might not make it home until Texas Jack rode to his rescue. According to Franc's journal entry:

I had just drank the last of my whiskey & water & intended to go 100 yards farther & then to discharge my rifle when I heard the faint report of a gun in the direction of the ranch; this aroused me as I knew it was a signal for me, I answered it with 3 shots in quick succession which is the usual distress signal & then laid full length on the ground feeling confident that help would soon come.

I fired again at intervals in order to give them the precise spot where I laid & after 15–20 minutes of anxious listening & waiting I heard the clatter of horses hoofs & looming up through the darkness came a man on horseback with another saddle horse beside on a dead run towards me in a moment he was beside me this gave me new life & I forgetting that I was half dead I jumped in the saddle & keeping in advance of the other man I made a bee line for the ranch as fast as my lively pony could run, on coming in to the ranch I was welcomed with cheers which I gaily responded to, jumped out of the saddle and fell headlong to the ground.

A vigorous rubbing of the temples with whiskey brought me to in a few moments & an administration of some milk punch in very small doses soon strengthened & unloosened my tongue so that I was able to give an account of my adventures.

They had begun to feel concerned about me when I had not made my appearance at dinner time as they knew I had not been well & as it is very easy to get lost in the labyrinth of valley & narrow gulches which I traversed, they ascended a hill close by & kept firing guns at intervals all afternoon and evening but I was too far away to hear

*them; they were glad as myself to see me reach home safely & said I
had looked like a ghost.*[4]

After resting a few days, the group pressed north, eventually reaching
present-day Thermopolis, Wyoming:

*We descend into the basin & camp at the Bighorn River, from the
entrance of Wind River into the canyon it is called Bighorn River,
the canyon is 18 miles long . . . in the distance we see what we suppose
to be the smoke of a camp fire, we conclude to reconnoiter & find out
what it is whether the camp of Indians or white men.*

*We approach carefully taking good care not to be seen by those in
the supposed & get within a 1/2 mile from it when the wind brings
us a strong smell of sulphur & the smoke turns out to be steam. On
arriving at the place we find it to be a mammoth hot sulphur spring.
It comes out at the foot of a hill where it forms a basin 25 feet wide
& of great depth; the water is darkened & very clear, the outlet is a
swift running stream 6 feet wide & 2 feet deep it runs 250 yards &
falls over a bank 75 feet high into the Wind River. In falling it forms
several sulphur pillars of fantastic design, for a great distance around
the ground is formed of sulphur sediments showing that the outflow
changes its course very often.*

*The water is very hot, so that we could not hold our hands in it,
the spring throws out a thousand or more gallons in a minute. On the
opposite of the river are the remains of another now extinct mineral
spring it is in the shape of a dome of transparent matter & of yellow
& crystal clear icicles. . . . [W]e saw several recently deserted Indian
camps with arrangements for drying meat & the Bannock Indians
have been in here shortly before us securing enough meat to enable
them to go on the war path, that accounts for the remarkable absence
of game.*[5]

Franc and his brothers had been involved in a profitable fruit-
importing business in New York, but during a trip to see to business
interests in South America, the count had been stricken with malaria,

inevitably leading to a decline in his health. Franc believed a trip to the more-arid American West would improve his spirits and health alike. As they viewed elk and buffalo grazing on the tall grass of the region, Franc asked Omohundro if he thought cattle would thrive here as they did in Texas. The old cowboy replied that he believed a man could make a fortune raising cattle in the Bighorn Basin.[6]

Franc returned home to New York, where he eventually convinced his brothers to invest in a cattle operation in Wyoming. Purchasing stock in Montana, Franc drove his animals south and established a ranch near present-day Meeteetse, Wyoming. His cattle operation grew to several thousand head, and he soon bought out his brothers' interest in the operation. In 1893, Otto hired two ranch hands named Butch Cassidy and Al Hainer, afterwards accusing them of stealing three of his horses. Though the men protested their innocence, Cassidy was convicted and spent time in prison before he was pardoned by Governor William Richards. During his eighteen-month internment at the Wyoming State Penitentiary, Cassidy's interactions with fellow inmates persuaded him to become a full-time outlaw after his release, and before the year was out he had recruited Harry "Sundance Kid" Longabaugh, and together they commenced the longest string of successful train and bank robberies in American history with their "Wild Bunch." Franc's Pitchfork Ranch holdings eventually ballooned to over 300,000 acres, and in the 1950s the Meeteetse ranch was selected by the Leo Burnett advertising company as the perfect site to film a new advertising campaign for a cigarette company, welcoming smokers to "Marlboro Country."

In early October, with Jack's long expedition with Franc and Ferber complete, the *Chicago Tribune* reported that "Mr. John B. Omohundro, who is familiarly known to the juvenile part of the population as 'Texas Jack,' the border scout, unerring marksman, scalp-lifter, etc., hove to at the Sherman House yesterday afternoon, laid his rifle across the counter, pushed back his copious hair, and put himself on record. He is on his way East."[7]

After traveling to the Billerica farm to see his wife, Jack quickly set off to Pittsburgh to join Doc Carver for a series of shooting exhibitions. Though Carver and his later biographer Raymond Thorp would cast

Texas Jack as the sidekick and "second fiddle" to Doc, the fact that newspaper advertisements gave the men equal billing speaks to the reality of the arrangement. After shooting in Pittsburgh and other cities in Pennsylvania, the pair traveled south to Wilmington, North Carolina. Carver had married Josephine Dailey in August, as Omohundro trekked across the Bighorn Mountains of Wyoming with the count, and now the new Mrs. Carver joined her husband and Texas Jack for the Southern portion of their tour, bringing with her a herd of elk that her husband purchased from the West to show Southern spectators.

Arriving in Wilmington, North Carolina, the local *Daily Reviewer* newspaper reported that "Dr. Carver and Texas Jack were the centre of attraction to the boys this morning until the elks appeared on the streets. . . . [A] little fellow thought Texas Jack was Santa Claus with his reindeers and ran home to announce the arrival of the mythical potentate to his little sister."[8] The next day, while Carver and his wife set off on a visit to Macon, Georgia, Omohundro remained in Wilmington, and the local *Wilmington Sun* dryly noted that "The warm weather, Texas Jack, and the Lumberton breeze were the principal topics of discussion yesterday."[9]

For the better part of the next two weeks, Omohundro remained in Wilmington, entertaining children, hunting with locals, and preparing for the shooting exhibition Carver had told the local papers he intended to put on when he came back from Georgia. When Omohundro received word from Carver that he had decided not to shoot in Wilmington and urging Jack to join him in Atlanta, Omohundro expressed his frustration at having disappointed the locals who were looking forward to the show. The local paper noted, "Texas Jack intends to leave the city tomorrow, as his pard, Dr. Carver, has decided not to give an exhibition of his shooting in this city. 'Texas' is a good, warm hearted fellow and has made many friends in the city."[10]

Shooting exhibitions in Atlanta and Macon, Georgia, along with at least a dozen more stops across the south, were much like those in New York, with Carver raking in accolades for his marksmanship while Texas Jack continued to receive the attention of reporters, spectators, and—to the increased frustration of Doc Carver, who had played the role of stilted lover when Ena Palmer's attentions had belonged to Omohundro—Doc's wife, Josephine. Carver told his biographer that in Atlanta, Mrs. Carver "mothered" Texas Jack. Jack's skill with Carver's elk also bothered him, as did reports of "Texas Jack's elks" appearing in newspapers along their exhibition route. When Carver decided to take his shooting skills to Europe for a series of exhibitions, Omohundro was not invited.

Carver biographer Raymond Thorp, pulling from interviews with Doc as well as Carver's notes and personal recollections, wrote that Omohundro, perhaps the greatest of the frontier scouts, had turned his back on his true calling when he headed east with Buffalo Bill:

> *Texas Jack Omohundro put his worst foot out (as later events proved) and became a benedict. Mme. Morlacchi, who had been imported from Europe by the infamous Jim Fiske, caught Jack's eye as she danced on Eastern stages, and from that time on the erstwhile plainsman was no good either for Cody's enterprises or buffalo hunting. After the marriage, which Doc unsuccessfully tried to prevent, Jack, who had sundered his prairie ties, was equally unsuccessful in obtaining show employment. Many years later Doc salvaged what was left of his old friend.*[11]

Thorp further claims that Doc Carver insisted on Omohundro's sobriety while they toured together and notes that by the time the pair appeared on October 29, 1878, at the Georgia State Fair in Macon, "Texas Jack [was] now completely rehabilitated and his old self again." Carver's sobriety, much like Ned Buntline's, seems to be a creation of self-promotion more than a deeply held and personally adhered-to belief. It is unlikely that either man swore off the bottle for any duration during their time together.

William Carver went on to greater fame in the years after his tour with Texas Jack, having challenged and defeated his main rival Adam Bogardus in nineteen out of twenty-five contests in a highly publicized series of shooting matches. Buffalo Bill Cody and Doc Carver would eventually join forces for a brief and highly contentious show entitled *The Wild West: Buffalo Bill and Dr. Carver's Rocky Mountain and Prairie Exhibition*, the failure of which spawned Cody's enduring partnership with promoter Nate Salsbury in a venture destined to shape America's perception of the frontier West forever, *Buffalo Bill's Wild West*.

Carver's competing show, *Wild America*, toured the United States as well as Europe and Australia before disbanding in 1893. Carver continued to give shooting exhibitions until 1896, when he gave a final performance in Lincoln, Nebraska. A local paper reporting on the event noted that Doc, who had for so long lied about his age to lend credence to his frontier claims, looked fifteen years younger than the age printed in his exhibition materials.

Carver went on to tour with a smaller show, having added to the horseback-riding and shooting performances the unique act of diving horses. Eventually the diving-horse performance became Carver's sole endeavor, and he toured with the animals and his daughter, son, and daughter-in-law across America. In June of 1927 one of Carver's favorite horses drowned following a dive into the Pacific Ocean, and Carver's health went into a quick decline. He died that August.

Carver's daughter-in-law Sonora was involved in an accident while diving in 1931 when her horse "Red Lips" was off balance when hitting the water tank they used in the act, causing Sonora to hit the water face-first. The impact caused retinal detachment in both of her eyes, but she continued to perform with the act for the next eleven years, even though she was now blind. The Walt Disney movie *Wild Hearts Can't Be Broken* is based on her life.

CHAPTER TWENTY-SEVEN

The Final Tour

THE TEXAS JACK COMBINATION OPENED ITS 1879 SEASON JUST BEFORE New Year's at Troy, New York, before settling in for a week at the Olympic Theatre in New York City with *The Trapper's Daughter*, once again well received by New York audiences. According to the *Evening Telegram*, the show

> *drew a very large and enthusiastic audience. The gallery was crowded with the rising generation, who always believe that one scout can kill ten Indians and are not satisfied unless a certain number of aborigines are duly killed off before the fall of the curtain. The business was remarkably good and the acting considerably above the average of these dramas. Mr. Donald McKay as Old Stoat was capital, and conducted very largely to the success of the play. Mr. Irving as the Quaker played a low comedy part in a most praiseworthy manner. Miss Mayer acted the part of Betty Modaney in a forcible manner and received frequent applause. The red fire, the raging Indians, the frequent bear and the stock villain, all came in for commendation, and when the crowded house dissolved itself like a sudden thaw, and perambulated Broadway, every tall, truculent looking man was pointed out by delighted youngsters as Texas Jack, who was evidently the "hero of the enemy" to those who had chosen the Olympic as their place of amusement.*[1]

Notable here is that for the first time since 1873, Giuseppina Morlacchi did not appear alongside her husband in his combination. While

Jack was demonstrating his skill with pistol, bow and arrow, and lasso to audiences with Doc Carver, Morlacchi had planned a tour of her own, once again performing in *The French Spy* for audiences across the country and once again receiving acclaim everywhere she went. When she performed in Fort Wayne, Indiana, a glowing review noted that "Mlle. Morlacchi has now established herself in the hearts of the Olympic's patrons as the finest attraction the theatre has ever had, and during the remaining three nights of her engagement here should be greeted with a rousing house."[2] The pair established a pattern of exchanging weeks at a theater, with Texas Jack and his combination performing for a week at a venue and then Morlacchi's troupe performing there the following week. They arranged their schedules to overlap, allowing the couple to spend time together and to make special appearances in each other's shows.

In March, the *Advertiser*, a local newspaper in the small mid-state hamlet of Addison, New York, reported, "The Texas Jack troupe busted in this place."[3] A lack of advertising and bad weather had resulted in poor receipts, and the combination was unable to pay its debts for printing, theater rental, actors' fees, and board bills. Despite this bust and the fact that he was anxious to return to his wife, Jack continued to travel to each scheduled show.

In April, a paper from Auburn, New York, reported that "Texas Jack played to a six-dollar house at Johnson Hall Monday night. Several of his creditors were looking for their money, but they were swindled."[4] That night, the various members of the combination went their separate ways, leaving their baggage and stage effects at their hotel as security for their board. Omohundro pawned one of his favorite revolvers for a paltry $15 to pay his hotel bill. As a personal favor to Texas Jack, the hotel's landlord furnished the two ladies of the tour money to purchase train fare back to New York.

Where the combination was advertised in advance, it seems to have found success, but receipts from the show's bigger audiences were taken by the manager, who had bought the rights to the show outright. In Syracuse, the Texas Jack Combination was initially so popular that the company was persuaded to stay for an additional week of shows, but with the manager taking the lion's share of the profits. During the last performance in Syracuse, the local newspaper reported that Omohundro's manager presided over the ticket office, "and after the performance, folded his greenbacks and silently stole away."[5] Texas Jack paid his performers out of pocket, and the troupe traveled to Boston for one last week-long run at the Howard Aetheneum. With apologies to the actors in the company, Omohundro called an abrupt end to the dramatic season and returned to Lowell to spend time with his wife.

Well before her husband's combination broke up, Morlacchi had told Boston newspapers that she and her husband planned to leave the stage after the current season was done in the spring. The *Chicago Tribune* released an article stating "[T]he stage is going to lose its Texas Jack. He will shortly play a season of farewell engagements, and then he and his wife, Mlle. Morlacchi, will retire."[6] Despite this announcement, Omohundro was approached by British novelist Bracebridge Hemyng—famous for his Jack Harkaway character and series of stories—to provide the cowboy with an entirely new drama, one that would showcase Omohundro's skills as an actor beyond the role of Texas Jack. Omohundro tentatively agreed to stage Hemyng's piece, perhaps as a farewell to the audiences of Boston, so close to his adopted hometown of Lowell. Plans were made to stage the new play at Stetson's Athenaeum in Boston when Jack and Morlacchi ended their stay in Leadville, Colorado.

At home in Lowell, Omohundro received a somewhat strange request, which he was happy to accept. The local *Lowell Courier* reported that Al Watts, the dogcatcher for the city of Boston, came to Jack to ask for training with the use of a lasso. Jack gladly obliged, fashioning a lariat and teaching the man to handle it properly. Newspapers across the country picked up on the story, and Watts became the most renowned dogcatcher in America, giving men in the same position in other cities demonstrations of the lasso techniques he had learned from the cowboy, Texas Jack.[7]

As summer approached, Jack reestablished himself touring not with his usual cast, but utilizing the house talent during weeklong runs at Toronto's Royal Opera House, Cleveland's Theatre Comique, and Detroit's Coliseum, each with full houses and positive reviews. Notably absent from his shows were his old stage partner Donald McKay, who had returned to the world of medicine shows, and Arizona John Burke. Coincidentally finding themselves in Detroit with their own engagements, Texas Jack was joined for his last show in the city by both Donald McKay and Ira Paine. The trio staged an impromptu shooting match, with Jack managing to destroy more glass balls than either of the other gentlemen in their last appearance together.

With his scheduled shows completed for the summer and no Western trip to occupy his time, Jack and Josephine traveled together to Buffalo and Niagara Falls without the pressing business of touring to occupy them. In the fall, they exchanged weeks at theaters in Philadelphia, where they had shared the small house just south of the park during the Centennial Exhibition. While Morlacchi continued to receive glowing reviews for her return to the stage as a featured ballerina, Jack appeared before full houses in *Texas Jack in the Black Hills* at the Standard Theatre. Notable on this trip were continued mentions by the press both of the couple's planned retirement from acting and comments that Omohundro had matured into quite a good actor, beyond simply playing the part of himself. The shows no longer included the deaths of scores of Indians, but free from the tight reins of outside management had developed into dramatic scenes closer to the reality of life on the rapidly shrinking Western frontier.

A *Philadelphia Times* reporter noted that "Mr. Omohundro . . . performed numerous heroic feats that awakened admiration, which was voiced in deafening applause, and the curtain fell upon vice punished and virtue rewarded in the most approved style. It will be a big week at the Standard, for the boys will all be there."[8] For Jack, a return to the full houses and packed galleries that had been the rule must have been a welcome change from the nearly empty venues he had played during his mismanaged prior spring.

The tour continued through late fall, with shows in New York City and Cincinnati, where once again, a local newspaper commented that "Texas Jack shows improvement in his acting,"[9] noting that the audience at each show was both full and excited. Next came stops in Louisville and Baltimore, where after a quick visit to see family in Virginia, Omohundro staged both *The Trapper's Daughter* and *Texas Jack in the Black*

Texas Jack Omohundro in stage costume, between 1878 and 1880. (BUFFALO BILL CENTER OF THE WEST, CODY, WYOMING)

Hills during a weeklong residency at the latter city's Front Street Theatre, again to favorable reviews and eager audiences. For many of these shows, marksman and sharpshooter Captain Joseph Rainbolt appeared with Omohundro, and together the two men demonstrated shooting targets over their shoulder using a mirror.

From mid-December through January 1880 in Chicago, the couple spent alternating weeks at that city's Academy Theatre, Mueller's Hall, and Lyceum. At the end of January, Jack played the Globe Theatre in St. Louis while Morlacchi appeared in *The French Spy* at another venue in the city. Spending the winter in the Windy City, Jack and Josephine must have reminisced about the day they had first met in that city, seven years earlier. As they had sporadically on their joint tour, the couple appeared together onstage in Chicago, performing the now-standard *The Trapper's Daughter*, but by early January appearing in a new play entitled *Little Billy; or, Adventures in Texas*, with new material based on Texas Jack's life as a cowboy in the Lone Star State.[10] The *Spirit of the Times* noted that the opening show for their Chicago run was so successful that patrons had to be turned away. Soon another piece, *The Sioux Spy of the Black Hills*, was added to the repertoire, showcasing Morlacchi and based on Omohundro's experiences scouting for General Terry during the Sioux conflict of 1876.

The pair filled engagements in St. Louis, Kansas City, and Denver as they headed toward Leadville, Colorado, where Josephine was booked for a substantial engagement. In Denver, Texas Jack and Morlacchi performed *The Trapper's Daughter*—not the same *The Trapper's Daughter* they had been performing for years, but a retitled version of the play *Fonda; Or, The Trapper's Dream*, written by Captain Jack Crawford. In his book about the "Poet Scout," *Ho! For the Black Hills*, Paul Hedren writes that, "Crawford also wrote a handful of plays, all of which were performed during his lifetime but none more spectacularly than when John B. 'Texas Jack' Omohundro staged and starred in *Fonda* in Denver in 1880."[11] Though the pair of Jacks, Omohundro and Crawford, never got the chance to act together onstage, they had remained friends, and Crawford was on hand to see the play—written while Crawford recuperated from the gunshot wound inflicted onstage with Cody—performed by Omohundro. The two parted in Denver, and Texas Jack and Josephine headed high into the Rocky Mountains of Colorado, to Leadville.

Morlacchi had agreed to star for nine weeks in both *The French Spy*, James Fenimore Cooper's *The Wept of Wish-Ton-Wish*, and Leadville's inaugural performance of *The Black Crook*—the very show she had competed against when first induced to travel to America—while Jack took *The Trapper's Daughter* to the Chestnut Street Theatre to the delight of the silver boomtown's denizens.

Chapter Twenty-Eight

Leadville, Colorado

Leadville, Colorado, was a textbook boomtown when Texas Jack and his wife arrived at the end of March 1880. The city had grown out of the ashes of another boomtown named Oro City, though to call that small mining town a city had been more than a little ambitious. Oro City was the result of a gold discovery at California Gulch during the Pike's Peak Gold Rush, leading one hundred thousand Americans to pick up stakes and set off for the region with dreams of gold. Within months nearly ten thousand prospectors had settled in Oro City. The area was immediately prosperous, and up to $2.5 million of gold was extracted from the region by the end of 1859. This bounty was not to last, however, and the Pike's Peak or Bust '59ers soon busted as the diminishing placer gold that had brought them to Oro City proved too difficult to separate from the heavy black sand that filled prospectors' sluice boxes.

Within a year, the population dwindled to only a few hundred enterprising souls still searching for gold flakes in the cold creek waters. In 1874 these remaining prospectors commissioned an assay of the dark, gritty sand and determined that it was cerussite, a mineral the miners called lead-spar. The cerussite sand flowing in the gulch at Oro City contained an unusually high concentration of silver, and when the prospectors managed to trace the cerussite back to its source in 1876, they discovered several silver-lead streaks. On May 3, 1878, the owners of the "Little Pittsburg" mine struck a massive silver lode and the Colorado Silver Boom began. Over the next fourteen years, some $80 million worth of silver was mined from the ground of the Centennial State.

Miners soon established a new city as close to the silver deposits as possible, and locals referred to their new community as Slabtown, until the establishment of a post office necessitated a name change. Leadville was named after the other more-prominent metal pouring from the mines.

Miners and prospectors who had departed when the placer gold dried up now rushed back to the area, overcrowding hotels that could now charge any price they wanted for their limited rooms. The price of silver skyrocketed as a result of the recently passed Bland-Allison Act of 1878, which required the federal government to purchase between $2 to $4 million of silver each month from the Western silver mines and to circulate silver dollars as currency.

By the end of 1878, mine owners and town founders Horace Austin Warner Tabor and August Meyer had convinced the rest of Park County to make Leadville the county seat. The city grew, as did the shantytowns that surrounded it, with names like Finn Town, Poverty Flats, and Boughtown, so named for the pine boughs busted miners used to roof their simple dwellings. The bitter cold and thin air above ten thousand feet meant many of these miners did not survive the city's harsh winters.

Horace Tabor first came to the area following the gold boom of 1861. A stonemason by trade, the enterprising Tabor journeyed from his native Vermont to Kansas after working in quarries across New England. In Kansas, he was elected to the Topeka Free-State Legislature, before President Franklin Pierce dismissed it in favor of the pro-slavery legislature elected under the supposed influence of Missouri "border ruffians." Tabor retreated to Maine, married the daughter of a former boss, and convinced his new wife to come with him to strike it rich in Colorado. First in the small town of Buckskin Joe and later in Oro City and Leadville, the couple owned and operated general stores and postal services, with Tabor's wife, Augusta, handling daily maintenance while her husband prospected in the mines.

In late 1877, Horace Tabor outfitted the prospecting team of August Rische and George Hook on a contingency arrangement, and when their "Little Pittsburg" mine hit the load, Tabor used his one-third stake to invest in other mining teams. Tabor eventually sold his stake in the Little

Pittsburg for $1 million, immediately investing a portion of his new wealth into a mine of his own, called the "Matchless Mine."

In later years, Tabor divorced his wife in favor of his mistress and was elected to the US Senate. By then, the Sherman Silver Purchase Act, which superseded the Bland-Allison Act, forced the federal government to purchase yet more silver at prices that ultimately proved untenable. After a financial crisis that was resolved only when the Rothschild banking family and J. P. Morgan himself intervened, the federal government repealed the Sherman Act and immediately ceased buying silver. The consequences to Colorado, to Leadville, and to Horace Tabor were both devastating and swift. Tabor spent his last years nearly destitute, serving as the postmaster for Denver.

Tabor's second wife, "Baby Doe" Tabor, who created quite a scandal as a home-wrecker when she married Horace, spent the last thirty years of her life living in the supervisor's cabin at the Matchless Mine. She moved there after the death of her husband, telling anyone who would listen that his dying words to her were, "Hold onto the Matchless mine, it will make millions." The mine was sold in 1927 to satisfy a long-standing debt, but the new owners allowed the now-destitute Tabor widow to remain in the cabin she occupied on the site. After a particularly brutal snowstorm during the winter of 1935, several neighbors noted that there was no smoke coming from the cabin's chimney and rushed over to find "Baby Doe" dead, frozen to the cabin's floor.

During his life, Horace Tabor spent much of his wealth improving the city of Leadville. By the time Texas Jack and Morlacchi arrived in the early spring of 1880, the city contained twenty-eight miles of paved streets, six major banks, five churches, three hospitals, gas streetlights, and regulated water mains. The town's *Chronicle* newspaper was the first in America to employ a female reporter full-time. The first theater in the city was "the Coliseum Novelty," which provided guests with clean rooms and entertainment, including dog- and cockfights, gambling, wrestling, and boxing matches, all under one roof. The Coliseum surpassed William Nye's popular saloon, where a sign over the piano read, "Please do not shoot the pianist. He is doing his best." The Coliseum was surpassed by Ben Wood's Chestnut Street Opera House, the first genuinely upscale venue in the city. A formal dress code was strictly enforced, with gentlemen doffing their hats inside and refraining from smoking around the fairer sex.

Wood's was the most popular venue until Tabor's Opera House opened on November 20, 1879. The massive three-story stone and brick building was the costliest structure in the state when it opened its doors. The interior was decorated in red, gold, white, and a pale sky blue, illuminated by seventy-two individual gaslights. Actors, writers, and musicians from around the world, including such notables as John Philip Sousa and Oscar Wilde, would entertain from the theater's massive stage.

Wilde recalled that on his trip to Leadville he was entertained one evening by miners who invited him to a three-course dinner. The menu was carefully prepared. According to Wilde, "The first course was whisky, the second course was whisky, and the third course was whisky." On the Tabor Theatre's stage, Wilde read from the autobiography of Italian artisan Benvenuto Cellini and found the audience much delighted. When the pleased audience asked the author why he didn't bring the Italian man with him, Wilde explained that Mr. Cellini had been dead for some time. One concerned voice from the crowd asked, "Who shot him?" When locals failed one evening to drink Wilde under the table, an impressed group of rowdy miners loaded the author—dressed in a purple Hungarian smoking jacket, knee breeches, and a pair of black silk stockings—into a bucket, lowering him into the mine, where they proceeded to name a newly discovered silver lode "The Oscar" in his honor.[1]

"When Texas Jack . . . arrived in Leadville he was greeted with a warm reception and crowds flocked around him to obtain a good view of the famous scout," wrote a reporter. "His piercing black eyes, long dark hair, white sombrero hat and athletic build, coupled with his splendid reputation, made him an object of curiosity from the start. . . . [W]henever Texas Jack showed himself on the streets he was followed by a large crowd of curiosity seekers."[2] Children asked for the famous cowboy to shoot coins from the air, ladies commented on the handsome actor, and men offered to buy the scout a pour of his beverage of choice at nearby saloons.

Omohundro's long struggle with the bottle had continued as he'd made his way to Leadville the preceding winter. When his theatrical troupe played in Greenville, Pennsylvania, a reviewer wrote, "The Texas Jack company played to a small audience at the Opera House, last Friday evening. The performance consisted chiefly of an exhibition of Texas Jack's drunkenness, and was not worthy, even of the small audience assembled."[3] Thirty-seven years later, a Leadville local named E. J. Riggs wrote that "one of the sights of Leadville was Texas Jack buying a quart of whiskey and sitting down on the floor in Ed Murray's saloon on Chestnut street with a twelve-hundred-dollar overcoat on and not getting up until the whiskey was gone."[4]

Perhaps most telling is a letter written by Jack's old friend Buffalo Bill Cody to Captain Jack Crawford. In the letter, written from the Maxwell House Hotel in Nashville, Tennessee, after a theatrical appearance on November 25, 1879, four months before Omohundro's arrival in Leadville, Cody writes, "I ran across Texas Jack in Louisville, busted flat. I got him on the road again to see if he can do anything. Whisky is killing him."[5]

Some reports have insinuated that Omohundro and his wife chose Leadville as their destination in order to combat Jack's consumption, as pulmonary tuberculosis was called at the time. Diagnosing the disease more than 140 years after the fact is impossible, but several factors lend some credence to the idea that John Omohundro was not only suffering from the affliction that had taken his mother at the age of forty, but was relying on alcohol in part to assuage his constant pain. A hasty retreat to the more-arid West was often the prescription for consumption, and patients were occasionally urged to seek higher altitudes to combat its symptoms.

Doc Holliday, another famous Western figure and sufferer of tuberculosis, was told that if he stayed in Georgia he would be dead within six months, but that by heading west he might extend that period to two years. Like Omohundro, Holliday eventually made his way to Leadville, spending some time there before heading to a sanatorium in nearby Glenwood Springs to die. If Jack was suffering from tuberculosis, his lifelong habit of regularly smoking a cheroot or his meerschaum pipe must have aggravated the condition.

As early as the middle of May, scattered newspapers reported that Omohundro was ill in Leadville of erysipelas.[6] Also known as St. Anthony's fire, erysipelas is a painful, acute, and potentially serious skin disease. Modern descriptions of the condition routinely list alcohol abuse as a significant risk factor. Though Omohundro may well have been suffering from erysipelas as a consequence of his reliance on hard drink, an alternate explanation exists: Multiple documented cases of *Mycobacterium tuberculosis* infections have been routinely misdiagnosed as erysipelas, including a prominent case study in 2011.

In this context, Jack and Morlacchi's repeated announcements that they planned on leaving show business at the end of the year may be taken as confirmation of their concerns over Texas Jack's health, which had been an issue for some time. In an 1877 letter to a cousin, composed while he was hunting in Wyoming, Jack wrote: "My health is getting better than it has been for several years; not been sick an hour since I left the settlement."[7] An interviewer reporting on a conversation with Morlacchi in Denver just before the couple traveled to Leadville mentioned that her husband was sick.

Regardless of his health, Jack was not content to remain idle in Leadville, staging a series of his own dramatic shows in the city for two weeks at the Chestnut Street Theatre while his wife trained local dancers to join her Grand Ballet Troupe for forthcoming performances of *The Black Crook* at the Grand Central. Jack's shows were well received by the citizens of Leadville, who had not had the benefit of being a stop on any prior Buffalo Bill or Texas Jack tour. Between shows, Jack joined the Tabor Light Cavalry, a ceremonial militia unit of local men tasked with keeping peace in the city.

One evening at his favorite saloon, Jack overheard a trio of inebriated strangers discussing a plan to hold up the departing stagecoach the following day. One of the men had learned that a mine owner who had recently struck it rich had cashed out his silver and sold his mine for a substantial sum and planned to leave town with his accumulated wealth the next morning. The men devised a plan to hide near a curve in the road down the mountain. When the coach was forced to slow its speed to navigate the curve, they would relieve the man of his purse.

Texas Jack recruited a pair of fellow Tabor guards to ride out with him that night, arriving at the spot well in advance of the would-be bandits. As Leadville's veteran stage driver rounded the corner, the low rumble of the coach's wheels and the pounding of horses' hooves was interrupted by one of the aspiring thieves shouting "Hands up!" as his partners appeared from the nearby woods, pointing their shotguns at the coach, its frightened passengers nervously peering out the windows. As two of the bandits slipped from their mounts to relieve the travelers of their wealth, a low voice boomed behind them, demanding that they drop their guns. The startled men turned to find themselves staring into the barrel ends of Texas Jack's revolvers, along with those of his companions. The three outlaws were relieved of their weapons and bound to the top of the coach for the long ride down the mountain, where they found an officer waiting for them.[8]

One Leadville inhabitant recalled another time that Jack became involved in a local matter:

> Around the post office there was a crowd of impertinent young fops somewhat like the gang of shabby genteel tramps usually seen on a fine afternoon around the Diamond building at the junction, and whom the police would be justified in "running in" under the vagrancy act. The mission of the former, like that of the latter, was to stand in people's way as much as possible, giggle at the ladies as they pass by, and, through awkwardness, squirt tobacco juice on their dresses.
>
> One of the Leadville gang, more audacious than the rest, insulted a young woman as she was passing into the post office. Texas Jack observed the proceeding and he instantly made the young blood get down, kiss the slightly upturned soles of the lady's shoes, and then made him fairly lick the surface of them as well as to tender her a most humiliating apology—about as near eating dirt as a man could get.[9]

While Jack was busy deterring local thugs, his wife performed first *The Wept of Win-Ton-Wish* and then *The Black Crook* at the Grand Central

Theatre while she offered dance lessons to the city's young ladies and prepared to launch *Around the World in 80 Days*. The *Leadville Weekly Herald* offered a portrait of Morlacchi's educational endeavor:

> *M'lle Morlacchi . . . the famous dancer, surrounded by wee little bits of humanity, from two to six years of age, and energetically teaching them the comical movements of the Chinese Ballet. It was a perfect bewilderment to the beholder. First, a little two-year-older would hoppity kickity up and down the room, joined by others, apparently at arranged periods, until the whole crowd—twenty in number—were bobbing, jumping, gesticulating first with one hand, then the other, intermingled with laughing words of reproof, in various languages, till the Babel was quieted, and "now we'll try it over again."*
>
> *M'lle Morlacchi is a versatile linguist, and her pupils seemed to task her powers to the utmost. She kept up a running fire of instructions in German to one, in French to another, Spanish to a third, and Italian to one in particular. Each hearer, as addressed, seemingly becoming more proficient in understanding and celerity of movement. "Oh, it eez so hard! But they are such good children—they like to learn—it eez fun for them," said the lady.*[10]

When some critics intimated that Leadville could not possibly stage an elaborate production such as *The Black Crook* with the same high standards as Eastern cities like Boston and New York, a reporter reminded readers that "Mlle. Morlacchi has been for years the acknowledged head of her profession, and is eagerly sought after by all our western managers when a spectacular ballet is to be formed. In the whole United States no better dancer or teacher can be found, and her title, 'The Peerless Morlacchi,' which was given by professional companions, and is not a self constituted assumption, has never been disputed even by her would-be rivals in the Terpsichorean art."[11]

As he had at Fort McPherson, Nebraska, and Lowell, Massachusetts, Rochester, New York, and Wilmington, North Carolina, Jack spent time entertaining the local children of Leadville, shooting coins out of the air and demonstrating his skill with the lasso. Here was the cowboy, the hunter, the actor, the scout, the guide, the famous Texas Jack preventing stagecoach robberies and the harassment of young women, showing the town's young men how to fashion a lasso and shoot a revolver. Here was everything they had read about in the dime novels, come to life before them and walking the streets of Leadville.

CHAPTER TWENTY-NINE

Curtain Call

THE COFFIN, DRAPED IN THE STARS AND STRIPES, SAT IN THE MIDDLE of the stage at the Tabor Opera House, covered in flowers imported for the occasion, blossoms being rare in Leadville above ten thousand feet. The silver plate on the coffin's side read "J. B. Omohundro."

Near the end of May, 1880, Jack's already declining health took a decided turn for the worse. Obituaries reported that he had caught a cold, which he had ignored until it turned into pneumonia. Some speculated pneumonia had quickly turned into consumption, laying waste to the once-strong scout high in Colorado's Rocky Mountains. When he died at 7:30 in the morning on Monday, June 28, 1880, Texas Jack Omohundro was a month shy of his thirty-fourth birthday.

At the funeral, the reverend rose—garbed in the official blue and gold regalia and carrying the sword befitting his status as chaplain of the Tabor Light Cavalry—and began the service. Fay Templeton's operatic company sang hymns, and hundreds of citizens took the opportunity to view the body of the famous Texas Jack. As the crowd proceeded to the street, Morlacchi haltingly approached the coffin, embraced it, and pressed her lips against the glass that covered her husband's face. She wept until she fainted and was carried to the waiting carriage by concerned locals. A brief prayer later, and the reverend mounted his horse and led the funeral procession to Leadville's Evergreen Cemetery, where a musket volley was fired to salute Omohundro's military service.

The procession consisted of a fifty-piece brass band with members of the Grand Central band, Gardner's minstrel band, the Coliseum band,

and the Wood's Theatre band. On its march, the band was followed by Fay Templeton's operatic company acting as a choir. Businesses in Leadville closed, and miners filed out of the mines and into town where citizens gathered to watch the procession pass. One local paper commented that "Men and women thronged upon sidewalks—packed them. One could really have walked on the heads of the people and nobody would have noticed it."[1]

Around the country, newspapers ran obituaries and notices about the death of the frontier hero and stage star. The vast majority of these offered pneumonia as the cause of death. Firsthand accounts of Jack's death are rare. The *Leadville Daily Chronicle's* obituary reported that:

> *John Baker Omohundro, better known under the sobriquet "Texas Jack," died at the residence of Major Howard, on Fourth Street, at 7:30 o'clock this morning. The primary cause of death was pneumonia contracted from exposure, which commenced a month since, but last week developed into rapid consumption. Dr. Cook was called in attendance day before yesterday and succeeded in rallying the patient to such a degree that his friends deemed a temporary cure would be effected, but at three o'clock this morning a sudden change occurred and he sank rapidly, unconscious to the last.*[2]

Other accounts were written well after the fact. Simpson Stilwell, known to his friends as Judge Jack or Comanche Jack, claimed to be in Leadville when Omohundro died and wrote that he had comforted his friend in his final days. A scout at Fort Hays and Fort Harker in Kansas, Stilwell may have met Jack Omohundro for the first time with Wild Bill and California Joe in Hays. Stilwell, who also claimed to have been in Deadwood for Wild Bill's assassination, later recalled the painful experience of watching Texas Jack die of consumption in Colorado.

Simpson's younger brother Frank would achieve some notoriety as a member of the Cochise County Cowboys in the Arizona Territory when he was suspected of murdering Morgan Earp on March 18, 1882. Two days later, Frank was shot and killed by Morgan's brother, Deputy US Marshal Wyatt Earp, in a Tucson train yard during Earp's vendetta ride with another man known as Texas Jack, John Wilson Vermillion. When Vermillion was asked why he was called Texas Jack, he answered that, like the other Texas Jack, John Omohundro, he was called Texas Jack "because I'm from Virginia."

When Simpson Stilwell died of Bright's disease in 1903, it was at the ranch of Bill Cody, where he'd spent the last five years of his life tending Cody's interests in Wyoming while Buffalo Bill was on tour.[3]

Seventeen years after Texas Jack Omohundro died in Leadville, an article appeared in the *Galveston Daily News* in Texas. The author prefaced his story by admonishing readers that he had "refrained from telling the story of the tragic end of Jack Omahundro [*sic*]—better known wherever the English language is written or spoken as Texas Jack—through consideration for the sensitive nature of his beautiful widow." Having read a report on Morlacchi's later death, the reporter abandoned his vow of silence, recalling "the terrible scene in the Sisters' hospital at Leadville."

The journalist wrote, "I first met Jack in Philadelphia over twenty years ago, when he was giving border plays at a second-class theater in conjunction with that other hero of my boyhood and friend of later days, Colonel William F. Cody. Jack's future wife . . . was a famous premier danseuse, with a wide fame in Europe, where dancing is appreciated . . . and was one of the most beautiful women I ever saw. I prefer to remember her by the name we gave her in Leadville—Mrs. Jack. It was a case of mutual love at first sight, if there ever was one, between her and Jack, and no one who saw them at that time could blame either. She was a perfect example of the luxuriant, tropical type of southern beauty (especially of southern Europe), and what is more rare in women of her vocation, she was educated, refined, and sensible.

"As for Jack," the author continued, "he was positively the handsomest thing in the way of physical manhood I ever saw. He stood over six feet, straight and lithe as an Indian; big, honest, boyish eyes, a silky moustache and a wonderful mane of brown curls that fell over his shoulders. While he was a giant in stature, his movements were as quick and graceful as those of a panther. His manner was gentle, frank and honest, and he was as guileless in the ways of the world as a schoolgirl—and more so.

"Jack . . . threw his dollars around with a lavish recklessness . . . [s]urrounded by saloons and lured into dissipations of which he had never dreamed in his wild, free life on the plains," the author lamented. By the time the cowboy arrived in Leadville, Jack was both "a heavy drinker and almost a total physical wreck. . . . His devoted wife, who had stood by him through it all and fought to save him from himself, as a mother fights to protect her child, concluded that the only hope to redeem him from his habits of civilization . . . was to get him back under the blue skies into the untainted air of the glorious [W]est: back where men's hearts grow big from contact with nature; where manhood asserts itself and virtue is respected and where agnosticism is impossible, because God's presence broods on the boundless plains and whispers in the canons of the eternal Rockies."

According to this author, Jack's return to the wilderness of the high Colorado mountains soon revealed that Texas Jack's efforts onstage had "blazed the way for that civilization that had ruined him. . . . He began life as a cowboy, but soon took to Indian fighting as a trade, and old frontiersmen have assured me that he never had his equal as a scout. . . . Jack had sold himself to the rum habit, and the foreclosure was rapidly approaching. He had gotten down to acting as a guide for hunting parties composed of Englishmen and back east tenderfeet and these associations were not calculated to better his malady."

In Leadville, "Jack made an honest effort to get sober and brace up, but he had chosen the wrong place for the effort. . . . He was plied with invitations to drink a hundred times a day, and was too weak to resist all of them. His wife had been reduced to playing in variety theaters so as to be [as] near him as possible and was then filling an engagement at the Grand Central theater in Leadville. She tried to hold him within bounds but failed. Mrs. Jack appealed to me for help, and I spent a day with him. . . . [He was] unable to eat anything and was keeping on his feet through the aid of milk punches. He consented to cut down his allowance of these, and when we parted he promised to drink nothing until he met me in town the following day. . . . He kept his appointment and his promise," the author continued, "but he was shaking pitiably when I found him in Charley Hall's beer cellar drinking seltzer and lemon. I was compelled to ride to the head of Iowa gulch, but he promised to meet me at the theater at night."

According to author of this article, by the time he'd returned to the city he was told that Texas Jack had fallen violently ill and had been taken to the Sisters' hospital. "I hurried there and was not surprised to learn that his attack was one of delirium tremens. The hospital did not have a regular straightjacket, but Jack's hands were strapped loosely to the four posts of the bed and five men were trying to control his convulsions. At the head of the bed, her big black eyes twice their normal size, the olive skin of her face corpse-like and waxen, rigid in terror, stood his wife. At the foot of the bed kneeled a sweet-faced young nun, praying rapidly. A young physician was administering a hypodermic injection of morphine, when he started back with a warning cry. Six of us sprang on Jack, as, with a terrible scream, his muscles contracted for a supreme physical effort. The straps on his wrists snapped like threads and the six men went hurtling against the walls of the room, and Jack fell back—dead.

"There were a few seconds when no one breathed," the author remembered, "and the silence oppressed like the weight of fathoms of water. Then came a shriek that hurt the brain like a blow and stopped the beating of the heart. The wife had flung herself on the corpse and was trying to tear it from the bed. She fought like a tigress when we tried to secure her, and I carry the marks of her teeth in my arm to this day. After she was bound hand and foot she sang lullabies to her lost boy all night as though he were her baby who had gone to sleep. She was sent to an insane asylum the next day and that was the last I ever heard of her until I saw the notice of her death the other day."[4]

John Sprogle Jr., the piece's author, lived in Leadville in 1880 and may well have been present at Omohundro's death. Denver's Sixth Annual City Directory in 1880 lists him as a journalist. In early 1881, a bulletin in the local *Leadville Daily Herald* mentions Sprogle as being presented with an expensive saddle in appreciation of his work on the staff of Brigadier General C. C. Howell. This may be the same Major Howard whose home Jack and Josephine had shared during their stay in Leadville. The same newspaper references Sprogle as a journalist in the area in November of 1880. He worked as a journalist in Leadville,

Denver, Colorado Springs, and Chicago before moving back to his native Philadelphia, where he reported for the *Philadelphia Inquirer*. In Chicago, he published a colorful account of an interview with Jay Gould and a number of reporters that was reprinted nationally.

Sprogle's *Recollections of a Reporter* piece about Texas Jack was published in *Lippincott's Monthly Magazine*, a Philadelphia-based literary journal, in January of 1899. Sprogle was assigned to Galveston by 1897 as a correspondent for the *Philadelphia North American* and was placed in charge of that paper's relief expedition after the deadliest hurricane in US history struck the island in September of 1900. In one report after the storm, Sprogle is called "the last of the foreign newspaper men to leave the Island city, and then not until the last of the American's relief had been turned over to Miss Clara Barton and the Red Cross Society for disposition." Sprogle's brother Howard served as the district attorney in Leadville as early as 1883 and was well connected in the area before that. Sprogle's father is listed as an owner of several mine stakes with his sons, which partially accounts for their presence in the city during the boom.

Enough of Sprogle's account rings true that it merits serious consideration. It seems that the journalist was at the time considering writing a memoir about his time as a reporter in frontier Colorado, and his story about the death of one of America's most well-known celebrities would have attracted much attention. Jack's fondness for whiskey is well documented. From Cody's letter to Crawford reporting that he had just seen Jack and that the "whisky [was] killing him," to Lord Dunraven's comment that "In the morning, Jack after the manner of his race, takes a good square honest drink of whisky 'straight,'" there are too many accounts of Omohundro's taste for strong drink to be dismissed.

Dunraven also noted that Omohundro was "of course also smoking— he is always smoking, except when he is eating, and the few moments he is obliged to devote to mastication are grudgingly given." If Dunraven's description of Texas Jack's habits on the hunt are typical, and no other accounts offer reason to suspect that they are not, then we are left with a picture of a man who drank often, smoked heavily, and ate sporadically at best. The US National Library of Medicine states that "Delirium tremens can occur when you stop drinking alcohol after a period of heavy drinking, especially if you do not eat enough food. Delirium tremens may also be caused by head injury, infection, or illness in people with a history of heavy alcohol use."

In its report of the cowboy's death, the *Cincinnati Enquirer* stated that "the primary cause of death was pneumonia contracted from convivial indiscretion and exposure, which commenced a month since, but last week it developed into rapid consumption."[5] According to the World Health Organization, heavy alcohol usage results in a threefold increase in the likelihood of tuberculosis infection; tobacco smoking doubles that increase.[6] References to pneumonia in Leadville at the time are numerous, and later visitor Doc Holliday was laid low by the disease at least four times in the two years he spent in the city. In 1880 alone, three hundred deaths were blamed on pneumonia, and one local paper accused city officials of burying the deceased under cover of night to prevent a panic.

Talk of a pneumonia epidemic was dismissed by city officials even then. At a meeting of the Arapahoe County Medical Society in 1884, doctors recorded the opinion that pneumonia was "not unfavorably affected by a high altitude, nor of more common occurrence." One doctor opined that pneumonia was "rare here, and . . . the frequency and fatality in Leadville was on account of the class of men who were found there."[7] Another doctor added simply that "all drunkards die in Leadville if they had pneumonia." In his *History of Leadville*, Marshall Conant Graff wrote that "in 1880, 300 died from pneumonia and this fact has given Leadville a reputation for pneumonia which it does not deserve. These deaths were due to lack of shelter, the life the people led, etc., and not to altitude."[8]

Leadville's death rate in 1880 was reported to be less than half of the death rate in Denver over the course of the same year. Leadville's first citywide directory in 1879, published just before Texas Jack and his wife arrived, went as far as to say that "No contagious or infectious diseases exist, and the greater number of deaths thus far have been from pneumonia; this, however, must not be attributed so much to climate and local causes as to the careless manner in which many persons have lived."[9]

An article in the *History of the Arkansas Valley* noted that in 1880, the year Jack died, "in nine cases out of ten, pneumonia was caused by drunkenness and the consequent exposure. The man, who, in Leadville, becomes drunk, and throws himself down on the floor, or in a gutter, to sleep off his debauch, is exceedingly likely to be frozen to death, or receive a fatal attack of pneumonia. On the other hand, there is not on record, in the practice of any physician, of a single instance of an attack of pneumonia upon men who clothe themselves and sleep warmly, and take ordinary precautions against exposure."[10]

Tuberculosis, heavy drinking to assuage the pain brought on by the consumptive disease, and exposure to the elements in the high Rocky Mountain air had together accomplished what Union Army rifles and cannons, sinking ships, stampeding cattle, lassoed buffalo, injured grizzly, and hostile Comanche, Sioux, and Nez Perce had failed to do. They had felled one of the strongest and most legendarily indefatigable heroes of the plains.

Epilogue

Newspaper reporters around the country told readers that Josephine would not survive her husband's passing. For days she refused to eat or drink. A month after the cowboy's funeral, a benefit was put together for Morlacchi in Leadville, but in her grief the widowed dancer was swindled out of the money the benefit had raised.[1] She returned home to Lowell and the home she and her husband had shared. The New Orleans *Times-Picayune* reported that she tried to commit suicide soon after arriving in Massachusetts.[2] A full year later, newspapers in Boston and New York claimed that the ballerina had gone insane, having fallen under the spell of spiritualism in an attempt to communicate with Texas Jack from beyond the grave.

Two years after her husband's death, the same papers wondered if she would ever grace the stage with her dancing again. Although sporadic newspaper announcements during the next five years declared that Morlacchi was at long last poised to return to the stages of Boston or New York, each report proved false. Josephine never toured again.

At home, Morlacchi the Peerless, the greatest danseuse of her time, offered free dance lessons to the poor women working the mills of Lowell, Massachusetts, and their daughters. Each year at Christmas, no matter where in the world he was, Bill Cody sent Morlacchi a reminder of his friendship with and affection for her husband, and the holiday season they had all spent on that stage together in Chicago years before.[3] Josephine nursed her sick sister, Angelina, who died in 1885. On July 25, 1886, Giuseppina Morlacchi Omohundro died of stomach cancer at her Billerica farm. The beautiful ballerina was laid to rest at St. Patrick's Cemetery in Lowell, over two thousand miles from the final resting place of her beloved husband. According to one report she left $25,000 worth of diamonds, gifts from her adoring husband, to the Boston actors' fund.[4]

Among the mourners at her funeral was John M. Burke, her former business manager and suitor, fellow actor and friend. Burke, ever the promoter of his goddess, told newspapers in New York that Morlacchi was so well regarded in Lowell that, though she was a devoted Catholic, local Methodist, Presbyterian, Baptist, and Episcopalian congregations had each turned out to pay their respects, closing businesses in town so that owners and workers alike could attend the funeral.

The truth was more in keeping with the private life Josephine had maintained since her husband passed away six years earlier. A handful of her friends from the local Catholic church and several of the mill workers she had taught to dance gathered at her grave to bid farewell to the woman who a decade before had been the single most famous dancer and actress in the nation. Josephine's grave is now largely ignored, and tours of the largely Irish cemetery often fail to stop by her monument. Brander Matthews, writing in *Appleton's Journal*, a New York literary magazine, summed up her lasting legacy in dance this way:

> *Of the two styles of modern dancing—the Taglioni exquisite in its chastity and severe in its beauty, and the Vestris full of languorous fire and aiming at an enervating sensation—of each of these schools we have had recent opportunities of seeing excellent representatives. To the first class belongs [a] style of exquisite beauty, chaste, almost to coldness, lacking only that smile which . . . is the dance of the features as the dance is the smile of the limbs. To the second school, of fiery and voluptuous art aiming at the senses rather than the intellect belong [other dancers], of superb technique, graceful gestures, and rounded attitudes, revealing the results of hard work and sound teaching.*
>
> *Mademoiselle Morlacchi united the best characteristics of these two dissimilar schools; she had skill, and style, and poetry; she was a fine pantomimist; she loved her art, and she felt fully that it is an art; she had the tact and the taste to conceal all trace of effort, knowing the hiding of artifice is the supreme proof of art.*[5]

In her despair over her husband's death, Morlacchi left only a simple wooden slab to mark Jack's grave. The wooden marker was inscribed in Josephine's hand, and bore the inscription:

John B. Omohundro
Dio guardia mia cara alma
Died June 28, 1880
Tuva hasta pronto
Texas Jack
Giuseppina Morlacchi[6]

The words were in Italian, and translate as:

John B. Omohundro
God guard my dear soul
Died June 28, 1880
I'll see you soon
Texas Jack
Giuseppina Morlacchi

Years later, Josephine expressed her regret that she hadn't provided a fitting memorial to her beloved husband. In her will, she set aside money to purchase a permanent monument in the Evergreen Cemetery, but for unknown reasons, the executor of her estate failed to fulfill her wish. Talking with a local reporter just two years after Jack's death, John M. Burke expressed his horror at the condition of the gravesite, and the wooden marker, now faded by summer sun and winter heat. "Do you know," Burke told the reporter, "I cannot bear to see his grave thus unmarked, and shall at once set about having a suitable monument erected to mark where lies the noblest work of God, 'a man.'"

In time the wooden marker over the cowboy's grave was taken by some souvenir hunter. The initial memorial inscribed by his wife was replaced with another one featuring a carving of a cartridge belt, crossed pistols, sheathed bowie knife, and Winchester rifle. Underneath these was a depiction of Yellow Chief, one of Omohundro's favorite horses and the one most often featured in dime novels about the scout. An inscription read:

Sacred to the Memory of
TEXAS JACK
(J. B. OMOHUNDRO)
Died June 28, 1880
[Age] 39, Pneumonia

The monument overstated his age by six years. When he died, he was one month shy of his thirty-fourth birthday. This memorial, too, was removed, and for the next decade a simple cross and a white wooden slab inscribed "Sacred to the memory of Texas Jack, John B. Omohundro" and bearing the dates of his birth and death marked his grave.

On the first day of September 1908, and twenty-six years after mentioning his disappointment at Jack's grave marker, John Burke, in his capacity as Buffalo Bill Cody's advance press agent, returned to Leadville. He hung his posters and gave interviews with newspapers and then walked to Evergreen Cemetery and the grave of Texas Jack. Reminiscing, he told local children stories about *The Scouts of the Plains* and tales of Buffalo Bill Cody, Texas Jack Omohundro, and Wild Bill Hickok hunting together in the mountains of Colorado. One local reporter thought it "probable that the sight of the simple cross which now marks Jack's resting place will prompt [Cody] to start some action with reference to the much discussed movement of substituting a monument more substantial and worthy of one of the bravest frontiersmen of the plains."[7]

That evening Cody assembled the cowboys of his Wild West show and marched them to Evergreen Cemetery, where they gathered around the final resting place of the first cowboy to star in the yellowed pages of dime novels, the well-trod boards of theatrical stages, and the imaginations of American citizens. The trip to Leadville in 1908 to pay his respects to his old friend and to purchase the memorial stone that still graces the grave of John B. Omohundro today was the first one Cody made to the city. In the thirty-six years since the pair had thrown caution to the wind and departed the Nebraska frontier to join Ned Buntline in Chicago, Cody had partnered with many other names that would be forever enshrined in the annals of the Wild West. Wild Bill Hickok, Kit Carson Jr., Captain Jack Crawford, Doc Carver, Nate Salsbury, Buck Taylor, Sitting Bull, Pawnee Bill, Tom Mix, Johnny Baker, and Annie Oakley would all spend time in some incarnation of Buffalo Bill's show, either on the stage or with the outdoor exhibitions Cody pioneered with Doc Carver before their falling-out. None of them seem to have left the impression on Buffalo Bill that Texas Jack did.

By the time Cody visited Leadville in 1908, he was the most prominent entertainer—and one of the most recognized men—in the world. From that humble start at Nixon's Amphitheatre, he went on to perform before presidents, kings and queens, and the Pope on stops on both sides of the Atlantic, spreading the myth of the American West wherever he went. In enshrining the cowboy as central to his version of the Wild West, Bill Cody ensured that even if they had forgotten his friend's name, America would remember Texas Jack. Buffalo Bill lived long enough to ensure that his own name lived on, but his long life equally guaranteed that the qualities he saw present in his friend would be forever associated with that man's profession. Without William F. Cody, there would not be an NFL team called the Buffalo Bills, but without Cody's Wild West show and its veneration of the cowboy profession embodied by his friend Texas Jack Omohundro, there might not be a team called the Dallas Cowboys.

On January 6, 1917, Buffalo Bill stepped onto the train at Glenwood Springs, where he had spent the week before resting and trying to recover from illness. Seventy years old, Cody suffered from both a bronchial infection and advanced kidney failure. Though he assured a reporter that he wasn't visiting the sanatoriums at Glenwood Springs to die, he certainly realized that his time at the springs was his last hope of getting well. Attended by his personal physician, a nurse, and his daughter, the old scout decided suddenly to return to Denver to visit his sister before heading home to Cody, Wyoming, the town he had founded at the gateway to his old friend Texas Jack's familiar haunts in Yellowstone Park.

The train stopped in Leadville late in the evening on January 6, and Cody sat up and waved to spectators for a moment. He spoke to his daughter and nurse about Texas Jack, and the monument he had placed at his partner's grave.[8] Not well enough to leave the train due to his declining health, Cody was unable to walk across town to Evergreen Cemetery and the monument he had generously erected for his friend. As the train pulled out of the station, Cody waved good-bye for the last time to the people of Leadville and his old pard, Texas Jack. Four days later, Buffalo Bill was dead.

Epitaph for the Cowboy

THE IDEA OF COWBOYS FIGHTING INDIANS ON THE OUTSKIRTS OF CIVI-lization is so permanently ingrained in our collective consciousness that as a scenario it seems not merely plausible but clichéd. The tropic cowboy captures all of American virtue reduced to a central mythic figure comprising a set of beliefs: The cowboy fought Indians. The cowboy was a rugged individualist. The cowboy played a major role in American history. The cowboy fought in gunfights. The cowboy's life was full of excitement.

We believe these truths about cowboys because Bill Cody presented his Wild West show as gospel truth in its depictions of the American West. In his show, cowboys rode to the rescue alongside Buffalo Bill, just like the real cowboy Texas Jack had on that April morning in 1872 when his well-placed shot saved the life of his friend, the scout. Texas Jack demonstrated his skills with pistol and rifle, from Thomas Edison's hotel window, on stages with Donald McKay, on street corners with Wild Bill Hickok, and at fairgrounds with Doc Carver. Texas Jack explored the wilds of Yellowstone Park, the mountains of Colorado, Wyoming, and Montana, and the hunting grounds of the Wind River, Sweetwater, and Bighorn regions. Texas Jack witnessed the end of the Civil War, the closing of the frontier, and the end of the cowboy era.

We believe that cowboys fought Indians because Texas Jack fought Indians. We know the cowboy was a rugged individualist because Texas Jack was a rugged individualist. We understand that the cowboy played a major role in American history because we see Texas Jack present at so many moments crucial not only to our shared history, but to our understanding of that history. We are sure that the cowboy fought in gunfights because of Texas Jack's proficiency with his weapons. We are certain that the cowboy's life was full of excitement because in the life of Texas

Jack we see a cowboy fighting on the battlefields of Virginia, riding the cattle trails of Texas, exploring the wildest regions, romancing the most beautiful and sophisticated woman in the country, befriending some of the most legendary figures of his day, braving the bullets and arrows of hostile enemies, and living a life as full of excitement as any dime-novel character.

The American West that Texas Jack explored and exemplified was also subtly shaped by him. The Earl of Dunraven, who joined Jack on hunts in 1872 and 1874, would go on to own over one hundred thousand acres of Estes Park, Colorado, much of it now preserved as Rocky Mountain National Park. His book about his trek through Yellowstone Park with Texas Jack spurred Europeans to visit the park and the American West. Wyoming, which includes "The Cowboy State" among its nicknames, was shaped by the men Jack took there for hunts. Sir John Rae Reid, who explored and hunted with Jack along the Sweetwater and Wind rivers in 1877, went on to cofound the Anglo-American Cattle Company and the Western Cattle Company, controlling as many as four hundred thousand acres of land, fifty thousand head of cattle, and several thousand horses. Count Otto Franc von Lichtenstein returned to Wyoming after his 1878 trip there with Omohundro to start the Pitchfork Ranch near Meeteetse, Wyoming, one of the most important cattle operations in the Bighorn Basin, and the shooting location for the famous Marlboro Country ads. Texas Jack's love of the West and his cowboy stories shaped not only the perception of his former career, but the reality of cowboy life afterward.

In America after the Civil War, people needed a new kind of hero. Readers and theatergoers made known by their consumption of dime novels, penny dreadfuls, and Wild West shows their desire for something new—some unifying national icon as far removed from the heroes of the war as it was from the confines of those people's daily lives. America needed a hero that didn't ride the streetcars of New York or the carriages of Atlanta. The nation found its new national identity on the back of a horse, with a six-shooter in his holster and a lasso in the air. In the cowboy, America found what D. H. Lawrence called "the essential American soul . . . an isolate, almost selfless, stoic, enduring man." The cowboy became an icon of the American ideal, both the American knight and the American hero.

The shadow cast by Texas Jack was far-reaching. Doane Robinson, the state historian of South Dakota credited with conceiving the Mount Rushmore National Memorial, originally wanted the huge sculpture to include Texas Jack Omohundro, along with Buffalo Bill Cody, Wild Bill Hickok, Chief Red Cloud (Maȟpíya Lúta), Meriwether Lewis, and William Clark. Robinson's initial plan was to have sculptor Lorado Taft carve these figures into The Needles, a series of granite pillars in present-day Custer State Park, to attract tourism to South Dakota. When the project was handed over to Gutzon Borglum, it was decided that the stone of The Needles was too fragile for such a sculpture, and that the project would attract more government funding if it depicted presidents rather than frontier heroes.

During William Howard Taft's presidency, he visited Sherman, Texas. While in town, Taft was introduced to a young banker named Sale Omohundro. "Omohundro! Omohundro!" exclaimed the president. "Are you any relation to the great Texas Jack Omohundro?" When the man informed the president that the two were distant cousins, Taft told the man how he had seen Texas Jack with Buffalo Bill in Cincinnati in his youth, and how much he'd enjoyed reading the Texas Jack dime novels as a young man.

When the fledgling Boy Scouts of America commissioned illustrator Will Crawford to create a piece showing where their organization hoped to fit into the pantheon of frontier scouts, they specifically asked that "the Boy Scout of the Confederacy," Texas Jack Omohundro, be included. The piece that Crawford returned, entitled *A New Scout on the Old Trail*, shows Jack, along with Buffalo Bill Cody, Davy Crockett, California Joe, Kit Carson, and Daniel Boone greeting a Cub Scout standing outside his pup tent before his small fire, and saying, "Put it thar, Pard! Yer do us proud!"

Texas Jack's legacy never achieved the heights of those other men. While books about Cody, Crockett, and Boone number in the hundreds, only one biography of Omohundro, Herschel Logan's *Buckskin and Satin*, was ever published, and it has been quietly out of print since its release in

Texas Jack Omohundro. (COWAN'S AUCTIONS)

1954. Jack's partner Buffalo Bill achieved his greatest success when he stepped off the stage boards and brought the Wild West by train into cities across the country and to countries across the world. Cody's legacy lives on in the city that bears his name in Wyoming, where visitors flock yearly to learn about the West, that was on their way into and out of Yellowstone National Park, where Texas Jack explored with the Earl of Dunraven and dodged arrows launched by Chief Joseph and the Nez Perce. Cody's gravesite on Lookout Mountain, high above Golden, Colorado, is visited by upward of four hundred thousand visitors each year, while the memorial that Cody erected in memory of his departed friend eighty-six miles away in Leadville gets only a few dozen visitors, mostly family who continue to decorate the grave on the anniversary of the scout's death.

This isn't to say that Texas Jack has been completely forgotten. In 1980 attorney and history buff Frank Sullivan, who first discovered Jack in the pages of the Earl of Dunraven's book *The Great Divide*, met Malvern Hill Omohundro Jr. at a meeting of the Sons of the American Revolution. When Sullivan asked Malvern if he was related to the frontier scout of the same last name, he was pleased to learn that Malvern was Texas Jack's nephew, the son of his youngest brother. Within four years, an informal gathering of just over a dozen Omohundro relatives and historians met in Cody, Wyoming, and after organizing as a nonprofit under the guidance of Dennis and Julie Greene, have been holding roundups every two years since. The Texas Jack Association maintains a website with information about Texas Jack Omohundro and his legacy and distributes a regular newsletter to members.

In Fredericksburg, Texas, near the heart of Omohundro's cowboy stomping grounds, is Texas Jack Wild West Outfitter. Mike Harvey, who started the company as a muzzle-loading shop in the late 1970s, is a prodigious collector of original period firearms as well as Texas Jack memorabilia. One of the most substantial and well-regarded private firearms collections in the world, it contains one piece of Jack Omohundro's history that he regards above all the others:

> *I would have to say that my most prized item is Texas Jack Omohundro's Smith & Wesson Model 3 American, U.S. marked first model, with the inscription on the side that says "Texas Jack, Cottonwood Springs, 1872." Recently I acquired Texas Jack's cane that he presented to a fellow named Booth. It's an ivory cane, scrimshawed with the names of many frontier icons. It is the real deal . . . a great piece of history.*[1]

This gun, now in Mike's possession, was once purchased at an auction by collector Herschel Logan and provided the impetus for his own biography of Omohundro. In talking to Mike Harvey, it is evident that his admiration of Texas Jack extends well past his firearm collection. He told me a story about being at an auction in Cody when an original photo card was presented. When the auctioneer read the description, "Lady in an Indian outfit," Mike told me, "I rushed to see it and it was Morlacchi in her 'Pale Dove' character costume taken during the making of 'Scouts of the Prairie.' I bought it for $65. No one else knew who it was."[2]

In March of 1994, the National Cowboy and Western Heritage Museum posthumously awarded Texas Jack Omohundro its Wrangler Award, inducting him into the Cowboy Hall of Fame with such stars as John Wayne, Gregory Peck, Clint Eastwood, and Ronald Reagan. Texas Jack is both the earliest stage actor, as well as the earliest-born person, to receive this honor, given to individuals who, through their outstanding individual works in film, television, and stage works, have kept the American West in the public's collective eye, thus perpetuating its legacy and enduring mythology.

In the 1960s men like Yuri Gagarin, Alan Shepard, and John Glenn opened to the world another frontier, and the Baby Boomer generation began to set their own Western stories in space. One hundred years after Texas Jack arrived at Fort McPherson on horseback and met Buffalo Bill, Neil Armstrong and Buzz Aldrin arrived at the Sea of Tranquility on the *Eagle*, establishing a frontier that would dominate the popular fiction of the next generation. Science-fiction magazines replaced the Western magazines that had superseded the dime novels, but the heroes remained explorers of the frontier.

There is a reason that so many American heroes have come from the frontier, no matter whether that frontier was the mountains of Tennessee, the missions of Texas, or the plains of Nebraska. The fact that Gene Roddenberry in his epic science-fiction series *Star Trek* described space as "the final frontier" was no accident. The draw of the frontier is a freedom that levels all men to a common rank. Without the trappings of civilization, we celebrate not the qualities a person can attain by virtue of their wealth or their family's status, but those that are inherent to their character: courage, determination, and loyalty. In the heroes of the frontier, real and imagined, from Davy Crockett to Lewis and Clark, from Buffalo Bill to Captain Kirk, from Neil Armstrong to Texas Jack Omohundro, we look for people who face the frontier and the potential of danger and then put heel to horse and ride ahead.

More than fifty years after Texas Jack's death, the *New York Times Magazine* summed up his place in the history of the American West:

> *He was the Mustang King—the Conqueror of Cayuses without a rival. Horses came to him on the end of a lariat, and when he chose the wrong one in the dark, he could not coax it to go home. He was a Knight in Silvered Sombrero, defender of women, subduer of bullies. . . . He fought Comanches by the tribe—and put them to death, or flight. He led cavalry to the rescue of wagon trains. He saved officers'*

ladies from prairie fires . . . he had a heart so soft that it never failed the innocent and the friendless.[3]

Texas Jack Omohundro was a living bridge between the civilized world of the stages he played and the savagery of the Western frontier he hunted and explored. He was a connection between the boys in the gallery at the Bowery Theatre and the buffalo herds that roamed the plains. He was the juxtaposition of the top hat and silk cravat and the buckskin breeches and sombrero. On both stage and horseback, he was cast as the prototypical American hero. He filled the role so well that he sacrificed his own fame in service to it.

John B. Omohundro died, and people forgot his name, but Texas Jack lives on—in every tourist who tries on a Stetson, every child playing cowboys and Indians. In every Western, whether book, television show, or movie, you can find Texas Jack wherever you find a cowboy.

NOTES

Introduction

1. Warren, Louis S. *Buffalo Bill's America: William Cody and the Wild West Show.* New York: Vintage Books, 2006, 206.
2. Ibid.
3. Cody, William F. "The Dead Shot Four; or, My Pards of the Plains. A Romance of Wild Careers and Heroic Manhood in Dark Days Camp," *Beadle's Weekly*, No. 752, April 10, 1897.
4. Warren, 517.
5. *Herald Democrat* (Leadville, Colorado), September 6, 1908.
6. Ibid.
7. Ibid.

Chapter 1: Cowboys and Indians

1. Bill, Buffalo. *The Life of Hon. William F. Cody, Known as Buffalo Bill.* Hartford, CT: Frank E. Bliss, 1879, 313.
2. Ibid., 251.
3. Ibid., 253.
4. Letter from Charles Meinhold to J. B. Johnson, April 27, 1872, "Buffalo Bill's Great Plains," accessed August 8, 2017, http://buffalobill.unl.edu/items/show/41.
5. *North Platte Democrat* (North Platte, Nebraska), May 2, 1872.
6. *Atchison Daily Patriot* (Atchison, Kansas), May 11, 1872.
7. Cody, *The Life of Hon. William F. Cody*, 315.
8. *Enterprise and Vermonter* (Vergennes, Vermont), May 16, 1873.
9. Street & Smith's *New York Weekly*, June 10, 1872.
10. Ibid.
11. *Inter Ocean* (Chicago, Illinois), December 17, 1872.
12. Cody, William F. *Story of the Wild West, and Camp-Fire Chats.* Philadelphia, Pennsylvania, Historical Publishing Co., 1888, 641.
13. Cody, Louisa Frederici. *Memories of Buffalo Bill.* New York: D. Appleton and Company, 1919, 246.

Chapter 2: *The Virginian*

1. Omohundro, Malvern Hill. *The Omohundro Genealogical Record: The Omohundros and Allied Families in America; Blood Lines Traced from the First Omohundro in Westmoreland County, Virginia, 1670, through His Descendants in Three Great Branches and Allied Families Down to 1950.* Staunton, VA: Manufactured for the author by McClure Print. Co., 1951, 512.
2. Ingraham, Prentiss. *Texas Jack, The Mustang King.* New York: Beadle and Adams, 1891.
3. *Spirit of the Times*, April 14, 1877.
4. Thrapp, Dan L. *Encyclopedia of Frontier Biography: In Three Volumes.* Lincoln: University of Nebraska Press, 1991, 1082.
5. Grant, Ulysses S. *Personal Memoirs.* New York: C. L. Webster, 1885–86, 181.
6. Snead, Virginia J. *Fluvanna County Sketchbook, 1777–1963: Facts and Fancies of Fluvanna County in the Commonwealth of Virginia.* Richmond, VA: Whittet & Shepperson, 1963, 103.
7. Harris, Joel Chandler. *On the Wing of Occasions.* New York: Doubleday, Page & Co., 1900, 65–66.
8. Wellman, Manly W. *Giant in Gray.* New York: Scribner, 1949.
9. Wittenberg, Eric J. *Glory Enough for All: Sheridan's Second Raid and the Battle of Trevilian Station.* Washington, DC: Brassey's, 2001.
10. Ibid.
11. *West Chester Local News* (West Chester, Pennsylvania), August 11, 1873.
12. *Memphis Daily Appeal* (Memphis, Tennessee), July 8, 1880.
13. Winik, Jay. *April 1865: The Month That Saved America.* New York, NY: Harper Perennial, 2008, 191.
14. *Texas Jack Scout*, July 2012, 27.

Chapter 3: *Texas Jack*

1. Omohundro, *The Omohundro Genealogical Record*, 496.
2. *Spirit of the Times*, March 3, 1877.
3. Ibid., April 14, 1877.
4. Ibid., March 24, 1877.
5. *Pomeroy's Democrat* (New York, New York), August 30, 1873.
6. Tyree, Larry, *Texas Jack's Cowboy Days.* Texas Jack Scout Volume XXI, Number 3, November 2016.
7. https://www.tshaonline.org/handbook/entries/cattle-rustling
8. Cox, James. *Historical and Biographical Record of the Cattle Industry and the Cattlemen of Texas and Adjacent Territory.* New York, NY: Antiquarian Press, 1959, 69.
9. Omohundro, *The Omohundro Genealogical Record*, 523.
10. *Frontier Times Magazine*, January 1932.
11. *Spirit of the Times*, March 24, 1877.
12. Ibid.
13. Rathmell, William. *Life of the Marlows: A True Story of Frontier Life of Early Days as Related by Themselves.* Ouray, CO: Ouray Herald Print, 163.

14. Omohundro, *The Omohundro Genealogical Record*, 524.
15. *Sunday Mercury* (New York, New York), April 6, 1873.
16. *Saint Paul Globe* (St. Paul, Minnesota), July 20, 1902.
17. Yost, Nellie Irene Snyder. *Buffalo Bill: His Family, Friends, Fame, Failures, and Fortunes.* Chicago: Swallow Press, 1980, 33.

Chapter 4: Holding Down the Fort

1. Memorandum, March 20, 1924, in W. F. Cody 201 File, RG 407, National Archives and Records Administration.
2. Omohundro, *The Omohundro Genealogical Record*, 514.
3. Ibid., 514–15.
4. *Omaha Bee* (Omaha, Nebraska), June 22, 1872.
5. Buffalo Bill. *An Autobiography of Buffalo Bill.* New York: Cosmopolitan Book Corporation, 1920, 190.
6. Cody, *Memories of Buffalo Bill*, 179.
7. Ibid., 183.
8. Ibid., 185–86.
9. Ibid., 189.
10. Warren, *Buffalo Bill's America*, 104.
11. Kingsley, George H., and Mary Henrietta Kingsley. *Notes on Sport and Travel.* London: Macmillan, 1900, 138–39.
12. Warren, *Buffalo Bill's America*, 103.
13. *Spirit of the Times*, April 14, 1877.
14. Dunraven, Windham Thomas Wyndham-Quin. *Hunting in the Yellowstone.* New York: Macmillan, 1925.
15. Kingsley and Kingsley, *Notes on Sport and Travel*, 139.
16. Undated article entitled "Life in the Western Wilds" in Morlacchi scrapbook, collection of David Gindy.
17. Ayers, Nathaniel M. *Building a New Empire.* New York: Broadway Publishing, 1910, 179–80.

Chapter 5: Ned Buntline

1. Bricklin, Julia. *The Notorious Life of Ned Buntline.* Helena, MT: TwoDot, 2020.
2. Monaghan, Jay. *The Great Rascal: The Life and Adventures of Ned Buntline.* Boston, MA: Little, Brown and Company, 1952, 6.
3. Bill, *The Life of Hon. William F. Cody*, 263.
4. "Arkansaw Traveler, Wild Bill's Humorous Interview with Hiram Robbins," as quoted in Joseph Rosa's *They Called Him Wild Bill*, 244.

Chapter 6: The Grand Duke

1. Saul, Norman E. *Concord and Conflict: The United States and Russia, 1867–1914.* Lawrence: University Press of Kansas, 1996.

2. Douglas D. Scott, Peter Bleed, and Stephen Damm. *Custer, Cody, and Grand Duke Alexis: Historical Archaeology of the Royal Buffalo Hunt.* Norman: University of Oklahoma Press, 2013. Letter from Albert Bierstadt to William T. Sherman, July 3, 1871.
3. Buffalo Bill, *An Autobiography of Buffalo Bill*, 230.
4. Smith, Greg. "Russian Duke Hunted in Hayes County," *McCook Daily Gazette*, Nebraska Centennial Edition, 1867–1967, http://negenweb.net/NEHayes/hist/RUSSIAN.htm.
5. Saul, *Concord and Conflict*, 70.
6. Otero, Miguel A. *My Life on the Frontier, 1882–1897.* Albuquerque: University of New Mexico, 1939.
7. Street & Smith's *New York Weekly*, August 26, 1872.
8. "May the Grand Duke Alexis Ride a Buffalo to Texas," Nola History, Edward Branley, https://web.archive.org/web/20170305114800/http://gonola.com/2011/01/19/nola-history-may-the-grand-duke-alexis-ride-a-buffalo-to-texas.html

Chapter 7: The Grand Buffalo Hunt

1. Kunhardt, Philip B., Jr., Philip B. Kunhardt III, and Peter W. Kunhardt. *Barnum: America's Greatest Showman.* New York: Alfred A. Knopf, 1995.
2. Letter dated February 22, 1872, in Niagara Falls Museum Collection, Niagara Falls, Ontario, Canada.
3. Ibid.
4. Ibid.
5. Ibid.
6. *Omaha Weekly Herald* (Omaha, Nebraska), June 12, 1872.
7. All excerpts from Ena Palmer from the *Journal of Ena Palmer* in the Ballantine Family Collection of the Nebraska State Historical Society.
8. *Lincoln Daily State Journal* (Lincoln, Nebraska), June 23, 1872.
9. Street & Smith's *New York Weekly*, August 26, 1872.
10. *Rochester Democrat and Chronicle* (Rochester, New York), March 27, 1877.
11. *Wakeda Record* (Carrollton, Missouri), July 5, 1872.
12. Letter, February 22, 1872, Niagara Falls Museum Collection.
13. Hardin, John W. *The Life of John Wesley Hardin: From the Original Manuscript.* Seguin, TX: Smith and Moore, 1896.
14. Smarsh, Sarah, and Robert B. Smith. *Outlaw Tales of Kansas: True Stories of the Sunflower State's Most Infamous Crooks, Culprits, and Cutthroats.* Helena, MT: TwoDot, 2016, 25.
15. *Niagara Falls Gazette* (Niagara Falls, New York), August 28, 1872.
16. *Toronto Globe* (Toronto, Ontario, Canada), August 28, 1872.

Chapter 8: Indians and Cowboys

1. National Archives and Records Service.
2. *Journal of Ena Palmer.*

3. Smith, D. Jean. *Medicine Creek Journals: Ena and the Plainsmen*. North Platte, NE: Old Hundred and One Press, 2003.
4. *Journal of Ena Palmer.*
5. *Spirit of the Times*, March 26, 1877.
6. Letters received by the Office of Indian Affairs, Pawnee Agency, 1870–72.
7. *Forest & Stream*, vol. 48, xii.
8. Letter from J. B. Omohundro to Ned Buntline (E. Z. C. Judson), printed in Street & Smith's *New York Weekly*, August 26, 1872.
9. Receipt from Department of the Interior, dated September 26, 1872, in Morlacchi scrapbook, collection of David Gindy.

Chapter 9: *The Earl of Dunraven*
1. *Weekly Missouri Democrat* (St. Louis, Missouri), April 16, 1867.
2. Cody, William F. *Life and Adventures of "Buffalo Bill."* Chicago, IL: Stanton and Van Vliet, 1917, 254.
3. *The Nineteenth Century: A Monthly Review*, October 1880.
4. Kingsley and Kingsley, *Notes on Sport and Travel*, 137–38.
5. Dunraven, Windham Thomas Wyndham-Quin. *The Great Divide: Travels in the Upper Yellowstone in the Summer of 1874*. London: Chatto and Windus, 1876, 31.
6. Letter from Sheridan to Omohundro, dated October 26, 1872, in Morlacchi scrapbook, collection of David Gindy.
7. Cody, *Life and Adventures of "Buffalo Bill,"* 248.
8. *Journal of Ena Palmer.*

Chapter 10: **The Scouts of the Prairie**
1. Bill, *The Life of Hon. William F. Cody*, 259.
2. Cody, *Memories of Buffalo Bill*, 230.
3. Ibid., 231.
4. *Spirit of the Times*, October 20, 1877.
5. Undated article entitled "Texas Jack Bull-Dozing on the Borders," in Morlacchi scrapbook, collection of David Gindy.
6. Cody, *Memories of Buffalo Bill*, 233–34.
7. Ibid., 234.
8. *Chicago Tribune* (Chicago, Illinois), May 21, 1872.
9. Cody, *Memories of Buffalo Bill*, 236–37.
10. Monaghan, *The Great Rascal*, 250.
11. Cody, *Life and Adventures of "Buffalo Bill,"* 262.
12. Cody, *Memories of Buffalo Bill*, 233–34.
13. Ibid., 240–41.
14. *Chicago Tribune* (Chicago, Illinois), December 14, 1872.
15. Bill, *The Life of Hon. William F. Cody*, 325.
16. *Chicago Times* (Chicago, Illinois), December 19, 1872.
17. Cody, *Memories of Buffalo Bill*, 248.

18. *Chicago Tribune* (Chicago, Illinois), December 19, 1872.
19. Cody, *Memories of Buffalo Bill*, 241–43.

Chapter 11: The Peerless Morlacchi

1. *New York Herald* (New York, New York), October 19, 1867.
2. *Courrier des États-Unis* (New York, New York), October 24, 1867.
3. *Courrier des États-Unis*, November 11, 1867.
4. *Indianapolis Journal* (Indianapolis, Indiana), March 15, 1885.
5. *Boston Daily Evening Transcript* (Boston, Massachusetts), December 9, 1867.
6. *Christian Register* (Boston, Massachusetts), February 22, 1868.
7. *Springfield Republican* (Springfield, Illinois), February 5, 1868.
8. *Boston Herald* (Boston, Massachusetts), November 12, 1911.
9. *Mitchell Capital* (Mitchell, South Dakota), September 3, 1886.
10. Barker, Barbara Mackin. *American Careers of Rita Sangalli, Giuseppina Morlacchi and Maria Bonfanti: Nineteenth-Century Ballerinas.* New York: Dance Horizons, 1980.
11. *Mitchell Capital* (Mitchell, South Dakota), September 3, 1886.
12. *New York Times* (reprinted in *Times-Picayune*, New Orleans, Louisiana), March 22, 1870.
13. *Boston Post* (Boston, Massachusetts), August 9, 1870.
14. *Rochester Democrat and Chronicle* (Rochester, New York), August 16, 1873.
15. US Census, 1870.
16. *Leadville Daily Herald* (Leadville, Colorado), September 21, 1882.
17. *Chicago Tribune* (Chicago, Illinois), January 28, 1996.
18. Ibid.
19. Street & Smith's *New York Weekly*, February 24, 1873.
20. Harris, Andrea. "Sur la Pointe on the Prairie: Giuseppina Morlacchi and the Urban Problem in the Frontier Melodrama," *Journal of American Drama and Theatre*, vol. 27, no 1 (Winter 2015).

Chapter 12: The Scouts on Tour

1. *Chicago Tribune* (Chicago, Illinois), December 29, 1872.
2. Sagala, Sandra K. *Buffalo Bill on stage.* Albuquerque: University of New Mexico Press, 2008.
3. *Indianapolis News* (Indianapolis, Indiana), January 11, 1873.
4. "Texas Jack Bull-Dozing on the Borders."
5. *Hartford Daily Courant* (Hartford, Connecticut), February 27, 1873.
6. *Daily Graphic* (New York, New York), April 8, 1873.
7. Cody, Louisa. *Memories of Buffalo Bill.* 245-246.
8. *New York Herald* (New York, New York) April 1, 1873.
9. *Weekly Tribune & Republican* (Omaha, Nebraska), December 21, 1872.
10. *Weekly Herald* (Omaha, Nebraska), January 1, 1873.
11. *Richmond Daily Dispatch* (Richmond, Virginia), February 26, 1873.
12. *Missouri Democrat* (St. Louis, Missouri), May 4, 1873.

13. Wills, Garry. *John Wayne's America: The Politics of Celebrity*. New York: Simon & Schuster, 1997, 302.
14. Ibid.
15. *Cincinnati Daily Gazette* (Cincinnati, Ohio), December 30, 1872.
16. *Indianapolis News* (Indianapolis, Indiana), May 15, 1873.
17. *Daily Herald* (Omaha, Nebraska), July 17, 1873.

Chapter 13: End of the Pawnee Lifeway
1. Blaine, Martha Royce. *Pawnee Passage, 1870–1875*. Norman: University of Oklahoma Press, 1990.
2. Riley, Paul D. *"The Battle of Massacre Canyon," Nebraska History* 54 (1973): 220–49.
3. Ibid.
4. Ibid.
5. *Rochester Democrat and Chronicle* (Rochester, New York), August 30, 1873.

Chapter 14: Payday
1. Cody, *Memories of Buffalo Bill*, 251–52.
2. *Cairo Bulletin* (Cairo, Illinois), April 22, 1873.
3. *Daily Alta California* (San Francisco, California), August 12, 1873.
4. Ibid.
5. Cody, William Frederick. *Story of the Wild West and Camp-fire Chats*. Philadelphia: R. S. Peale Co., 1888, 652.
6. Rosa, Joseph G. *They Called Him Wild Bill: The Life and Adventures of James Butler Hickok*. Norman: University of Oklahoma Press, 1974, 246.

Chapter 15: Romance for Texas Jack
1. *Sunday Mercury* (New York, New York), April 6, 1873.
2. *Indianapolis Sentinel*, quoted in *Cincinnati Enquirer* (Cincinnati, Ohio), January 15, 1873.
3. Ibid.
4. *Rochester Democrat and Chronicle* (Rochester, New York), August 20, 1873.
5. Ibid., September 1, 1873.
6. *Inter Ocean* (Chicago, Illinois), September 2, 1873.
7. Cody, *Memories of Buffalo Bill*, 252–53.
8. Fellows, Dexter W., and Andrew A. Freeman. *This Way to the Big Show: The Life of Dexter Fellows*. New York: Viking Press, 1936, 18.
9. *Journal of Ena Palmer*.
10. Untitled clipping in *Journal of Ena Palmer* in the Ballantine Family Collection of the Nebraska State Historical Society.
11. *Detroit Free Press* (Detroit, Michigan), September 21, 1873.
12. *Sunday Times* (Chicago, Illinois), May 17, 1874.

Chapter 16: The Scouts of the Plains

1. Bill, *The Life of Hon. William F. Cody*, 329.
2. Ibid.
3. Buel, James W. *Heroes of the Plains or Lives and Wonderful Adventures of Wild Bill, Buffalo Bill, Kit Carson, Capt. Payne, "White Beaver," Capt. Jack, Texas Jack, California Joe.* St. Louis, MO: Historical Publishing Co., 1883, 160–61.
4. Cody, *Memories of Buffalo Bill*, 259–60.
5. Buel, *Heroes of the Plains*, 161.
6. Ibid., 158–59.
7. Ibid.
8. *Boston Herald* (Boston, Massachusetts), October 2, 1927.
9. "Arkansaw Traveler, Wild Bill's Humorous Interview with Hiram Robbins."
10. Cody, *The Life of Hon. William F. Cody*, 330.
11. *Wayland Register* (Wayland, New York); Walter Noble Burns, "Frontier Hero: *Reminiscences of Wild Bill Hickok* by his old *Friend Buffalo Bill," Blackfoot Optimist* (November 2, 1911).

Chapter 17: A Season Offstage

1. *Democrat and Chronicle* (Rochester, New York), February 13, 1925.
2. *Lowell Sun* (Lowell, Massachusetts), January 26, 1889.
3. Dunraven, *The Great Divide*, xii.
4. Ibid., xiii.
5. Ibid., 32.
6. Ibid., 33–34.
7. Ibid.
8. Ibid., 36.
9. Ibid., 50–51.
10. Ibid., 146–47.
11. Dunraven, Windham Thomas Wyndham-Quin. *Canadian Nights: Being Sketches and Reminiscences of Life and Sport in the Rockies, the Prairies, and the Canadian Woods.* London: Smith, Elder, 1914, 73.
12. Dunraven, *The Great Divide*, xii.
13. Dunraven, *Canadian Nights*, 75.
14. Dunraven, *The Great Divide*, 155–56.
15. Article titled "Texas Jack's Experience of Three Months on the National Park in the Yellowstone Region," from *Boys of the World*, clipping in Morlacchi scrapbook, collection of David Gindy.
16. Ibid., 173.
17. *Spirit of the Times*, April 14, 1877.
18. "Texas Jack's Experience of Three Months on the National Park."
19. Dunraven, *The Great Divide.* 348.
20. *Forest & Stream* (New York, New York), November 27, 1879.
21. Ibid., 375.

22. Dunraven, *Canadian Nights*, 57.
23. *Spirit of the Times*, April 14, 1877.

Chapter 18: Last Ride with Buffalo Bill
1. Letter from William F. Cody to Buckskin Sam Hall, July 5, 1879, MS6.0050 in Collection of the Buffalo Bill Center.
2. Image titled "Portrait of Non-Native Man, Jim Spleen, from Baxter Springs, KS, Who Took on the Alias of Kit Carson in Order to Enter West Point," n.d., NAA INV 01612617, in the National Anthropological Archives of the Smithsonian Museum.
3. Sagala, *Buffalo Bill on Stage*, 79.
4. *Times-Democrat* (New Orleans, Louisiana), December 14, 1875.
5. *Buffalo Evening Post* (Buffalo, New York), April 4, 1876.
6. *Daily Courier* (Lowell, Massachusetts), May 1, 1876.
7. Wetmore, Helen Cody. *Last of the Great Scouts: The Life Story of Col. William F. Cody*. Duluth, MN: Duluth Press Printing Co., 1899, 192.
8. *Daily Gazette* (Wilmington, Delaware), June 5, 1876.
9. Philadelphia City Directory, 1876.

Chapter 19: Centennial 1876
1. *Philadelphia Times* (Philadelphia, Pennsylvania), March 14, 1876.
2. *Philadelphia Inquirer* (Philadelphia, Pennsylvania), February 10, 1876.
3. Ibid., June 21, 1876.
4. *Philadelphia Times* (Philadelphia, Pennsylvania), July 5, 1876.
5. *Daily Evening Bulletin* (San Francisco, California), September 8, 1876.
6. *Philadelphia Times* (Philadelphia, Pennsylvania), September 25, 1876.
7. Ibid., September 22, 1876.
8. Ibid., October 3, 1876.
9. *Chicago Tribune* (Chicago, Illinois), February 23, 2017.
10. Dobrow, Joe. *Pioneers of Promotion: How Press Agents for Buffalo Bill, P. T. Barnum, and the World's Columbian Exposition Created Modern Marketing*. Norman: University of Oklahoma Press, 2018.

Chapter 20: General Custer and Wild Bill
1. *Gazette & Bulletin* (Williamsport, Pennsylvania), November 17, 1874.
2. *Philadelphia Press* (Philadelphia, Pennsylvania), July 8, 1876.
3. *Critic-Record* (Washington, DC), July 12, 1876.
4. *Rochester Democrat and Chronicle* (Rochester, New York), July 10, 1876.
5. *The Sun* (New York, New York), July 11, 1876.
6. Letter from Cody to Omohundro, printed in *Public Ledger* (Memphis, Tennessee), July 27, 1876.
7. Rosa, *They Called Him Wild Bill*, 281.
8. Ibid.

9. Included in poem "Wild Bill's Grave" by Captain Jack Crawford, printed in *Virginia Evening Chronicle*, August 4, 1877.

10. *The Herald* (New York, New York), March 2, 1877.

11. Kuykendall, William Littlebury. *Frontier Days: A True Narrative of Striking Events on the Western Frontier*. Denver, CO: J. M. and H. L. Kuykendall Publishers, 1917.

12. *Sunday Morning News* (Wilkes-Barre, Pennsylvania), November 11, 1877; unmarked newspaper clipping in Morlacchi scrapbook, collection of David Gindy.

13. *San Francisco Chronicle* (San Francisco, California), October 10, 1876.

14. *Memphis Daily Appeal* (Memphis, Tennessee), October 15, 1876.

15. Hedren, Paul. *First Scalp for Custer: The Skirmish at Warbonnet Creek, Nebraska, July 17, 1876*. Lincoln: Nebraska State Historical Society, 1980; rev. ed., 2005, 27.

Chapter 21: On the Hunt

1. *Spirit of the Times*, March 7, 1877.

2. Ibid.

3. *Santa Fe New Mexican* (Santa Fe, New Mexico), January 27, 1877.

4. *Spirit of the Times*, March 7, 1877.

5. Ibid.

6. Ibid.

7. *National Republican* (Washington, DC), February 25, 1877.

8. *Morristown Gazette* (Morristown, Tennessee), February 28, 1877.

9. *Wild Life on the Plains and Horrors of Indian Warfare by a Corps of Competent Authors and Artists Being A Complete History of Indian Life, Warfare and Adventure in America Making Specially Prominent the Late Indian War with Full Descriptions of The Messiah Craze, Ghost Dance, Life of Sitting Bull, the Whole Forming an Authentic and Complete History of the Savage Races In America—Their Illustrious Leaders, Their Beliefs, Manners and Customs, Comprising Terrible Battles, Wonderful Escapes, Thrilling Tales of Heroism, Daring Exploits, Wonderful Fortitude, etc., etc*. St. Louis, MO: Excelsior Publishing Co., 1891, 464.

Chapter 22: The Texas Jack Combination

1. McMurtry, Larry. *The Colonel and Little Missie: Buffalo Bill, Annie Oakley, and the Beginnings of Superstardom in America*. New York: Simon & Schuster, 2006, 109.

2. Kasson, Joy S. *Buffalo Bill's Wild West: Celebrity, Memory, and Popular History*. New York: Hill and Wang, 2000, 46.

3. *The Times* (Philadelphia, Pennsylvania), October 2, 1876.

4. Clark, Keith, and Donna Clark, eds. *Daring Donald McKay, or the Last War Trail of the Modoc*. Portland, Oregon: Portland Historical Society, 1971.

5. *Pittsburgh Daily Post* (Pittsburgh, Pennsylvania), June 7, 1875.

6. *Dispatch* (New York, New York), April 3, 1877.

7. *New York Sun* (New York, New York), April 5, 1877.

8. *Daily Journal of Commerce* (Kansas City, Missouri), May 17, 1877.

9. *Inter Ocean* (Chicago, Illinois), May 1, 1877.

10. *Spirit of the Times*, April 14, 1877.
11. *New York Times* (New York, New York), October 27, 1877.
12. Ibid.
13. *New York Daily Herald* (New York, New York), February 24, 1878.
14. Letter from Omohundro to Crawford in the collection of the Denver Public Library.

Chapter 23: Return to Yellowstone
1. *Spirit of the Times*, October 13, 1877.
2. *Weekly Clarion* (Jackson, Mississippi), August 8, 1877.
3. *Chicago Tribune* (Chicago, Illinois), September 13, 1877.
4. *Cheyenne Daily Leader* (Cheyenne, Wyoming), August 10, 1877.
5. *Chicago Tribune* (Chicago, Illinois), September 13, 1877.
6. Carpenter, Frank D. *The Wonders of Geyser Land: A Trip to the Yellowstone National Park, of Wyoming . . . with a Thrilling Account of the Capture by the Nez Perces Indians, and Subsequent Escape of the National Park Tourists, of Radersburg and Helena, Montana, in August, 1877.* Black Earth, WI: Burnett & Son, 1878.
7. *Chicago Tribune* (Chicago, Illinois), September 13, 1877.
8. Ibid.
9. *The Times* (London, England), August 27, 1878.
10. *The Sun* (New York, New York), October 21, 1877.
11. Ibid., October 22, 1877.
12. *Weekly Journal* (Sioux City, Iowa), October 23, 1877.
13. Unmarked newspaper clipping in Morlacchi scrapbook, collection of David Gindy.
14. Carpenter, *The Wonders of Geyser Land.*

Chapter 24: Texas Jack's Troubles
1. *Sunday Morning Times* (Syracuse, New York), October 7, 1877.
2. Schroth, Raymond A. *The Eagle and Brooklyn: A Community Newspaper, 1841–1955.* Westport, CT: Praeger, 1974.
3. *Daily Eagle* (Brooklyn, New York), March 17, 1878.
4. Ibid., March 18, 1878.
5. *Morning Herald* (Oswego, New York), July 18, 1879.

Chapter 25: Dr. Carver
1. Carver, William F. *Life of Dr. William F. Carver of California, Champion Rifle-shot of the World . . . Truthful Story of his Capture by the Indians When a Child, and Romantic Life among the Savages for a Period of Sixteen Years. To Which is Appended, a Record of His Remarkable Exhibitions of Skill with a Rifle.* Boston, MA: Press of Rockwell and Churchill, 1878.
2. Ibid.
3. *Public Ledger* (Memphis, Tennessee), June 14, 1878.

4. *State Sentinel* (Indianapolis, Indiana), July 10, 1878.

5. Thorp, Raymond W. *Spirit Gun of the West; The Story of Doc. W. F. Carver; Plainsman, Trapper, Buffalo Hunter, Medicine Chief of the Santee Sioux, World's Champion Marksman and Originator of the American Wild West Show.* Glendale, CA: A. H. Clark Co., 1957, 90.

6. *The Sun* (New York, New York), July 5, 1878.

7. *The Herald* (New York, New York), July 6, 1878.

8. Ibid., July 8, 1878.

9. *New York Times* (New York, New York), July 7, 1878.

10. *The Sun* (New York, New York), July 6, 1878.

11. *Daily Eagle* (Brooklyn, New York), July 7, 1878.

12. Ibid.

Chapter 26: The Cowboy, the Count, the Wizard, and the Doctor

1. Dyer, Frank Lewis, and Thomas Commerford Martin. *Edison: His Life and Inventions.* Honolulu, HI: University Press of the Pacific, 2001.

2. Letter from Omohundro to the New Orleans Crescent City Gun Club, printed in the *New Orleans Daily Democrat* (New Orleans, Louisiana), July 17, 1878.

3. Entry, Monday, July 29, 1878, Journal #5 of Otto Franc von Lichtenstein, Buffalo Bill Center of the West.

4. Ibid. (Friday, August 23, 1878).

5. Ibid. (Saturday, September 14, 1878).

6. *Progressive Men of the State of Wyoming.* Ann Arbor, MI: UMI, 975, 628.

7. *Chicago Tribune* (Chicago, Illinois), October 6, 1878.

8. *Daily Review* (Wilmington, North Carolina), October 25, 1878.

9. *The Sun* (Wilmington, North Carolina) October 26, 1878.

10. Ibid., November 10, 1878.

11. Thorp, *Spirit Gun of the West,* 75.

Chapter 27: The Final Tour

1. *Evening Telegram* (New York, New York), January 28, 1879.

2. *Daily Gazette* (Fort Wayne, Indiana), February 19, 1880.

3. *Addison Advertiser* (Addison, New York), March 13, 1879.

4. *Evening Auburnian* (Auburn, New York), April 4, 1879.

5. *Daily Courier* (Syracuse, New York), April 5, 1879.

6. *Chicago Tribune* (Chicago, Illinois), May 27, 1879.

7. *Lowell Courier* (Lowell, Massachusetts), June 20, 1879.

8. *Philadelphia Times* (Philadelphia, Pennsylvania), September 16, 1879.

9. *Cincinnati Enquirer* (Cincinnati, Ohio), October 22, 1879.

10. *Inter Ocean* (Chicago, Illinois), January 5, 1880.

11. Crawford, Jack, and Paul L. Hedren. *Ho! for the Black Hills: Captain Jack Crawford Reports the Black Hills Gold Rush and Great Sioux War.* Pierre: South Dakota State Historical Society Press, 2012.

Chapter 28: Leadville, Colorado

1. Friedman, David M. *Wilde in America: Oscar Wilde and the Invention of Modern Celebrity.* New York: W. W. Norton & Co., 2015.
2. *Kansas City Times* (Kansas City, Kansas), May 15, 1884.
3. *Advance Argus* (Greenville, Pennsylvania), March 6, 1879.
4. *The Herald* (New York, New York), February 13, 1917.
5. Letter from Cody to Crawford in the William A. Bell Family Collection of the Buffalo Bill Center of the West.
6. *Daily Leader* (Cheyenne, Wyoming), May 14, 1880.
7. Letter to Sidney Omohundro, dated July 22, 1877; unmarked newspaper clipping in Morlacchi scrapbook, collection of David Gindy.
8. Cattermole, E. G. *Famous Frontiersmen, Pioneers and Scouts: The Vanguards of American Civilization . . . Including Boone, Crawford, Girty, Molly Finney, the Mcculloughs . . . Captain Jack, Buffalo Bill, General Custer with His Last Campaign against Sitting Bull, and General Crook with His Recent Campaign against the Apaches.* Chicago: Elder Publishing Co., 1888, 507–08.
9. *Kansas City Times* (Kansas City, Kansas), May 15, 1884.
10. *Leadville Weekly Herald* (Leadville, Colorado), April 24, 1880.
11. *Leadville Daily Herald* (Leadville, Colorado), May 9, 1880.

Chapter 29: Curtain Call

1. *Daily Democrat* (Leadville, Colorado), June 30, 1880.
2. *Daily Chronicle* (Leadville, Colorado), June 28, 1880
3. Ahlquist, Diron Lacina. *"Simpson Everett 'Jack' Stilwell," Lawmen & Outlaws.* Lawmen.GenealogyVillage.com, https://lawmen.genealogyvillage.com/outlaws/stilwell.htm, retrieved May 12, 2011.
4. *Daily News* (Galveston, Texas), May 31, 1897.
5. *Cincinnati Enquirer* (Cincinnati, Ohio), June 30, 1880.
6. "Tuberculosis." World Health Organization. https://www.who.int/tb/areas-of-work/treatment/risk-factors/en/.
7. *Denver Medical Times.* Denver, CO: Medical Times Publishing Co., 1883.
8. Graff, Marshall Conant. *A History of Leadville, Colorado.* Madison: University of Wisconsin, 1920.
9. Leadville Colorado City Directory, 1881.
10. O. L. Baskin & Co. *History of the Arkansas Valley, Colorado.* Chicago: O. L. Baskin & Co., 1881.

Epilogue

1. *Item* (New Orleans, Louisiana), August 19, 1880.
2. *Times-Picayune* (New Orleans, Louisiana), July 25, 1880.
3. *Harrisburg Telegraph* (Harrisburg, Pennsylvania), November 6, 1890.
4. *Richmond Dispatch* (Richmond Virginia), August 21, 1886.

5. *Appleton's Journal of Literature, Science and Art*, vol. 4. New York: D. Appleton & Co., 1869—1872.

6. *Daily Herald* (Leadville, Colorado), September 21, 1882.

7. *Herald Democrat* (Leadville, Colorado), September 2, 1908.

8. *Semi-Weekly Spokesman-Review* (Spokane, Washington), January 7, 1917.

Epitaph for the Cowboy

1. "The Story of Cimarron Firearms, Part 1: The Guns." https://www.youtube.com/watch?v=WxVDzCC-sPA.

2. Correspondence with Mike Harvey, Texas Jack Wild West Outfitter, October 3, 2016.

3. *New York Times Magazine* (New York, New York), January 4, 1931.

INDEX

Italicized page numbers indicate photographs.

Acknowledgments

I WOULD LIKE TO EXTEND MY APPRECIATION TO THE FOLLOWING PEOPLE:

The editorial staff at TwoDot Books and Rowman & Littlefield

Archivists at newspapers.com, genealogybank.com, the Library of Congress' Chronicling America, HathiTrust, JSTOR, archive.org, and online state newspaper archives

Nicholle Gerharter, Karen Roles, Linda Clark, and Mack Frost at the Buffalo Bill Center of the West

John Rakowski and Steve Plutt at the Pikes Peak Museum

Janine Whitcomb at the University of Massachusetts–Lowell Center for Lowell History

Andrea Faling at the Nebraska State Historical Society

Rachel Castro at the University of Arizona Special Collections

Jessica Munson at the National Museum of Dance

Hanna Parris and Roger Dudley at the Denver Public Library

Jeff Malcomson at the Montana Historical Society

Erika Van Vraken at the State Historical Society of Missouri

Julia Chambers and Abby Houston at Syracuse University

Dolores Colon at Yale University

Mike Harvey and Jamie Wayt at Texas Jack Outfitters and Cimarron Firearms

Julie Greene, Carole Brown, Larry Tyree, Rene Tyree, and Rick Omohundro at the Texas Jack Association

Dr. John Lehman

Jay Haddad at the Actors Fund

Larry Hardesty

David Gindy, owner of the Morlacchi Scrapbook

Guy Lefebvre

Eric Duncan at Cowan's Auctions

Jamie Rigsby at the Buffalo Bill Museum and Grave

Daisy Njoku at the Smithsonian Institute

Douglas Seefeldt, Jeremy Johnston, and Frank Christianson at the William F. Cody Archive

Delia Cioffi

Sandy Sagala

Joe Dobrow

Robert Aquinas McNally

Julia Bricklin

Betty Woomer

Mads Madsen at Colorized History for colorizing the cover image

My family: Jaime, Jonah, Cherith, and Emaline; my brothers, Morgan and Michael; my parents, Bill and Leesa

About the Author

Matthew Kerns is a historian, web developer, and digital archivist who lives with his wife and children in Chattanooga, Tennessee. His most recent public project is the Walter Becker Media Project (walterbecker-media.com), as reported in *Rolling Stone*. He manages a blog, YouTube channel, the popular Western podcast *Dime Library* (dimelibrary.com), and the Texas Jack Facebook page (facebook.com/jbomohundro). He has had multiple articles about Texas Jack published in *The Texas Jack Scout*, the triannual publication of the Texas Jack Association.

9 781493 055418